Conferences with

Literary Conversations Series
Peggy Whitman Prenshaw
General Editor

Photo credit: © Photofest

Conversations with Ray Bradbury

Edited by
Steven L. Aggelis

University Press of Mississippi
Jackson

www.upress.state.ms.us

The University Press of Mississippi is a member of the Association of American University Presses.

Copyright © 2004 by University Press of Mississippi
All rights reserved
Manufactured in the United States of America

12 11 10 09 08 07 06 05 04   4 3 2 1
∞
Library of Congress Cataloging-in-Publication Data

Bradbury, Ray, 1920–
  Conversations with Ray Bradbury / edited by Steven L. Aggelis.
    p. cm. — (Literary conversations series)
Includes index.
  ISBN 1-57806-640-9 (cloth : alk. paper) — ISBN 1-57806-641-7 (pbk. : alk. paper)
  1. Bradbury, Ray, 1920– —Interviews. 2. Authors, American—20th century—Interviews.
3. Science fiction—Authorship. I. Aggelis, Steven L. II. Title. III. Series.
  PS3503.R167Z466 2004
  813'.54—dc22   2003025136

British Library Cataloging-in-Publication Data available

Books by Ray Bradbury

Novels

The Martian Chronicles. Garden City, New York: Doubleday, 1950; revised as *The Silver Locusts*, London: Rupert Hart-Davis, 1951.
Fahrenheit 451. New York: Ballantine, 1953; abridged edition, London: Rupert Hart-Davis, 1954.
Dandelion Wine. New York: Doubleday, 1957; London: Rupert Hart-Davis, 1957.
Something Wicked This Way Comes. New York: Simon and Schuster, 1962; London: Rupert Hart-Davis, 1963.
Death Is a Lonely Business. New York: Alfred A. Knopf, 1985; London: Grafton, 1986.
A Graveyard for Lunatics: Another Tale of Two Cities. New York: Alfred A. Knopf, 1990; London: Grafton, 1990.
Green Shadows, White Whale. New York: Alfred A. Knopf, 1992; London: HarperCollins, 1992.
From the Dust Returned. New York: Avon, 1998.
Let's All Kill Constance: A Novel. New York: William Morrow/HarperCollins Publishers, 2003.

Short Story Collections

Dark Carnival. Sauk City, WI: Arkham House, 1947; abridged edition, London: Hamish Hamilton, 1948.
The Illustrated Man. Garden City, New York: Doubleday, 1951; revised edition, London: Rupert Hart-Davis, 1952.
The Golden Apples of the Sun. Garden City, New York: Doubleday, 1953; revised edition, London: Rupert Hart-Davis, 1953.
The October Country. [Illustrated by Joseph Mugnaini]. New York: Ballantine, 1955; London: Rupert Hart-Davis, 1956.
A Medicine for Melancholy. New York: Doubleday, 1959; revised as *The Day It Rained Forever*. London: Rupert Hart-Davis, 1959.
R Is for Rocket. Garden City, New York: Doubleday, 1962; London: Rupert Hart-Davis, 1968.
The Machineries of Joy. New York: Simon and Schuster, 1964; abridged edition, London: Rupert Hart-Davis, 1964.

S Is for Space. Garden City, New York: Doubleday, 1966; London: Rupert Hart-Davis, 1968.
Twice 22. New York: Doubleday, 1966.
I Sing the Body Electric! New York: Alfred A. Knopf, 1969; London: Rupert Hart-Davis, 1970.
Long After Midnight. New York: Alfred A. Knopf, 1976.
A Memory of Murder. New York: Dell, 1984.
The Toynbee Convector. New York: Alfred A. Knopf, 1988; London: Grafton, 1989.
Quicker than the Eye. New York: Avon, 1996.
Driving Blind. New York: Avon, 1997.
One More for the Road. New York: William Morrow/HarperCollins Publishers, 2002.

Plays, Radio and Musical Scores

The Flying Machine. Woodstock, Illinois: Dramatic Publishing Company, 1953; 1981.
The Anthem Sprinters and Other Antics. New York: Dial Press, 1963.
The Day It Rained Forever: A Comedy in One Act. New York: Samuel French, 1966.
The Pedestrian: A Fantasy in One Act. London; New York: Samuel French, 1966.
The Wonderful Ice Cream Suit, and Other Plays. Toronto; New York: Bantam, 1972; London: Hart-Davis, MacGibbon, 1973.
Madrigals for the Space Age, for mixed chorus and narrator with piano accompaniment. [Music by Lalo Schifrin, text by Bradbury]. New York: Associated Music Publishers, 1972.
Pillar of Fire and Other Plays. New York: Bantam, 1975.
Forever and the Earth: Radio Dramatization. Athens, Ohio: Croissant, 1984.
A Device Out of Time. Woodstock, Illinois: Dramatic Publishing Company, 1986 [*A Device Out of Time: A One-Act Play* 1965].
Ray Bradbury's Falling Upward. Woodstock, Illinois: Dramatic Publishing Company, 1988.
The Day It Rained Forever: A New Musical. [Music by Bill Whitefield, lyrics by Bradbury and Whitefield, and additional music and lyrics by Tom Gire]. Woodstock, Illinois: Dramatic Publishing Company, 1990.
Christus Apollo: Cantata Celebrating the Eighth Day of Creation and the Promise of the Ninth. [Illustrated by D'Ambrosio]. Newport Beach, California: Gold Stein Press, 1998.

Juvenile Fiction

Switch on the Night. [Illustrated by Madeleine Gekiere]. New York: Pantheon, 1955; reprinted [Illustrated by Leo and Diane Dillon]. New York: Alfred A. Knopf, 1993, 2000.
The Halloween Tree. [Illustrated by Joseph Mugnaini]. New York: Alfred A. Knopf, 1972; London: Hart-Davis, MacGibbon, 1973.

Dinosaur Tales. Toronto; New York: Bantam, 1983.

Fever Dream. [Illustrated by Darrel Anderson]. New York: St. Martins Press, 1987.

The April Witch: A Creative Classic. [Illustrated by Gary Kelley]. Mankato, Minnesota: Creative Education Company, 1987.

The Fog Horn: A Creative Classic. [Illustrated by Gary Kelley]. Mankato, Minnesota: Creative Education Company, 1987.

The Other Foot: A Creative Classic. [Illustrated by Gary Kelley]. Mankato, Minnesota: Creative Education Company, 1987.

The Veldt: A Creative Classic. [Illustrated by Gary Kelley]. Mankato, Minnesota: Creative Education Company, 1987.

The Smile. Mankato, Minnesota: Creative Education Company, 1991.

Ahmed and the Oblivion Machines: A Fable. [Illustrated by Chris Lane]. New York: Avon, 1998.

Contents

Introduction xi

Chronology xxvii

The Market Is Not the Story: An Interview with Ray Bradbury
   R. Walton Willems 3

Sum and Substance: With Ray Bradbury and Herman Harvey
   Herman Harvey 8

A Portrait of Genius: Ray Bradbury   Show 17

Ray Bradbury: Cassandra on a Bicycle   *Pierre Berton* 31

An Interview with Ray Bradbury   *William B. Allen* 39

Ray Bradbury: On Hitchcock and Other Magic of the Screen
   Arnold R. Kunert 54

Ray Bradbury: Space Age Moralist   *William F. Nolan* 80

The Bradbury Chronicles   *Shel Dorf* 85

It's Up, On, and Away   *Barbara Newcomb* 100

Ray Bradbury: The Science of Science Fiction   *Arthur Unger* 107

Ray Bradbury: An Interview   *Abraham Drassinower and
   Cheryl Kemkow* 112

The Romance of Places: An Interview with Ray Bradbury
   Rob Couteau 122

Interview with Ray Bradbury   *Donn Albright* 139

A Few Words with Ray Bradbury: The "Fahrenheit" Chronicles—It Did
   Happen Here   *Judith Green* 145

Bradbury Talk Likely to Feature the Unexpected *Anne Gasior* 147
Playboy Interview: Ray Bradbury *Ken Kelley* 150
Science-Fiction Supernova *Sandy Hill* 170
An Interview with Master Storyteller Ray Bradbury *Jason J. Marchi* 175
Ray Bradbury *Joshua Klein* 184
Future Tense Sci-Fi Legend Bradbury Going Strong *Jim Cherry* 191
Conversation with Ray Bradbury *Steven L. Aggelis* 194
Index 203

Introduction

Ray Bradbury considers himself a child of his time. He was born Ray Douglas Bradbury on August 22, 1920, in Waukegan, Illinois, and began reading voraciously at the age of eight, about the time Hugo Gernsback's pulp magazine *Amazing Stories* first appeared. He came to maturity just prior to World War II, when the V-1 and V-2 rockets were used against the British, and began writing in the nascency of the space age. Since his first professional sale in 1941 of "Pendulum," written with Henry Hasse for *Super Science Stories*, Bradbury has written and published hundreds of essays, short stories, novels, dramas, operas, teleplays, poems, and screenplays. Over the course of his career, he has been interviewed more than 335 times.

The Bradbury family's American roots run back three hundred years. The early Bradbury immigrants came from a little community outside London, England, and settled around 1630 in Salisbury, Massachusetts. Later, members of the family moved to Illinois. Bradbury's father's full name is Leonard Spaulding Bradbury. Ray combined his middle name and his father's to create one of his pseudonyms, Douglas Spaulding, also the name of one of his characters. Bradbury's great-grandfather in Waukegan was involved in the printing trade, making up small booklets and doing odd printing jobs at the same time that he was editor and publisher of two newspapers. Much of the Bradbury family money was lost by his paternal grandfather's ill-fated expeditions, including his desperate enterprises in gold and silver mining in Canada and Nevada. Bradbury's childhood was filled with such stories of family misadventure.

Esther Marie Moberg, Bradbury's mother, was two when her family migrated to America from Stockholm, Sweden, as part of the movement of the Swedes to the steel mills in Worcester, Massachusetts. When steel and iron foundries moved into the vicinity of Chicago, her family migrated there. In Illinois, Esther met Leonard, and they were married in Waukegan, where Bradbury and his older brother Leonard were born. Bradbury had another brother, Leonard's twin, Samuel, who died in the Asian flu epidemic in 1918, two years before Ray's birth. This tragedy was followed by the death of a sister, Elizabeth, in 1927, when Ray was only seven. Consequently, Esther Bradbury was overcautious in rearing Ray, making him, he readily admits in a video biography, *Ray Bradbury: An American Icon*, a "mama's boy," who was bottle-fed until the age of six and spoon-fed until he was thirteen or fourteen years old. Bradbury did not leave the nest until he was twenty-seven years old.

The early deaths of these siblings most assuredly contributed to Bradbury's fascination with death, one of his major themes. In the 1962 Harvey interview, Bradbury comments on how he came to see the value of horror films such as *Dracula* as a way of "making do with death." According to Bradbury, Count Dracula is a symbol for death and the unknown, and the stake, cross, and Bible are symbols used to conquer death. With these sure-fire vampire-extinguishing symbols, the reader or filmgoer can self-project into the text or film and release his or her tension about the horror of the unknown, in much the same way that the people of Mexico laugh at death in its face in their celebration of El Día de los Muertos (the Day of the Dead), on which Bradbury based his 1947 short story "El Día de Muerte," the English title for which is "The Day of Death."

Bradbury credits two people, his Aunt Neva and his father, for his literary interests. Aunt Neva—a painter, artist, dress designer, and, above all, a great lover of books, who was only ten years older than Bradbury—lived next door to him in his grandmother's house when he was a boy. Bradbury thoroughly enjoyed her company and conversation, at times looking upon her as a kind of surrogate mother. His natural mother was not particularly interested in literary things, and he went to his aunt for artistic stimulation. Of Aunt Neva, Bradbury says that she "helped bring me up in a world of let's-pretend, in a world of masks and puppets that she made, in a world of stages and acting, in a world of special Christmases and Halloweens. It was she who read me my first fairy tales, she who read Poe aloud to me when I was seven and taught me all about fabulous mythological country from which I never quite emerged" (*Show*).

His father's reading habits also influenced Bradbury. As he informs us in the 1961 recordings in his home by Craig Cunningham, compiled in the unpublished manuscript entitled *The Dogs That Eat Sweet Grass*, as the young Bradbury matured, the sight of his father "constantly sitting in the front room with a book in his hand" served as inspiration (4). Seeing his father "night after night in the living room, like a statue, saying very little to the family," contributed to Bradbury's picking up books and magazines and reading them throughout his developmental years. Throughout the interviews in this book, Bradbury is critical of the public educational system in the United States. He came to reflect in the 1999 Klein interview, surely drawing upon his own childhood experiences, that the developmental years, especially kindergarten and the first grade, demand the attention of anyone who wishes positive reform in education. "It's the teachers who have to do the job in kindergarten and first grade. Once you teach them to read and write, then the students will be curious. But the education system has failed, and all the money that Washington sends out in the next two years has got to go to local schools, first grade, and kindergarten. Then we can cure the problem." Bradbury's 1999 thinking had not strayed from his belief expressed nearly two decades earlier that if children do not know how to read and write certainly by the third grade, then they're not going to know how to think—since "the only way that you can learn to think is by knowing how to write" (Newcomb).

Films, comics, and books, all stimulations Bradbury loved, have been part of his writing, beginning with *The Hunchback of Notre Dame*, starring Lon Chaney, in 1923 when he was a mere three years old and *The Phantom of the Opera* when he was five. These two films set Bradbury off on a great, lifelong love affair with the cinema. Buck Rogers arrived in eight-year-old Bradbury's life, and he "lived in a state of near hysteria waiting for the comic to slap onto my front porch each night in the evening paper" (*Show*). With Buck Rogers came Tarzan and John Carter, Warlord of Mars, created by Edgar Rice Burroughs. He borrowed the Burroughs books from his Uncle Bion, read them numerous times, and virtually committed them to memory, chapter and verse. Aunt Neva's huge bookcase next door to him supplemented Bradbury's Burroughs readings with Lyman Frank Baum's "Oz" books. Bradbury reminisces, "Long before I went to the regular library, I picked up on those elements of fantasy which I think influenced me and changed my life" (Dorf). Later on, he prowled the Waukegan town library for volumes of Jules Verne, Robert Louis Stevenson, and H. G. Wells. Says Bradbury, "The library was the greenhouse in which I, a very strange plant indeed, grew up, exploding with seeds" (*Show*).

The young Bradbury kept moving from excitement to excitement. When Blackstone the Magician came to town, "that was incredible, too," says Bradbury. "I could hardly wait. I'd just go right out of my head waiting for Blackstone to show up. So all of that energy and passion and madness went right into my writing when I began to do it at the age of twelve" (Dorf). Bradbury decided to become a magician at the age of ten after Blackstone gave him his first live rabbit. The young Bradbury's meeting with Mr. Electrico was also inspirational. This meeting is recounted in the video biography, *Ray Bradbury: An American Icon*. When he was twelve, he attended Mr. Electrico's performance when the Dill Brothers Combined Shows set up their tents just outside Waukegan. With a charged sword, Mr. Electrico reached out and touched the boy Bradbury on both shoulders and then on his nose, and commanded him to "Live forever!" The following day, the enthralled Ray returned and met Mr. Electrico in his uncharged state, who revealed to Bradbury the behind-the-scenes mysteries of the carnival, introducing him to some of the carnival figures, such as the strong man and the fat woman. Then he told the boy they had had a memorable meeting in a previous incarnation during the battle of the Ardennes forest in France. Bradbury's extraordinary encounter with Mr. Electrico and his consequent insider's glimpse into carnival life loom large in his short stories such as "The Black Ferris," first published by *Weird Tales* in 1948, and "The Illustrated Man," released two years later, as well as his popular 1962 novel *Something Wicked This Way Comes*. For example, in the first of these works, the slick carnival man Mr. Cooger appears, dressed in sharp, bright clothes with a carnation in his lapel, his hair greased with oil, and a brown derby on his head.

Bradbury's inspiration to be a writer solidified at age twelve, when he began writing his first stories by hand on butcher paper. He was determined that his first "book" should be a sequel to a Mars volume by Burroughs. Bradbury's young talents not only included burgeoning writing skills, but also his thespian interests in performing magic shows and reading comics to children over radio air waves on Saturdays. Thus, Bradbury fused his passion for magic and comics and drama, which still flourishes. John J. McLaughlin, theater critic for *The Nation*, wrote the following in the January 25, 1965, edition about "The World of Ray Bradbury," an evening of three one-act plays: "The appearance of a theatrical company dedicated to producing his own work represents more than dabbling in a new literary form for Bradbury. It is a full commitment to put time, energy, and money into the theatre. He spent $20,000 out of his own pocket, gathered a professional group of actors and stage technicians, and set out to establish a permanent theatre where his plays can be staged for as long as he cares to write them" (92–93).

Continuing his writing and thespian propensities, at Los Angeles High School Bradbury studied short story writing under Jennet Johnson, whom he describes in the 1964 *Show* interview as "a kindly, patient, warm, and very human woman, whose influence must weigh heavy on the scales [of his development as a writer]. After her, my teachers were all established writers in the science-fiction field." At his high school, Bradbury became a scriptwriter, producer, and director of the school's *Roman Review*. During his senior year, he joined the Los Angeles Science Fiction League, founded in 1935 as a chapter of Gernsback's Science Fiction League, and he began friendships with Ray Harryhausen, Forrest J. Ackerman, Robert Heinlein, Hannes Bok, Jack Williamson, Edmond Hamilton, Henry Kuttner, and Leigh Brackett. The League met in Clifton's Cafeteria, where free meals were provided if someone was short of money. Heinlein, Hamilton, Kuttner, and Brackett, at one time or another, worked with Bradbury on refining his craft. Brackett, particularly, met with him every Sunday afternoon for about four years in Santa Monica. Bradbury soon reached the point where he was able to write well enough to chart his own direction.

In June 1939, when he was nineteen and had saved enough money, Bradbury traveled four days and nights in a Greyhound bus to the First World Science Fiction Convention in New York, where successful writers and editors in the field convened. On this trip, he acted as agent for Hannes Bok, a member of the League who was also an artist and whose illustrations Bradbury carried with him. Bradbury showed Bok's many oil paintings and illustrations to *Weird Tales*, *Astounding Science Fiction*, and similar magazines and was directly responsible for selling his friend's work. Bok continued doing artwork for the covers and interior illustrations for science-fiction magazines in the years following.

This 1939 trip to New York proved pivotal for Bradbury's professional ambitions. Beyond the thrill of meeting central figures in the science-fiction field and successfully promoting his friend Bok's illustrations, Bradbury was able to further his own writing career, sharing samples of his short stories and receiving editors' encouragement to continue writing his stories. In particular, the editor Walter Bradbury, no relation to Ray, planted the thematic seed that eventually germinated and became *The Martian Chronicles*. On this same trip Bradbury also formed a friendship with Julius Schwartz, who later became his first agent in the pulp field and was editor at DC comics starting in 1944. When "Julie" read his work for the first time, he told Bradbury it was not good enough, and he rejected Bradbury as a client. Bradbury was twenty-one before he presented a short story that met Mr. Schwartz's standards. "Pendulum," a collaborative effort with Henry Hasse, was sold to *Super Science Stories* and was Bradbury's first move into the pulp field for real money.

On Bradbury's momentous 1939 trip to New York, he also visited the New York World's Fair, which fueled his energies, imagination, and creativity with its exhibits of the future. Presented to him was a holistic view of a future community, complete with freeways and cloverleaf intersections, a fabulous concept to behold in that day. This fascination with the future and technology continued throughout Bradbury's writing, though, ironically, in his private life he has avoided driving, preferring to ride a bicycle, and has shunned e-mail in favor of more human, handwritten letters. Bradbury's rapture with things future is manifest in his involvement in city planning, including his participation in the development of Disney World's Experimental Community of Tomorrow (EPCOT) and Horton Plaza in San Diego. Bradbury's penchant for urban planning, which is a prevalent concern for him throughout his interviews, was framed by his philosophy to be part of the solution, not part of the problem. He perceives the active leadership role of the corporations, such as Walt Disney, in the development of ideal cities as the panacea for urban ills: "[T]he failure of cities is the failure of chambers of commerce and the failure of the mayors and the city councils who don't understand what cities are," he believes. "They're in for political power, they're not in to recreate the city, and make it better for everyone. So my dream has been, if they won't do it, some sort of corporate effort has to do it" (Couteau). This remedy-focused philosophical bent attracted Bradbury to the problem-solving genre of science fiction.

Unfortunately, amid the grand promises of what the world could be, within a few months of his New York trip, the United States was plunged into World War II. Poor eyesight kept Bradbury from the front lines, but his writing appeared in the major pulp magazines of the period: *Weird Tales, Famous Fantastic Mysteries, Thrilling Wonder Stories, Planet Stories, Super Science Stories, Detective Book Magazine, New Detective Magazine, Dime Mystery Magazine,* and *Astounding Science Fiction.* The pulp press is not without merit, he avowed to the *Show* interviewer: "Long before mass media began publishing or broadcasting material on the color problem, science fiction acted out such problems in the pulp magazines. I wrote a story in which the Negroes picked up and went off to Mars, leaving the entire South in the lurch, way back in 1949."

A major milestone occurred in Bradbury's writing in 1943, when he wrote "The Lake," which he considers to be his first story of literary value. It recorded a disturbing incident from his childhood, when he built sand castles with a little girl on the shore of a lake. She went for a swim and never returned. He trusted his subconscious and allowed his emotions to write the story, and as a

Introduction

result was able, at least partially, to purge from his system a demon that had long haunted him, the memory of her death. Bradbury has relied on his muse ever since, and he advises those who wish to be writers to follow their emotions, rather than economics. He discourages writers from being directed by profit, because "the cleansing process, the therapeutic process that should be going on between the writer and his typewriter, or his pen and ink, is cut across, then, by this commercial function. And he begins to lie. And as soon as he begins to lie in his work, it becomes noncreative, nontherapeutic to himself, and nontherapeutic to anyone that reads him" (Harvey). Paradoxically, Bradbury has become one of the most financially successful writers in America, sometimes by repackaging his works in different collections for redistribution.

Two events in 1947 proved monumental for Mr. Bradbury. He married Marguerite "Maggie" McClure and became a client of literary agent Don Congdon. Both relationships have persevered to this day. During the '40s, five of Bradbury's stories brought him critical acclaim. "The Big Black and White Game," "Powerhouse," "The Meadow," "I See You Never," and "Homecoming" were selected for prestigious awards. The latter became the nucleus of his 1998 novel *From the Dust Returned*. In John C. Tibbetts's March 20, 1991, interview with Bradbury for the *Christian Science Monitor*, which, regrettably, does not appear in this collection, Ray recalled how his story "Homecoming" was sold in the slick magazine market. *Mademoiselle* and *Vogue* "were women's magazines with fine story editors who published work by Katherine Anne Porter, Carson McCullers, and Eudora Welty," he remembered. "A young assistant at *Mademoiselle* found one of my stories in the 'slush pile.' It was about a family of vampires, called 'The Homecoming.' He gave it to the story editor and said, '. . . you must publish this!' That young man was Truman Capote, and *Mademoiselle* ended up changing the whole magazine to fit the story!" (17).

If the decade of the '40s solidified Bradbury's reputation in the pulp tradition with a scattering of prize-winning, non-pulp short stories, then the '50s introduced Bradbury to the major slick magazines. His work appeared in *Senior Scholastic, Maclean's, Esquire*, the *Saturday Evening Post, Argosy, Charm, Life*, and *Playboy*. Approaching the '50s, Bradbury's short works made the transition to hardcovers and paperbacks as compilations. His first hardcover collection, *Dark Carnival*, was published in 1947. The 1950 publication of *The Martian Chronicles*, a collection of short stories with the common thread of planet Mars accounts, which shed light on contemporary issues, established Bradbury's reputation in the sophisticated, speculative fiction field.

The literary critic Christopher Isherwood rendered the first major review of a Bradbury work when he critiqued *The Martian Chronicles* in *Tomorrow* magazine. Isherwood's analysis placed Bradbury more in the fantasy tradition, one of Poe's genres, than in the science-fiction field. Bradbury admits, "I'm not a science-fiction writer. I've only written one book that's science fiction, and that's *Fahrenheit 451*. All the others are fantasy." Bradbury is careful to differentiate between the two: "Fantasies are things that can't happen, and science fiction is about things that can happen" (Klein). Bradbury agrees with the critics' charge that he relies too much on fantasy and not enough on science to be labeled a science-fiction writer. He says in his 1996 *Playboy* interview with Kelley, "I use a scientific idea as a platform to leap into the air and never come back. This keeps them angry at me. They still begrudge my putting an atmosphere on Mars in *The Martian Chronicles* more than forty years ago." As evidence of this grudge by readers, Juliet Grimsley's essay in the December 1970 *English Journal* cites a student's response to Bradbury's Mars: "When an author can make his reader believe his story, I feel he is then a good writer. Ray Bradbury did this to me, and it makes me a bit angry to think I believed his 'fakey' story without any question" (1239).

Many critics point to Bradbury's prose collections of the '50s as among his best. *The Illustrated Man* was published in 1951, and like *The Martian Chronicles* it is a collection of short stories linked by a framing device, a tattooed man whose illustrations come alive to tell their stories. In 1953 Bradbury published his most influential and widely read work on censorship, *Fahrenheit 451*, a revision and expansion of his fifty-six-page novella, "The Fireman," which first appeared in *Galaxy*. *Fahrenheit* was sold to Hugh Hefner's new magazine, *Playboy*, in three installments. In the May 1954 edition of *Playboy*, readers' reactions to the *Fahrenheit* installments in "Dear Playboy" varied from "I've read a lot of stories in my day but this one is the worst. It *stinks!*" to "Ray has been a good friend for a number of years and gifted me with the original manuscript to F.451 a few months back. At that time I termed it a classic in the field and upon re-reading the first installment in your magazine my opinion seems justified." That accolade was made by William F. Nolan, whose interview with Bradbury is included in this collection. *Playboy* continued to publish Bradbury's fiction, essays, and poetry throughout his career.

Fahrenheit 451 is the quintessential fictional masterpiece on censorship and is discussed numerous times in Bradbury's interviews. Even though he abhors censorship, "when government controls things, and you cannot publish or

Introductionxix

sell or find in a library the books that you want" (Gasior), Bradbury paradoxically believes government may and should use discretion in selecting the art it wishes to fund, without being considered tyrannous: "[Government is] just saying that they're funding you just as a gallery does; a gallery has the right to choose what it wants to hang on its walls. That's not censorship—that's selectivity" (Albright).

As special interest groups and political correctness gained influence, Bradbury came to view these forces as menacing as despotism and the malleable masses, and he expanded his views on censorship. "So whereas back then [the early '50s] I wrote about the tyranny of the majority, today I'd combine that with the tyranny of the minorities. These days, you have to be careful of both. They both want to control you" (Kelley). "If we listened to all these groups then we wouldn't have anything to read or anything to look at. It's okay for them to speak up, but you don't have to listen to them 'cause if we censor all the things the gays want changed and all the women's lib things changed and all the Jewish groups want changed and all the Catholic groups, after a while you have empty shells" (Albright).

Bradbury's output for the rest of the '50s included *The Golden Apples of the Sun* and *The October Country*, both published in 1953, the latter containing many of the stories from *Dark Carnival* with some additions, and *A Medicine for Melancholy*, released in 1959. Each of these volumes gathered stories written from 1945 to 1959. In 1957 he also produced his semi-autobiographical novel, *Dandelion Wine*, which contains many previously published individual short stories. In his review of *Dandelion Wine*, literary critic Robert O. Bowen commented in the September 7, 1957, issue of the *Saturday Review* that "no other writer since Mark Twain has caught the vitality and innocence of small-town American youth with as fine and mature perception as Ray Bradbury's (18). In 1971 the Apollo 15 crew named a section of the moon Dandelion Crater after the title of this Bradbury novel.

Bradbury's work in 1954 crafting the screenplay for John Huston's film *Moby Dick* established him as a permanent fixture in Hollywood. *Moby Dick* set a conspicuous precedent for Bradbury's presence in television, cinema, and stage, and, no doubt, contributed to his financial success. In addition to his works appearing on all the major networks—ABC, CBS, NBC, BBC, and PBS—sixty-five of his teleplays for *The Ray Bradbury Theater* were produced for Home Box Office (HBO) and USA Network from 1985 through 1992. HBO viewers tuned into Bradbury's familiar description of the genesis of his ideas: "People ask 'Where do you get your ideas?' Well, right here [pointing to his cluttered 'office' that brings to mind the 'fabled attic or basement storehouse' he uses in the *Show* interview as a metaphor for the source of his *Dandelion Wine*]. All this is my Martian landscape. Somewhere in this room is an African veldt. Just beyond, perhaps, is a small Illinois town where I grew up. And I'm surrounded on every side by my magician's toy shop. I'll never starve here. I just look around, find what I need, and begin. I'm Ray Bradbury, and this is *The Ray Bradbury Theater*. Well, then, right now what shall it be? Out of all this, what do I choose to make a story? I never know where the next one will take me. The trip—exactly one half exhilaration, exactly one half terror."

In 1961 Bradbury composed the voice-over narration for the movie *King of Kings*. The following year saw the release of *Icarus Montgolfier Wright*, an eighteen-minute animated film conceived by Bradbury and the co-written with George C. Johnson. The film was nominated for an Academy Award as the best animated short subject of the year and received a Golden Eagle Film Award. Bradbury's first drama collection, *The Anthem Sprinters and Other Antics*, appeared in 1963, and director François Truffaut's film adaptation of *Fahrenheit 451* was released in 1966.

Though predictably critical of film versions of his works, Bradbury said in his 1972 interview with Kunert: "I thought François Truffaut did a fine job with *Fahrenheit 451*. I loved the adventure, the chase, the way he handled his actors." According to Bradbury, the film improves with multiple viewings: "There are many fine little throwaway items that one often misses on the first viewing. Truffaut probably didn't have the city congested with people, for example, because he wanted to suggest that everyone was inside—watching television." Bradbury regards many of the film's scenes as poignant: "For example, the first night that Montag reads a book, sitting by the television set, and using the light from the set to read is a great touch. That isn't even in my book. And the careful articulation of the words from Dickens, running his finger over every word, stumbling. This is a *great* scene." Bradbury counted the conclusion of the film among the most beautiful in the history of film: "These people at the ending of the film only articulate as walking metaphors what *we* are as people. Each of us has some part of some book in our heads. Some of us have good memories. Some of us have poor memories. But we all have memories of a book and how it changed our lives. So to me, that ending is beautiful. It's a lovely movie. It's a haunting movie."

Introduction								xxi

Bradbury's *Something Wicked This Way Comes*, a novel which includes many autobiographical episodes, was published in 1962 and was subsequently popularized in film by Walt Disney Studios in 1983. Its thirteen-year-old Will Halloway is essentially Douglas Spaulding from *Dandelion Wine*. Throughout the '60s Bradbury published several repackaged anthologies of previously written and compiled material, including *R Is for Rocket*, *The Machineries of Joy*, *The Vintage Bradbury*, *S Is for Space*, and *Twice 22*. Of *The Machineries of Joy*, literary critic Martin Levin writes in the February 16, 1964, *New York Times*' Reader's Report: "Mr. Bradbury is a smooth pitchman for his versatile collection, luring you into each story with a well-thrown narrative hook, and then confronting you with whatever exhibit takes his fancy" (38). The decade culminated in a 1969 collection of new Bradbury fiction, *I Sing the Body Electric!*

With the nation's successes in its space program in the late '60s, Bradbury shifted from thinking about space as a concept to thinking about it as a definite reality, and he welcomed the theological implications of such "blasphemies." "We are refashioning God into a new image so that He will stay conveniently out of the way. So that we can get the work done of going into space, of landing on God's moon, of landing on God's Mars, and going places where, a hundred years ago if we had tried to go there, we would have been burned at the stake for doing the job" (Berton). Bradbury believes in the divinity of man and not in the anthropomorphic God: "Man is a fusion of the human and the divine. I believe that the flesh of man contains the very soul of God, that we are, finally, irrevocably and responsibly, God Himself incarnate, that we shall carry this seed of God into space" (Nolan). In response to William B. Allen's query regarding whether "one finds much of Walt Whitman or Ralph Waldo Emerson in Bradbury," Ray admits, "Not too much. I read Emerson so many years ago that I can't really say that he rubbed off that much. Little of Whitman, and I was very young. But Whitman could have come to me through other people; people like Norman Corwin or Thomas Wolfe. I'm not sure how much Whitman Thomas Wolfe read; but there are echoes. Emerson could have come to me through other people too. But if I really listed influences, I don't think I would put them on the list anywhere."

Little new Bradbury fiction appeared in the '70s and '80s. Instead, Bradbury turned his energy towards publishing poetry—*When Elephants Last in the Dooryard Bloomed*, *Where Robot Mice and Robot Men Run Round in Robot Towns*, *The Haunted Computer and the Android Pope*, and *The Complete Poems of*

Ray Bradbury, released from 1973 through 1982. During this period, drama also received more of his attention. *Madrigals for the Space Age, Pillar of Fire, Dandelion Wine, Leviathan '99,* and *The Martian Chronicles* were all staged from 1973 through 1976, and *Pillar of Fire and Other Plays for Today, Tomorrow, and Beyond Tomorrow* came to print in 1975.

The three Bradbury short story collections released in the '70s and '80s, *Long After Midnight, The Stories of Ray Bradbury,* and *The Toynbee Convector,* gather the stories Bradbury wrote from 1943 through the '80s. Ralph A. Sperry in the December 1976 *Best Sellers* book review of *Long After Midnight* describes the story "The Better Part of Wisdom" as "the most sensitive, most restrained, most graceful treatment of homosexuality I've ever read, ought to be required reading for all gay writers." The critic Orson Scott Card, writing in the November 2, 1980, *Washington Post Book World,* said concerning *The Stories of Ray Bradbury*: "It is not the characters he expects you to identify with. Rather, he means to capture you in his own voice, expects you to see through his eyes. And his eyes see, not the cliché plot, but the whole meaning of the events; not the scenes or the individual people, but yourself and your own fears and your own family and the answer, at last, to the isolation that had seemed inevitable to you" (5).

Bradbury delved into the crime and detective genre early in his writing career, and these stories were collected in *A Memory of Murder*, released in 1984. In 1985 he published a second work within this genre, *Death Is a Lonely Business*. Set in 1949 Venice, California, this work contains many autobiographical dimensions. Bradbury admits that the crazy kid in the novel is a portrayal of Bradbury himself as a struggling writer for pulp magazines: "Events in my past life are in there, some people that I knew" (Couteau). The November 3, 1985, review of the book in the *Washington Post Book World* focuses on its romantic style: "Ray Bradbury's writing remains as rich and ripe as ever," Ross Thomas writes. "When describing a woman he has his Young Writer hero think of her as being 'a lovely chess game carved and set in a store window when you were a kid. She has a freshly built girl's gym, with only the faintest scent of the noon tennis dust that clings to golden thighs.'" The book is dedicated to the memory of "hard-boiled" writers Raymond Chandler, Dashiell Hammett, James M. Cain, and Ross Macdonald, among others.

The sequel to *Death Is a Lonely Business, A Graveyard for Lunatics,* was inspired by an incident in Bradbury's life, when he sailed to Europe and for four or five days observed a man with a horribly disfigured face. He began to

Introduction

write the book with the plot revolving around the man with the ruined face. The work is critical of the film industry for such things as control over the writer's material, because "once you sell those things to the studio, they can do anything with it that they want" (Klein). *Let's All Kill Constance*, Bradbury's 2002 novel, is the latest in this series. As Bradbury explains to Jason Marchi in a 1998 interview preceding the publication of this work, Constance has "been in my first two murder mysteries, and I killed her off in the first one. As I was revising that first murder mystery she came back and knocked on the door and said, 'I refuse to stay dead. Put me back in.' So I put her back in and now she's in three books." His murder mystery characters are paranoids, schizophrenics, neurotics, and perverts—all representative of the underbelly of mass culture.

Over the last decade, in addition to his late murder mysteries, Bradbury has published two novels—*Green Shadows, White Whale* (1992), a mosaic of his experiences in Ireland while working on the *Moby Dick* screenplay for John Huston, and *From the Dust Returned* (1998), a tapestry of exploits by the ghouls of his imagination. The Elliott family, featured in the latter novel, is based on Ray's childhood memories of his grandmother, his Aunt Neva, and his favorite Swedish uncle, Einar. The individual characters in the Elliott family threesome appear elsewhere in previously published short stories. Three compilations of short stories, written from 1947 through 2001, were published from 1996 through 2002—*Quicker Than the Eye*, *Driving Blind*, and *One More for the Road*. *Publishers Weekly* said of the twenty-one stories in *Driving Blind*: "Despite bizarre actions and abstract twists, all are grounded in the everyday. Here are sketches, vignettes, strange tales, colorful anecdotes, little tragedies, hilarious lies, and metaphysics too" (72). Hanna-Barbera Studios' animated version of Bradbury's *The Halloween Tree* earned an Emmy in 1993, and Walt Disney Studios released *The Wonderful Ice Cream Suit* on video in 1998. Bradbury wrote the screenplay for this movie and considers it "the best film I've ever made, and there's not one curse in the whole film. And it's about people who could very easily curse, you see? But you don't need those swear words" (Klein).

At eighty-three Mr. Bradbury continues to work from his wheelchair, his post-stroke command center. In a May 7, 2002, communication to me, he reminded me of his circumstances: "During the last two-and-a-half years, I've been recovering from a stroke. Not long ago I went completely blind in my left eye and my right eye is behaving poorly. I've had to learn to write again and to speak clearly, and there are many other medical problems that have occurred in recent months." At the time of my interview with him, he was awaiting the release of the remaking of his short story "A Sound of Thunder" in production in Prague and other Hollywood projects. His plays continue to be presented on the stage.

Of all the accolades Bradbury has received over his illustrious career, most notably the Nebula Grandmaster Award for his lifetime achievements and the National Book Foundation's 2000 Medal for Distinguished Contribution to American Letters, Bradbury would best like to be remembered as a teller of tales. In his own words, from the 1964 *Show* interview, he sends himself "on a journey back through the ages in a time machine. Arriving in Baghdad I would walk through the marketplace and turn down a street where sit the old men who are the tellers of tales. There, among the young who listen and the old who say aloud, I would like to take my place and speak when it is my turn. It is an ancient tradition, a good one, a lovely one, a fine one. If some boy visits my tomb a hundred years from now and writes on the marble with a crayon: He Was a Teller of Tales, I will be happy. I ask no more name than that." And Bradbury has most solidly earned that epigraph.

The interviews in this collection span more than five decades and appear in chronological order as they were conducted. Obvious grammatical and spelling errors have been silently corrected. Bradbury's responses to interviewers, over the years, are well crafted and generally consistent, with exceptions, some of which I have highlighted. This uniformity is due, in large part, to repetitive or similar questions being posed and his typically well-rehearsed responses. Some duplication of questions and answers occurs in the different interviews, but I have made every effort to cover the gamut with as little redundancy as possible. It is impossible to offer all the available interviews in one volume, but I wanted to assemble the "major," most representative, and most difficult-to-access interviews.

A number of people helped me with this project: Seetha Srinivasan and Walter Biggins from the University Press of Mississippi; Dr. R. Bruce Bickley Jr. and Dr. William T. Lhamon Jr., members of my doctoral committee, and Dr. Elisabeth Logan, associate dean and professor of library and information studies, Florida State University; Margaret J. Kimball, Stanford University archivist; Jon Edmondson, public services manager, UCLA Southern Regional Library Facility; Alva Moore Stevenson, UCLA Oral History Program; Dr. Peter Schramm, Ashland University; Dr. William B. Allen, Michigan State University; William F. Nolan, acclaimed author and Bradbury bibliographer; Jason J. Marchi, New Century Cinema Group; Arnold Kunert, retired communication arts teacher; Dr. Jonathan Eller, a Bradbury scholar, University of Indiana and Purdue University, Indianapolis; Donn Albright, professor in communications, Pratt Institute, and author of *The Ray Bradbury Bibliography*; and Shel Dorf, former lettering man on Milton Caniff's *Steve Canyon* comic-strip, who has two interviews with Milton Caniff included in the University Press of Mississippi's *Milton Caniff: Conversations*, edited by Robert C. Harvey, and who graciously served as my ambassador to personally meet and talk with Mr. Bradbury in San Diego. Special credit is given to my wife, Kitty Jo, and my mother, Zola Belle, for their professional assistance and continuing support.

Last, but not least, I am deeply grateful to Ray Douglas Bradbury, who made a personal commitment to my project and also granted me access to Craig Cunningham's interview with him entitled *The Dogs That Eat Sweet Grass*, 1965, maintained by the University of California Los Angeles Oral History Program. Echoing the words of Mr. Electrico to the young Ray Bradbury, my wish is that he may "Live forever!" And, indeed, he will—in the hearts and minds of his readers.

SLA
2003

Chronology

1920	Ray Douglas Bradbury is born on 22 August in Waukegan, Illinois, the third son of Leonard Spaulding Bradbury and Esther Marie Moberg Bradbury. Leonard and Samuel, twin older brothers, were born in 1916; Samuel died in the Asian flu epidemic in 1918.
1923	As a child of three, Bradbury sees the film, *The Hunchback of Notre Dame*, which leaves an indelible impression.
1925	Discovers *The Phantom of the Opera* at age five.
1926	Bradbury's family moves from Waukegan to Tucson, Arizona. Elizabeth, younger sister, is born.
1927	Elizabeth dies of pneumonia. Family returns to Waukegan.
1928	Bradbury begins reading *Buck Rogers*, along with *Tarzan* and *John Carter, Warlord of Mars* by Edgar Rice Burroughs. Simultaneously discovers Hugo Gernsback's pulp magazine *Amazing Stories*.
1929	Becomes acquainted with Lyman Frank Baum's "Oz" books.
1930	Meets Blackstone the Magician and Mr. Electrico.
1932	First stories written by hand on butcher paper. Family moves to Tucson. Bradbury discovers Jules Verne. Performs magic shows at Oddfellows Hall and American Legion. Reads comics to children on Saturdays on radio station KGAR.
1933	Family returns to Waukegan.
1934	Bradbury's Aunt Neva takes him to the World's Fair in Chicago, and he is enthralled by the Century of Progress exhibit. Bradbury's father, a power lineman having trouble gaining employment during the Depression, moves his family to Los Angeles.
1937	Becomes scriptwriter, producer, and director of the *Roman Review* at Los Angeles High School. Discovers science-fiction fandom. Joins the Los Angeles Science Fiction League, founded in 1935 as a chapter of Gernsback's Science Fiction League and begins friendships with Ray Harryhausen, Forrest J. Ackerman, Robert Heinlein, Hannes Bok, Jack Williamson, Edmond Hamilton, and Henry Kuttner.

1938	First short story, "Hollerbochen's Dilemma," published in *Imagination!*, an amateur fanzine. Graduates from Los Angeles High School and sells newspapers on Los Angeles street corners through 1942.
1939	Begins publishing his fanzine, *Future Fantasia*. Meets Julius "Julie" Schwartz, and they frequent the New York World's Fair. Attends the World Science Fiction Convention in New York. Joins Wilshire Players Guild, Laraine Day's drama group.
1941	Schwartz becomes Bradbury's agent and Bradbury, in collaboration with Henry Hasse, makes his first professional sale, "Pendulum," to *Super Science Stories*. Attends Robert Heinlein's weekly writing classes.
1942	Quits selling newspapers and writes full time. Discovers his writing style in "The Lake."
1945	Breaks into writing for the "slick" magazines, such as *McCall's*. Travels to Mexico to collect masks for the Los Angeles County Museum. "The Big Black and White Game" selected for *Best American Short Stories*.
1946	Leigh Brackett works with Bradbury on his writing techniques. He completes her "Lorelei of the Red Mist" for *Planet Stories*. Dramatic radio rendition of "Killer, Come Back to Me" for *Molle Mystery Theatre* (ABC).
1947	Many of Bradbury's early stories, written 1943–47, presented in a collection in his first book, *Dark Carnival*. Receives O. Henry Award for "The Homecoming." Dramatic radio renditions of "The Meadow" for *World Security Workshop* (ABC) and "Riabouchinska" for *Suspense* (CBS). Bradbury marries Marguerite McClure (27 September). Don Congdon becomes Bradbury's literary agent.
1948	Receives O. Henry Award for "Powerhouse." "I See You Never" selected for *Best American Short Stories*. "The Meadow" selected for *Best One-Act Plays—1947–48*. Dramatic radio renditions of "Summer Night" and "The Screaming Woman" for *Suspense* (CBS).
1949	Selected best author of 1949 by National Fantasy Fan Federation. Dramatic radio renditions of "The Lake" and "The Wind" for *Radio City Playhouse* (NBC). First daughter, Susan, born.
1950	*The Martian Chronicles* (revised as *The Silver Locusts* in the UK, 1951), a collection of linked stories, receives rave review by Christopher Isherwood in *Tomorrow*. "The Great Fire" selected for *Best Humor of 1949–50*. "The World the Children Made" selected for *Best*

Chronology

Saturday Evening Post Stories. Dramatic radio renditions of "To the Future," "There Will Come Soft Rains," "Zero Hour," "Mars Is Heaven," "The Martian Chronicles," and "And the Moon Be Still Bright" for *Dimension X* (NBC); "Mars Is Heaven" for *Escape* (CBS); "The Crowd" for *Suspense* (CBS); and "The Rocket" for *NBC Presents: Short Story*.

1951 *The Illustrated Man*, short story collection, published. Dramatic radio renditions of "Dwellers in Silence," "The Veldt," "Marionettes, Inc." and "Kaleidoscope" for *Dimension X* (NBC) and "The Earth Men" for *Escape* (CBS). Bradbury stories adapted for television by other writers include "Zero Hour" and "Marionettes, Inc." for *Tales of Tomorrow* (ABC); "Zero Hour" for *Light's Out* (NBC); and "The Man" for *Out There* (CBS). Second daughter, Ramona, born.

1952 "The Other Foot" selected for *Best American Short Stories*. Edits *Timeless Stories for Today and Tomorrow*, anthology. *No Man Is an Island*, an address delivered by Ray Bradbury before the Los Angeles Chapter of the National Women's Committee of Brandeis University, published. Bradbury stories adapted for television by other writers include "The Rocket" for *CBS Television Workshop* and "Summer Night" for *Suspense* (CBS).

1953 *Fahrenheit 451* (novel), *The Flying Machine* (play), and *The Golden Apples of the Sun* (short story collection, illustrated by Joseph Mugnaini) published. Two popular early science-fiction films, *It Came from Outer Space* and *The Beast from 20,000 Fathoms*, are loosely based on Bradbury short stories. (Writes extended treatment for *It Came from Outer Space*, and *The Beast from 20,000 Fathoms* credits Bradbury's short story "The Fog Horn.") Travels to Ireland for six months to work on screenplay for John Huston's film version of *Moby Dick*. Dramatic radio renditions of "Mars Is Heaven" and "The Whole Town's Sleeping" for *ABC Radio Workshop* and "Zero Hour" for *Escape* (CBS).

1954 Receives Benjamin Franklin Magazine Award for "Sun and Shadow" and two other awards—National Institute of Arts and Letters Award in Literature and Commonwealth Club of California Literature Gold Medal Award—for *Fahrenheit 451*, which is published in three installments in *Playboy*. Bradbury story "The Black Ferris" adapted as series pilot for Sam Goldwyn Jr.

1955	*The October Country* (short story collection, illustrated by Joseph Mugnaini) and *Switch on the Night* (juvenile fiction, illustrated by Madeleine Gekiere) published. Dramatic radio renditions of "Zero Hour," "The Whole Town's Sleeping," and "Kaleidoscope" for *Suspense* (CBS); and "And the Moon Be Still as Bright," "Mars Is Heaven," "The Veldt," "Dwellers in Silence," "To the Future," and "Marionettes, Inc." for *X Minus 1* (NBC). Bradbury story "Cora and the Great Wide World" adapted for television by other writer for *G.E. Theater* (CBS). Third daughter, Bettina, born.
1956	Receives Boys Club of America Junior Book Award for *Switch on the Night*, juvenile fiction. *Moby Dick*, screenplay by John Huston and Bradbury, released. Edits *The Circus of Dr. Lao and Other Improbable Stories*, anthology. Bradbury's teleplays include "Shopping for Death," based on his short story "Touched with Fire," for *Alfred Hitchcock* (CBS); and "The Marked Bullet" for *Jane Wyman's Fireside Theater* (NBC). Dramatic radio renditions of "Hail and Farewell" and "Season of Disbelief" for *CBS Radio Workshop*. Bradbury story "And So Died Riabouchinska" adapted for television by other writer for *Alfred Hitchcock* (CBS).
1957	*Dandelion Wine*, novel, published. Father dies.
1958	Bradbury's teleplays include "The Wonderful Ice Cream Suit" for *Rendezvous* (CBS); "Design For Loving," based on his short story "Marionettes, Inc.," for *Alfred Hitchcock* (CBS); and "The Gift" for *Steve Canyon* (NBC). "The Day It Rained Forever" selected for *Best American Short Stories*. Fourth daughter, Alexandra, born.
1959	Short story collection *A Medicine for Melancholy* (revised as *The Day It Rained Forever* in the UK) published. Writes the teleplay "Special Delivery," based on his short story "Come into My Cellar," for *Alfred Hitchcock* (CBS).
1960	Writes teleplay "The Tunnel to Yesterday" for *Trouble Shooters* (ABC). Stage production of "The Meadow" at the Huntington Hartford Theatre in Hollywood, California.
1961	Composes voice-over narration for the movie *King of Kings*.
1962	Publishes his novel *Something Wicked This Way Comes* and his short story collections *R Is for Rocket* and *The Small Assassin* (abridgment of *Dark Carnival*). *Icarus Montgolfier Wright*, an eighteen-minute animated film based on a Bradbury concept and co-written by

Bradbury and George C. Johnson, is released. Bradbury writes three teleplays: "The Faith of Aaron Menefee," based on the short story by Stanley Ellin, for *Alfred Hitchcock* (CBS); "The Jail" for *Alcoa Premiere Television* (ABC); and "I Sing the Body Electric!," which becomes a short story in 1969, for *The Twilight Zone* (ABC). Stage production of "Way in the Middle of the Air" at the Desilu Gower Studios in Hollywood, California.

1963 First collection of drama, *The Anthem Sprinters and Other Antics*, which contains "The Great Collision of Monday Last," "The First Night of Lent," "A Clear View of an Irish Mist," and "The Anthem Sprinters, The Queen's Own Evaders," published. The play *Yesterday, Today and Tomorrow*, which is derived from three stories ("A Medicine for Melancholy," "The Wonderful Ice Cream Suit," and "The Pedestrian"), is presented at Desilu Gower Studios in Hollywood, California. *Icarus Montgolfier Wright* is nominated for Academy Award for best animated short subject of the year and receives Golden Eagle Film Award.

1964 *The Machineries of Joy*, short story collection, published. The U.S. Government Pavilion at the New York World's Fair commissions Bradbury to compose the screenplay *American Journey*. Bradbury produces *The World of Ray Bradbury*, which consists of "The Veldt," "The Pedestrian," and "To the Chicago Abyss," at the Coronet Theater in Hollywood, California. Bradbury story "The Jar" adapted for television by other writer for *Alfred Hitchcock* (CBS).

1965 *The Autumn People*, Bradbury stories adapted for E.C. Comics by Albert B. Feldstein; *A Device Out of Time: A One-Act Play*; and *The Vintage Bradbury: Ray Bradbury's Own Selection of His Best Stories* published. *The Wonderful Ice Cream Suit*, a presentation of three one-act plays ("A Device Out of Time," "The Wonderful Ice Cream Suit," and "The Day It Rained Forever"), produced by Bradbury at the Coronet Theater in Hollywood, California. *The World of Ray Bradbury* runs again, this time in New York at the Orpheum Theater. "The Other Foot" selected for *Fifty Best American Short Stories: 1915–1965*. Bradbury receives Mrs. Ann Radcliffe Award from the Count Dracula Society.

1966 *Tomorrow Midnight*, Bradbury stories adapted for E.C. Comics by Albert B. Feldstein; two short story collections, *Twice 22* (which collects the stories in *A Medicine for Melancholy* and *The Golden Apples of the Sun*) and *S Is for Space*; and two plays, *The Day It Rained Forever: A Comedy in One Act* and *The Pedestrian: A Fantasy in One Act*, published. Director François Truffaut's film adaptation of *Fahrenheit 451* is released. The one-hour radio drama "Leviathan '99" is produced by British Broadcasting Company (BBC). Bradbury's mother dies.

1967 *Dandelion Wine* staged as a full-length musical drama at Lincoln Center, New York. *The Anthem Sprinters*, which consists of Bradbury one-act Irish plays ("The Great Collision of Monday Last," "The First Night of Lent," "A Clear View of an Irish Mist," and "The Anthem Sprinters") is staged at the Beverly Hills Playhouse in California.

1968 Receives Aviation Space Writers Association Award and the Robert S. Ball Memorial Award for the *Life* magazine science article "An Impatient Gulliver above Our Roofs." "Leviathan '99," the original one-hour radio drama, is broadcast over the BBC in London, England. *Any Friend of Nicholas Nickleby's Is a Friend of Mine* staged at the Actor's Studio West in Hollywood, California.

1969 *I Sing the Body Electric!*, short story collection, published. Director Jack Smight's film version of Bradbury's *The Illustrated Man* released. *Christus Apollo*, cantata, with music by Jerry Goldsmith and lyrics by Bradbury, is staged at Royce Hall, University of California, Los Angeles. *Any Friend of Nicholas Nickleby's Is a Friend of Mine* is staged at Rio Hondo College.

1970 "Mars Is Heaven" selected for the Science Fiction Hall of Fame by the Science Fiction Writers of America.

1971 *Old Ahab's Friend, and Friend to Noah, Speak His Piece: A Celebration*, verse, published. Panel discussion at California Institute of Technology with Ray Bradbury, Bruce Murray, Arthur C. Clarke, Walter Sullivan, and Carl Sagan published in 1973 as *Mars and the Mind of Man*. Bradbury receives Mrs. Ann Radcliffe Award from the Count Dracula Society.

1972 *Madrigals for the Space Age* (for mixed chorus and narrator with piano accompaniment, music by Lalo Schifrin, text by Bradbury), *The Wonderful Ice Cream Suit and Other Plays*, and *The Halloween Tree* (juvenile fiction, illustrated by Joseph Mugnaini) published.

Chronology xxxiii

Dandelion Wine is staged at California State College, Fullerton; and *Leviathan '99*, an adaption by Bradbury from his radio play, is performed at Samuel Goldwyn Studio Stage 9 Theater in Hollywood, California. Receives television screenplay credit under the pseudonym Douglas Spaulding, along with Ed Weinberger (Edwin Boyd), for *Picasso Summer*, which is based on Bradbury's "In a Season of Calm Weather," written in 1957. *The Screaming Woman*, a short story adaptation, is the Universal-ABC Movie of the Week.

1973 *When Elephants Last in the Dooryard Bloomed: Celebrations for Almost Any Day in the Year*, verse, and *Zen and the Art of Writing and The Joy of Writing: Two Essays*, published. *Madrigals for the Space Age*, with music by Lalo Schifrin and lyrics by Bradbury, is presented at Los Angeles Music Center, Dorothy Chandler Pavilion. *Pillar of Fire*, which includes "Pillar of Fire," "Kaleidoscope," and "The Fog Horn," is staged at the Little Theatre, California State College, Fullerton.

1974 *That Son of Richard III: A Birth Announcement*, verse, published. *Dandelion Wine* produced off-Broadway at the Phoenix Side Show.

1975 *Pillar of Fire and Other Plays* and *Ray Bradbury*, short story collection, published.

1976 *Long After Midnight*, a retrospection collection and World Fantasy Best Collection nominee (1977), and *The Best of Bradbury* published. Bradbury's teleplay "Murderer" is presented by WGBH-TV, Boston. Three dramatic productions: *Leviathan '99* at the Samuel Goldwyn Studios Stage 9 Theatre; *The Martian Chronicles* at the Cricket Theatre, Minneapolis; and *Dandelion Wine*, adapted for the stage by Peter John Bailey, in the Kreeger Theater at Arena Stage, Washington, D.C.

1977 *Where Robot Mice and Robot Men Run 'Round in Robot Towns: New Poems, Both Light and Dark* and *Man Dead? Then God Is Slain!* (illustrated by Hans Burkhardt), verse, published. Receives Lifetime Achievement Award from the World Fantasy Convention. *The Martian Chronicles* presented at the Colony Theatre in Burbank, California.

1978 *The Mummies of Guanajuato* (an illustrated version of Bradbury's story "The Next in Line," with photos by Archie Lieberman) and *Twin Hieroglyphs That Swim the River Dust* (verse collection) published.

The Bike Repairmen: A Poem (designed and printed by Pall Bohne for the Ray Bradbury Celebration, Oct. 23–31, Twentieth Anniversary of California State University) published.

1979 *The Attic Where the Meadow Greens* (verse collection), *The Poet Considers His Resources* (poem), *The Aqueduct: A Martian Chronicle* (story), and *Beyond 1984: A Remembrance of Things Future* (verse and essays) published. Receives two awards: the Aviation Space Writers Association Award for the ABC television documentary *Infinite Space: Beyond Apollo* and the Best Poet Balrog Award. Receives a D.Litt. from Whittier College.

1980 *The Stories of Ray Bradbury, The Last Circus and The Electrocution* (two stories, illustrated by Joseph Mugnaini), and *The Ghosts of Forever* (a large format illustrated book with an essay, a story, and five poems) published. The television miniseries *The Martian Chronicles* airs on NBC. Presented the Gandolf Award (Grand Master) from the World Science Fiction Society at the Hugo Award Ceremonies.

1981 *The Haunted Computer and the Android Pope* (collected verse) and *Then Is All Love? It Is, It Is!* (verse, illustrated by Scott Fitzgerald) published. *Dandelion Wine* performed at the Colony Theatre in Burbank, California.

1982 *The Complete Poems of Ray Bradbury* published. Bradbury co-authors the teleplays "The Electric Grandmother" (NBC Peacock Theater), "All Summer in a Day" (PBS), and "The Invisible Boy" (CBS Library: Robbers, Rooftops and Witches). Receives George Foster Peabody Award from the University of Georgia, an Emmy nomination from the Academy of Television Arts and Sciences, and American Film Festival Blue Ribbon Award for "The Electric Grandmother."

1983 *Dinosaur Tales* (juvenile fiction) and *The Love Affair* (a short story and two poems) published. Walt Disney Studios' *Something Wicked This Way Comes*, with screenplay by Bradbury.

1984 *A Memory of Murder* (crime fiction collection), *Forever and the Earth: Radio Dramatization*, and *The Last Good Kiss: A Poem* (illustrated by Hans Burkhardt) published. Receives Jules Verne Award and Valentine Davies Award from the Writers Guild of America for his cinema work.

1985 *Death Is a Lonely Business* (murder mystery) and *Long After Ecclesiastes: New Biblical Texts* (verse, illustrated by D'Ambrosio) published. HBO produces six television episodes of *Ray Bradbury Theater*. Receives Home Box Office (HBO) Ace Award for Writing a Dramatic Series. Presented Body of Work Award from PEN.

1986 *A Device Out of Time* (*A Device Out of Time: A One-Act Play* 1965) published.

1987 *Death Has Lost Its Charm for Me* (verse), *Fever Dream* (juvenile fiction, illustrated by Darrel Anderson), and *The April Witch, The Fog Horn, The Other Foot*, and *The Veldt* (*A Creative Classic* series, illustrated by Gary Kelley) published. "Walking on Air," an original teleplay, released.

1988 *The Toynbee Convector* (short story collection) and *Ray Bradbury's Falling Upward* (first produced in Los Angeles at the Melrose Theatre) published. USA Network produces fifty-nine episodes of *Ray Bradbury Theater* beginning in 1988 and ending in 1992. Receives Los Angeles Drama Critics Circle Award for *The Martian Chronicles*. Nominated for two Bram Stoker Awards: Best Short Story ("The Young Thing at the Top of the Stairs") and Best Collection (*The Toynbee Convector*).

1989 *The Climate of Palettes*, verse, published. Receives Nebula Grandmaster Award for his lifetime achievements.

1990 *Classic Stories 1: Selections from The Golden Apples of the Sun and R Is for Rocket, Classic Stories 2: Selections from A Medicine for Melancholy and S Is for Space, The Day It Rained Forever: A New Musical* (music by Bill Whitefield, lyrics by Bradbury and Whitefield, and additional music and lyrics by Tom Gire), and *A Graveyard for Lunatics* (novel) published.

1991 *On Stage: A Chrestomathy of His Plays* (10 one-act plays) *Yestermorrow: Obvious Answers to Impossible Futures* (essays), and *The Smile* (juvenile fiction) published.

1992 *Green Shadows, White Whale*, novel, published.

1993 *Switch on the Night* (illustrated by Leo and Diane Dillon) published. Hanna-Barbera Studios' animated version of *The Halloween Tree* wins an Emmy.

1995 *The World of Ray Bradbury* performed at the Colony Theatre in Burbank, California.

1996 *Quicker Than the Eye*, short story collection, published.

1997	*Driving Blind*, short story collection, published and nominated for British Fantasy Society Best Collection and World Fantasy Best Collection awards. *With Cat for Comforter* and *Dogs Think That Every Day Is Christmas*, verse, published.
1998	*From the Dust Returned* (novel), *Ahmed and the Oblivion Machine* (juvenile fable, illustrated by Chris Lane), and *Christus Apollo: Cantata Celebrating the Eighth Day of Creation and the Promise of the Ninth* (illustrated by D'Ambrosio) published. Disney's *The Wonderful Ice Cream Suit*, screenplay by Bradbury, is released.
1999	Bradbury suffers a stroke.
2000	Recipient of the National Book Foundation's 2000 Medal for Distinguished Contribution to American Letters. *Dandelion Wine* is performed at the Colony Theatre in Burbank, California.
2001	*A Chapbook for Burnt-Out Priests, Rabbis, and Ministers* (essays) and *Ray Bradbury Collected Short Stories* (juvenile fiction in the Great Author Series) published. *Dandelion Wine* is performed at the Colony Theatre in Burbank, California.
2002	*One More for the Road* (short story collection), *I Live by the Invisible: New and Selected Poems*, and *They Have Not Seen the Stars: The Collected Poetry of Ray Bradbury* published.
2003	*Let's All Kill Constance* (novel) and *The Best of Ray Bradbury: The Graphic Novel* (comic book) published.

Conversations with Ray Bradbury

The Market Is Not the Story:
An Interview with Ray Bradbury
R. Walton Willems / 1948

Writers' Markets & Methods, 15.3 (March 1948), pp. 8–9. Reprinted by permission.

Ray Bradbury started writing when he was twelve. The stories were sequels to Tarzan—ones he couldn't afford to buy. He spent the next nine years learning how to reach a larger audience.

Bradbury, today, still writes stories he would want to read. He doesn't write for the money market, for certain magazines, nor for a chosen audience. He writes the best story he can to sell where it may. Most of his stories are on the fantasy side.

"Most selling writers could produce a story of any type," Bradbury says, "but the author who prefers westerns, for instance, can write fine ones with a good deal of sincerity in them. This is a feeling he could not give a type of story he didn't like. The sincerity extends to the reader and improves the story immeasurably.

"Which doesn't mean there is anything wrong with writing for money, for those who prefer to do so. The money-writer is writing for a purpose and he's in some ways on sounder footing than many a writer who wouldn't think of writing for money. He knows what his objective is."

Bradbury believes the writer must know his objective, must know why he is writing. If it's money he wants, and only money, he should admit this to himself and go about finding ways to make it. But, if, like Bradbury, one considers artistic worth and reputation above all, then this, too, should be admitted and said author should resign himself to little money but great returns in reputation until his name is established, whereupon the money will begin appearing as reward for honest work well done. A goal to reach will bring out individuality and style that would not develop in a writer trying to fit first one, and then another, market.

He's got reasons for thinking writers shouldn't study markets too intensely.

"The writer who slants his material is striving to copy something. He should develop his own product, should know what it is, and should have some idea of where to sell. But he shouldn't be writing the typical *X Magazine* story. The editor can get that from his regular writers."

Not slanting has shown results. A science-fiction story Bradbury wrote, expecting it to land in a pulp, hit a top Canadian publication at twenty times the pulp price. Reason: He hadn't written down for pulp.

"Know what you have to offer. If you don't think it good don't submit it. If you think it your best don't be afraid of any market."

Bradbury learned courage in submissions the hard way. Several stories were on file for three years before he nerved himself to submit them. One, a psychological study of a neurotic boy with a Christ complex, finally went, and was sold, to *Charm*. Hardly a likely market. A vampire story went to *Harper's* and stayed there! Another vampire story sold to *Mademoiselle*. They were good enough to overcome editorial reluctance to stories so far afield. The vampire story was so unsuitable to *Mademoiselle* that the editor changed to a vampire issue to suit the story!

Again, "I See You Never" was in file for two years before submission. The *New Yorker* used it, and, a few weeks ago, it won a place in *The Best American Short Stories* of 1948.

Readers have found a Bradbury story doesn't change quality according to the magazine. The editor knows it is the best Bradbury can do regardless of rates. Giving only of the best is the surest way, Bradbury feels, for an author to hope to please both editors and readers.

"I don't know what a typical Bradbury story is," he admits. "I hope the one I write tomorrow is better than the one I write today, of course, because I expect the one today to teach me something more about writing.

"My stories are imaginative because that's my field. Sincerity is important. It's hard to make the reader feel something the author doesn't. . . . No, I never write down, and I'm not ashamed of anything I turn out. I make it my best work. . . . I don't use pseudonyms, but sometimes the editors will insist upon one."

Bradbury reads literature as an aid to writing. "This might sound strange for a writer whose work has gone mostly to the pulps. Yet, the masters of literature were, first, masters of telling a story well, and the writer can learn from them. The writer should do his best for the story, not for the market. His best is to provide entertainment to serve the purpose of the reader. If the writer has a message it must be secondary.

"The writer should strive for a well paced story, written as well as he can handle it. The writer's vocabulary need not be extensive—he shouldn't throw unusual words at the reader—but I do believe in using the right word. The reader should be given something more than the basic meaning by the use of words that are dynamic and colorful, that provide pictures for the reader.

"Every writer must be his character. Describe the character's reactions, feelings, sensations—what he smells, and whether, for instance, he feels extreme heat or cold. This brings the reader closer to the character. This must be done in moderation, though. The character's immediate circumstances must be kept in mind and what he is likely to notice taken into consideration.

"I try to enable the reader to *see*. Ray Bradbury should never come between reader and story. I want the reader to be there. The writer's personality or wit shouldn't come into the narration of the story. Flavor, color, humor or slang should come through actions and dialogue of the characters, not from intruding asides from the author."

Bradbury finds stories grow best from characters and ideas. The writer who works with these will create many new stories for each one he writes.

"I get dry spells, of course, but I have some protection against them. I usually take three to six months to finish a story. But I'm not working on it all that time. I try to keep twenty-eight stories in process during one year. I carry a story forward when I feel like working on that story. When I'm not as interested in it as I should be I put it away and work on something for which I can show some enthusiasm. There is always some story to fit the mood, and of course, with so many stories going I have the backlog and the momentum to go on when ideas are temporarily scarce.

"I believe the writer should work on something, *anything*, to be writing. I work five to eight hours a day, at least five days a week."

What many writers would consider a finished story often goes back in file for possible later revision.

"I get the most effective final copy when I'm not too objective about the first draft. I get words down so the idea is there, and the correct mood and tension. Revision is largely a matter of cutting to speed the pace and eliminate wordage that might be more important to the author than to the reader. Being too objective and critical, too analytical on the first draft sometimes freezes a writer. The writing doesn't come naturally, but is stiff and awkward— self-conscious."

Bradbury believes two things should be avoided by the beginning writer. First is collaboration. Here each writer hopes the other will do the work. Second, stay away from first person writing. Few stories are not better in the third person, and the writer always using the first person is working toward a thought-habit hard to break.

"Writers must know human behavior. They should learn how to create a character which the reader will accept as recognizably human. The writer should study people, naturally, and a few books on psychology should be read. But don't let the technical psychological terms enter your actual writing. Use your knowledge to motivate characters, not to impress the reader."

It's always interesting to find what a writer thinks a writer is. "They certainly aren't thinkers," Bradbury said. "They're not idea men or spreaders of knowledge. Not primarily, at least. The fiction writer is, first, an emotionalist. Whether he admits it or not. A story is not successful through logic, or beautiful thinking, or by its appeal to the intellect, though these elements must be present. It succeeds in its appeal to the readers' emotions. Many of the best loved stories are weak in plot and idea, implausible in conception. They are great because they get under the reader's skin, causing him to react sympathetically with the characters."

Bradbury sees nothing complicated about plotting. "I put my character at a turning point in his life, where he needs something. Then he will almost automatically be in conflict with someone trying to prevent him from getting it. The story grows from the conflict.

"No, I don't know any tricks to make writing easy. It's work and study and writing.... Method? Sit down and write.... In addition, I frighten the neighborhood by shouting for quiet so I can work."

Bradbury's idea file is unusual. Instead of filing ideas he writes an opening. The idea is in use, the mood is set, the story is started and ready to continue at any time.

"Some writers are sure their stories are not considered by the editors," Bradbury said. "Personally, I've submitted a lot of work to editors who'd never heard of me. Often they bought. Sometimes stories came back with letters telling why they weren't buying."

Bradbury knows discouragement, knows it mustn't be allowed to get the writer down. He wrote for four years before submitting his first story, then submitted for five years before selling. He learned much in this time and success came because he kept going.

He's found discouragement comes even with steady sales. The writer doesn't acquire seniority and the right to an income as does the employee. Each story is a new experience in writing, and selling must stand on its own.

Bradbury believes short stories are where the fiction writer should learn his trade. The short story is the easiest to sell, and principles learned here apply to all fields of writing and dramatic presentation.

He admits he doesn't plan the future of the story. "Working for the story itself is enough. I complete it as best I can. If it wins a prize award I'm happy, but a story can't be a planned prize winner. . . ."

And when the Hollywood studios come around interested in buying stories which the writer has almost forgotten about, that just bears out Bradbury's contention that it's worthwhile to put your best in every story.

Sum and Substance: With Ray Bradbury and Herman Harvey

Herman Harvey / 1962

Produced by Joseph Sands, directed by Jim Johnson, and created by Herman Harvey with the University of Southern California, KNXT Public Affairs. Reprinted by permission. [Transcribed by Steven Aggelis]

Herman Harvey: In the contemporary world of writing, there is a species which goes by the name of science fiction. And whether one argues that such literature is unique to our time or that, indeed, it is as old as the spoken word, there seems to be little question that among the very finest examples of such writing are the works of Ray Bradbury. To be certain, Ray Bradbury writes about rocket ships, about interstellar excursions, and about strange, incredible universes. But, he does this always within the context of man, of his needs and hopes, his understandable frailty, and the occasional impressive gesture of heroism. And it was of these that Ray Bradbury spoke when we met, when he ventured to describe what he had come to see as the "Sum and Substance."

There seems to be little question that Ray Bradbury is one of our most creative and provocative writers. In our characteristically mad rush to attach labels to everything and, possibly, thereby make life a little more safe, he has been called a science-fiction writer. If there must be a label, I prefer to think of Ray Bradbury as one of the long line of distinctly gifted people who once were called the "tellers of tales." To be sure, on occasion, he uses familiar ingredients—rocket ships, space travel, incredibly strange worlds—but usually that's entirely beside the point. For example, in a story he wrote some years ago called, incidentally, "Way in the Middle of the Air," he tells of the Southern Negroes' growing indignation, of how in a massive exodus they leave the South, settle on Mars, and Ray Bradbury deftly, perceptively, incisively sketches the economic chaos which explodes in the South. In a sequel to the story, Ray Bradbury makes it necessary for what is now a distinctly Caucasian Earth population to leave the Earth, and to seek refuge and safety on Mars, now, of course, populated by the Negro. What now develops is one of the most impressive explorations of both human frailty and human compassion that our literature has to offer.

For well over twenty years, this has been the nature of Ray Bradbury's writing—writing which, somehow, consistently addresses itself to matters of the human heart and spirit, of human dignity, of the love of one's fellow man, and the joy of simple, unadulterated living. And so these were the things we talked about when I met with Ray Bradbury. And as we talked, I asked him what it was that he now saw as meaningful and substantial in his own life, what he would want to say were he to give words to his own feelings of commitment and value—what for him represented ingredients which were substantial and enduring.

Ray Bradbury: Well, it's come to me, fairly late, perhaps, to consider that there are two honorable professions in this world. And if I could give back to the creative people of the world the sense I have received from a lifetime of doing and then thinking about it, I would like to say to the creative people—especially to writers; this is my field after all: "You are in the same profession as the doctors of the world." The doctors cure the bodies, and the aesthetic people come along, the writers come along, and help to cure the minds. They are working in the same field as with psychologists and psychiatrists. And if they're working at the top of their form, if they're on good terms with their subconscious, if they're creating out of a sense of fun and enjoyment in the world, then they are digging out of themselves things that they can offer to the world. When these things are offered in this way, they can then help people throughout the world even as medical people help with their medicines. It's taken me a long time to believe this. I may have begun to believe it some years ago, but I couldn't prove it, and now I've begun to observe ways of proving it, and trying to do this sort of thing with my work.

HH: Doesn't the creative person realize this?
RB: I think most creative people I have met have a strong sense of inferiority they're battling all the time. It's probably one of the reasons why they went into writing, or painting, or acting to begin with. So, they come late to maturity in many ways, and they come late to full and substantial belief in what they're doing. And it's taken me until about two years ago to begin to see the ways we work. For instance, this is the way I line it up. A good story, a good play, a good film does the following things: that we build a tension toward laughter, and at a given point in a good play, or a good film, or a good story,

we give permission to laugh, and people laugh and release that tension. In a tragedy, we build a tension all during the drama, or the film, or the story toward crying, and we then give permission to cry, and people may cry and release that tension. When it comes to love, if we see a beautiful thing, if we see a beautiful woman, if we're telling a love story let's say, and we have a tension build then for the fruition of this love, we give permission to love. We give permission for the pursuit and the conquering, and this tension is relieved. There are many other tensions. We have tensions for violence that build in us as people in this world. And then we say to people: "You have built such a tension about a given problem in the world today or in your own life, I give you permission to pick up that greatest of all villains and throw him off of the building at the end of this work of art and release that tension.

Now, there's another tension I would like to address myself to. It is not often enough discussed by creative people, and I think because we've ignored it we've come to a time in many of our plays, many of our novels, many of our short stories, where we've neglected to observe this theory of tensions I'm discussing here. And as a result, we've wound up being rather sick at times in the past, in the recent past. And this is the tension, then, of being sick. If we're going to write a play about a very unpleasant thing, let us say, if we're going to tell the worst there is to tell about human beings—and it must be told; I'm not saying that we shouldn't do it. But, if we say to people, "I'm going to tell you such a story, I'm going to write you such a play, or show you such a film that at the very end you'll want to be sick," then we must give permission to throw up. Now, not to know this is not to know yet another tension and finding ways to release that tension and allow people to be really ill, very decidedly ill, because only by being ill can we become well. We know this is a function of all dogs who throw up and then go out into the fields and eat sweet grass. So, this is one of the things a writer can do. If he knows what he's doing, fine. But, he cannot know during the process. I don't ask him to know during the process. But before and after, he can examine this piece of work that he has done, and if he decides it is a sick piece, then he must find ways of relieving this tension he's given people, rather than to throw down their throats and cram down into their stomachs a gigantic hairball which stays in their crop and they can't deliver forth.

We then wind up with a situation similar to the one we have in newspapers today. In other words, the newspaper functions the same way in most of our communities today as the artist who does not know how to create, doesn't know what he's creating, or how to go about relaxing tensions. The newspaper is the hairball of our time. And it creates these tensions. It thrusts them into our mind, and it winds up delivering us into the hands of a feeling which says, "Life is no damned good. We might as well blow our brains out. We might as well destroy Russia and ourselves on the same magnificent day." Well, any time you're playing around with a death wish in this way, any time you're playing around with the dark side of mankind, with the destructive side of mankind, it behooves you to know what you're playing with. Now, the newspapers are irresponsible, except for three or four in this country, and almost everywhere in the world, because they're playing upon this tension. They're increasing this tension continually. They are the people who are playing Russian roulette, but with us. They hand us the gun day after day and say, "Put it to your temple and keep pulling the trigger, not just once but continually."

So, this is, I think, the long way around to my point that you cannot in your art duplicate the "half function" that is going on in your society, in the newspapers and other places in your society, where a certain tension is not being relieved. It is up to the artist, then, to look to that tension and see if he can relieve it, not by playing the Pollyanna, not by giving happy endings, but by making sure that the sickness is a whole, and that the sickness finally results in a cleansing by being really sick. And this moves us suddenly into the field, to help build my point and show you where I'm going with it, of the horror film. I might bring this up as an example.

A really bad horror film does nothing for nobody. It's just there; it's silly. We see them on TV all the time. We go to the theaters because we expect we're going to see more than we wind up with. But here, too, the art form malfunctions by not realizing a good horror film partakes of philosophy, of religion, of the mystery of life. And then the writer or the creator in the horror film might say, "What are we trying to do here?" We're trying to make do with death. We're trying to make do with destruction. So, a good mythology like Dracula, it's a really fine mythological way of making do with death because what does this story do for us? It holds up before us a symbol of death and says, "Here's Count Dracula. Isn't he magnificent? And he is going to scare the hell out of you during the next two hours. He is going to represent the unknowable." Now, for centuries, our religions, our philosophies have tried to find a way for us to accept our position on this world. We have various approaches, and various religions, various philosophies. We have told ourselves ghost stories. We have the Grimm's fairy tales. All of these are ways of rearing up before us the unknowable at times, so that we can make do with death. Well, a horror film then says, "I parade before you a symbol of the unknown. We can't see death. It is a part of living. It is a cessation of life, and, therefore, since it is merely a cessation and not a thing, we have to find a symbol to act it out for us. So, we bring on Count Dracula, and at the end, then, of a really beautifully made horror film, we have another bit of magic, and we have a formula. We have a stake, or we have the cross, or we have the Bible, we have some symbolic thing that we can use to do death in. Then, symbolically, we can release our tension in regard to the horror of the unknown. And a good horror film allows us, then, to destroy death, and for a little while be on better terms with the unknown, just as a good parable in the Bible allows us to do the same thing. Or the good advice of a philosopher friend or a psychiatrist can help us do the same. We need varying attacks to these tensions on many levels. And to ignore one is to become a malfunctioning human being. And I believe the reason why I become prouder of writing—I didn't start out with this intent at all. I was just having a good time, but I am proud now to see that in my work and in the work of others I have helped people to cry. I have helped people to laugh. I have helped people to be violent. I have helped people to be a little sick. And then I have shown them the way to the fields where the dogs lie themselves down to eat the green grass. So, it's a long answer to a very short question. But this is the way I would sum up my life. And I would hope other writers could finally sum up their lives and look to their writing and see if, first of all, they're enjoying themselves in it, and if they are, then they'll automatically be performing some of these functions.

HH: There's a couple of things that intrigue me here, Mr. Bradbury. One, I think, as I listen to you develop these points, that you may be underlining with a very heavy pencil the fundamental social responsibility of the author. You are saying to them, are you not?: "Now, look, you have a responsibility. You should do things in a certain way." There is a therapeutic value, and I mean this in a very broad sense, therapy for one's soul, mind, or whatever. Is this true?
RB: Yes, it's definitely true, and it becomes political without having to be political. That's the good thing about it too. If you're functioning on all these levels, if you're releasing all these tensions, you invariably fall into political spheres. And, especially if you're working in science fiction, let's say, but you're not pontificating. You're automatically carrying out your responsibility to yourself, first of all, because you're trying to solve your own problems. And the sad thing about our culture today, and the one thing I would try to warn people about, if I were giving advice to young writers, or people moving into any field, is the fact that we have put the cart before the horse. We're far more interested in profit. Everyone is out for the fast buck. Everyone wants a big home and a nice

car. And, actually, these should come as rewards for work well done, later in life. And, as a result, they do work they think will sell in a given field—which means they begin to act unhealthy in their work. The cleansing process, the therapeutic process that should be going on between a writer and his typewriter, or his pen and ink, is cut across, then, by this commercial function. And he begins to lie. And as soon as he begins to lie in his work, it becomes noncreative, nontherapeutic to himself, and nontherapeutic to anyone that reads him. There is nothing of value, then, to be taken out for himself or for anyone else.

HH: I wonder how many writers that would be at all intrigued with the prospect of being referred to, essentially, as a "tension reduction station."
RB: Well, I don't know. [Laughs.] We shouldn't try to put too much of a label on this process. It's interesting to discuss; it's interesting to break it down. But, then, as soon as one is finished with the discussion, the main thing you want to say to people is: "Go and love very much in your work." And if you do not love the idea of being alive in this world to begin with, you really can't be a very good creative person. That means, love also means, hating in a certain special way. The greatest artists in the world, men like [Francisco] Goya, loved hating. And there was a delicious quality, a great sense of fun, in finding the proper enemy and attacking. And out of this passionate thing, this passionate dedication for the truth as they saw it, to go into battle and destroy kings and princes, and to make war against war, and to hate poverty. And a man like [Charles] Dickens came along and saw London the way it was, and enjoyed hating London the way he saw it, and penning it down. So, it doesn't mean just one attitude. And when I say "loving life," that means loving everything in it, paying attention to it, knowing it, and daring to put it down, and examining the dark things in great detail.

HH: The point that occurs to me in all of this is that, again, if one takes this from a general therapeutic standpoint, one says at one point or another: "This writing or this work is good for you in the therapeutic context." I think this also implies that, possibly, some writing is not good for you. I worry, then, about the censorship implication of keeping one and not the other. The other thing that intrigues me in this is the possibility that, really, perhaps, tension should be around and allowed to remain at a level. Perhaps, this is the kind of thing that galvanizes a reader into action—some kind of final fitting together of material that, perhaps, has not been resolved successfully.

RB: That's an excellent point. And there are many stories I've written over the years where I've had to make this very decision. If I want a certain action from my reader, or a reaction, do I get him to move by relaxing his tension at this point, or by giving it to him and making him keep it? I've used both approaches, and, then, I've used the in-between approach. Sometimes shock is a fabulous thing. I had a story in *Saturday Night Post* some years ago, about a boy and girl who fell under this spell of a television room. And the television room became the mother and father. And when the real mother and father, seeing that the function of the parents had been taken over by the room, tried to turn it off, the children killed the parents, using the room to destroy them. Well, now, this is a very shocking way of ending a story, a very horrible way. But, I called attention to certain problems going on in our society in such a way that, I think, you're unable to forget the story, and, maybe, some days later could relate it to the function of television in your own life. This is a case where I left the tension at a fairly high level, even though I destroyed the parents. But, there was no happy ending. There was no relaxation on other levels. And I hope people went away and thought about it. This problem rises again and again, and I have used varying solutions. If I wanted people to go off and think about the colored problem in America, I might want to keep them at the top of their tension. But there are other times, however, especially in the science-fiction field, I think you have to examine your total society. Let's put it this way: We've been living for quite a long while now in a state of tension in the world. And we don't like it. We don't like this uneasy peace. But, there's nothing we can do about it—that is, insofar as starting a war is concerned. That would relax the tension. It really would [laughs], in a tremendous way. So, we have to find other outlets. And, with our newspapers driving us toward suicide continually, it's a good time for writers to find ways of solving some of these problems on other levels for the reader, as a countermeasure to what the newspapers are doing. I don't believe in a suicidal time that art can be suicidal. It has to be more constructive. Conversely, in a much more quiet time, it is up to the writer to be a little more suicidal. In other words, if everything is running too peacefully, then the artist must come along and shake people up and say: "Bring yourself out of this stupor, for God's sake, or we'll destroy ourselves by inactivity." So, I think you look at your total time and say: "What is the—how does the boat ride right now? Do I bail out? Or do I pour a little water into the boat? One or the other. What kind of irritant should I be?"

HH: I see this from the outside—the view from outside. Might I ask something about, perhaps, the view from within, as it were? That, indeed, as a craftsman, these are things within your control—that, indeed, you use them beautifully and admirably, I grant. What happens to you when you write? What sorts of things, in terms of your own perceptions, your own development, your own growth—the questions that come to you?

RB: First of all, there is a great sense of elation. I think I'm one of the happiest writers I know, simply because I'm always going with my emotions. I write out of my emotions. I write out of my need to express myself. If I get good and mad at *Harper's Bazaar* magazine, let's say, for one of their strange issues, with their very odd people from another world—I think it's published on Mars, don't you? [Herman Harvey laughs.], *Harper's Bazaar*. I'm quite sure it is, and it's being rocketed into us every week here. Or if I'm particularly delighted with some new discovery or a relationship, let us say. I just wrote a story I'm very pleased with—I don't know if it's going to sell or not—but I finished it and sent it off. And I did it because I had to do it. I noticed the resemblance (I lived in Ireland for some time a few years ago.), and I was able to observe the Irish male and his position in the world, and the fact that he remained unmarried until he was forty, and lived in the pubs most of the time, or the cinema. And then I brought in a crew of six—a very elderly gentleman and five young men in their twenties—from Fire Island. And I had these six sort of twittering, birdlike males arrive in Ireland, to the despair and dismay of the local citizenry. And I then compared the Irish male and the male in his bright plumage brought over from Fire Island, and I did a story which is nothing more than going down the line and proving they're almost identical, except in final function. And I don't know if this story's going to wind up in *Playboy*—I hope it does; it'd be a nice change. But out of a sense of sheer delight at finding these similarities, I had to make the comparison and write the story. Then, if I get very mad at something—for instance, you get arrested in parts of L.A. for being a pedestrian; I don't like that—and I write a short story about that. If something upsets me with the colored situation, and I take the Negroes and I put them in rocket ships and send them off to Mars, in a short story, to rid myself of that tension. So, everything comes right off the top of my mind, and, as a result of writing, immediately, within the hour after I'm angry, or within the hour after I'm sick at something, or within the hour after being delighted. . . . I think I've kept myself moving and growing pretty well over the years, with an accumulation of acts of making this gigantic tapestry, I guess you'd say, of emotions noted and acted upon.

HH: You mentioned the anger in specific fashion. I imagine there are other dimensions of emotional response that motivate you.
RB: Yes, well, this sort of thing happened to me some years ago. I went to my doctor with a sore throat, and I said, "Would you look in there? It feels kind of funny all around." He looked at my throat, and he says, "Oh, it's a little red. It's normal." He says, "You know what you're suffering from?" And I said, "No. What?" He says, "You're suffering from a bad case of discovery of the larynx." [Both laugh.] And I said, "What he's saying, in other words . . . he's saying it's all normal." And I went out of there feeling all of my bones. And he said, "Well, you've got all kinds of bones in your body you've never noticed. Maybe you haven't felt the medulla, or the bone on the end of your knee, here, the knee cap, that moves around if you get it in a certain position." So I went home and immediately wrote a short story about a man who becomes terrified. Why does he become terrified? Because he discovered that within his flesh he has imprisoned a baroque symbol of horror, a skeleton. And he becomes terrified of his own skeleton inside of himself because he's seen all of these horror films as a child, and skeletons are always used as symbols of terror. So, I wrote a story—it's a short story—that's a competition between the flesh and the mind of this man and the symbol of death imprisoned within his flesh. And I sold it to *Weird Tales*—all as a result of my doctor saying I have discovered my larynx. So, this is the way I come upon ideas. And I don't deny them; I act on them immediately.

HH: So it was that I talked with Ray Bradbury, that he spoke of the writer who worked as the physician, who had the same demanding, unequivocal responsibility, who was sensitive to the inevitable human tensions and responsibly concerned with providing his culture some opportunity to deal with them, comfortably and effectively. And I remember that Ray Bradbury said, "I'm proud that I help people to cry, I help people to laugh, I help people to be violent, I help people to be a little sick. And then I show them the way to the fields where the dogs lie themselves down to eat the green grass." Such was the way that one man in the twentieth century came to view his universe. This man, Ray Bradbury.

A Portrait of Genius: Ray Bradbury
Show / 1964

Show, 4.11 (December 1964), pp. 52–55, 102–4. Reprinted by permission.

Show: Science fiction has traveled a popular road from H. G. Wells's *The War of the Worlds*, from the Frankenstein monster era, to the complex, highly successful formula that is today's science fiction. What are the differences between Wells's stories and, say, yours?

Ray Bradbury: Before I comment on the question, I feel I must argue with the way the question is set up. There can be no successful formula for writing science fiction or, for that matter, any kind of fiction. Any writer who sets out to write by formula turns away from himself, whatever truth he contains about the world, and any creativity he has to offer. A good writer creates out of need, hunger, excitement, a high sense of fun, zest, gusto, elation, call it what you will. He lives, or should live, by his passions. Passion does not allow for formula. The man who takes a Manual of Sex Instructions to bed should get out of bed immediately; he is in danger of severe malfunction. Writing and living are one and the same process. Formula endangers any natural process. So, finally, the best science fiction is written by those who see something they dislike in our society and explode on the spot about it.

A good example of this is my story "The Pedestrian." I have been stopped on numerous occasions for walking at night, for being a pedestrian. To express my outrage, I wrote a story about a future world where all walkers in the city, at night, are considered criminal.

As for any difference between Wells's writings and mine, I still feel a great kinship for his work. There are differences, of course, but we all come from the same moral vineyard where we worked under the kindly eye of our great-uncle, Jules Verne. I would have to re-read Wells to spot any large dissimilarities. I regret to say I have not re-read him for twenty years. Verne, on the other hand, I have re-read much in the past four years and know him to be of an exact and absolutely similar blood to my own.

Show: Are you a moralist? Are the science-fiction writers of today moralists?
RB: I think I am, above everything, for the question of morality rises again and again with each machine that we create. As each invention populates the world with itself, new laws must go on the books to control its direction. While machines are amoral, sometimes the very manner of their construction, and the power locked into their frame inspires man to lunacy, idiocy or evil. Some of the greatest liberals of our time are illiberal and demonic in a car. Some of the greatest conservatives become radical destructionists when they step on the starter and rampage off after murder. I once asked a class in design at the Art Center in Los Angeles to design a car that would cause men *not* to prove their masculinity every time they slung themselves into the bucket seat. How to induce a man *not* to use the maniac power engineered into a roadster there indeed is where morality, design, metal and human ingenuity meet, clash and often end up in destruction. Perhaps we need to invent a car that trembles more, roars more and makes men feel as if they were going eighty while only traveling forty. The problem remains unsolved. We must solve it. So too, architecture is a problem in morality as well as construction. The buildings of the future must be stages which produce, in their usage, human beings rather than unhappy beasts. *This* is the stuff of good science fiction!!

As for other science-fiction writers, it seems inescapable, the problem of morality that immediately arises as soon as a machine pops into the mind of its inventor. Long before the locomotive crossed the prairies and won the West, the human problems it would cause could have been anticipated by any writer capable of sitting and thinking on it for an hour. Touch any science-fiction writer working today and you will, nine times out of ten, touch a moralist.

Show: Why science-fiction stories at all?
RB: Because they are a convenient shorthand symbolic way to write of our huge problems. Smog, freeways, cars, atom bombs, most of mankind's trouble these days comes from an abundance of machinery and an undersupply of imagination applied to that machinery. Science fiction supplies the imagination whereby to judge, suggest alternatives and provide seedbeds for future improvements.

Show: Who is your favorite science-fiction writer? Why?
RB: Jules Verne. Because he was among the first and still remains one of the best—a writer of imagination, moral fiber and good humor who inspires as

he writes. He makes one proud to be a human being. He sets tests for mankind, dares him to lift himself by his bootstraps. He honors an old-fashioned virtue: work. He honors the searching mind, the inquiring eye and the capable hand. He gives rewards for work well done. He is in sum, admirable, and his novels will be around as long as boys need to become good, kindly and enthusiastic men. In an age which has often bankrupted its fund of ideals, Verne, from another age, calls out to better goals and warns man not to worry so much about his relationship with God, but rather to see his kinship with other men. Would that there were more like him writing today.

Show: Are there any restrictions on the science-fiction writer? Have you the freedom to write what you want?
RB: No restrictions I can think of. In fact, it is probably the freest field of all. During the McCarthy reign of terror, I wrote a novel titled *Fahrenheit 451* which was a direct attack on the kind of thought-destroying force he represented in the world. Yet few people attacked me for writing an anti-McCarthy novel. I was able to propagandize without getting myself stoned or pummeled. Later, the Russians pirated an edition of this same book, which I hear has sold very well in Russia. Obviously, because it is science fiction, they haven't gotten the message that I meant *all* kinds of tyrannies anywhere in the world at any time, right, left or middle. So I have been a subversive force, if you like, in the USSR, while being equally subversive here.

Show: Is there any form of censorship as to what you can or cannot write?
RB: Again, science fiction is freedom itself. Long before mass media began publishing or broadcasting material on the color problem, science fiction acted out such problems in the pulp magazines. I wrote a story in which the Negroes picked up and went off to Mars, leaving the entire South in the lurch, way back in 1949. Religious topics, usually verboten, are welcome in science-fiction magazines. I have written a number of stories about priests traveling in Space, searching for God or wondering if a Blue Fire-Balloon, encountered on Mars, were human or merely a hallucinatory light. There is hardly a subject, save sex, that hasn't appeared in the science-fiction magazines twenty years before it came into public notice in the larger quality magazines. And, of course, in the field of politics and philosophy, science fiction predates all the mouthings of our present politicos and space-scientist philosophers by anywhere from twenty to a hundred years. Every time a government official opens his mouth these days, something from a

1928 issue of *Amazing Stories* falls out. Today's astronomical theories, published in learned bulletins, were acted out in *Wonder Stories* in 1931.

Sex, as already indicated, has been the only missing subject. But even here, in recent years, the science-fiction story has dared tread on toes. Homosexuality as a solution for tensions of men on five-year rocket journeys has been dramatized not once but on numerous occasions by several writers. So now the last barriers have fallen, and science fiction incorporates, even today, most of the ideas you will never find in *McCall's*, *The Saturday Evening Post* or *Good Housekeeping*.

Show: How did you get into science-fiction writing? Are you a frustrated scientist? Were you influenced by a parent, friend, teacher or other writer?
RB: My aunt Neva helped bring me up in a world of let's-pretend, in a world of masks and puppets that she made, in a world of stages and acting, in a world of special Christmases and Halloweens. It was she who read me my first fairy tales, she who read Poe aloud to me when I was seven and taught me all about fabulous mythological country from which I never quite emerged. Ten years older than myself, she was more like an older and loving sister whose art-and-dressmaking studio I hung about sniffing the watercolors and oil paints. Halloweens, she dabbed me with makeup, dressed me as a witch or monster and let me scarify at her parties. She took me roller-skating on autumn nights, in the middle of empty and abandoned concrete streets far out on the edge of town where the houses had not as yet built themselves up. I went with her to collect pumpkins and cornshocks out in farmyards far beyond the city limits and helped fill her big old house with them on October evenings. When I decided to become a magician, at the age of ten, after Blackstone the Magician gave me my first live rabbit, it was Neva who watched my first pitiful illusions, who paid enthusiastic attention. Later, she let me watch her create the costumes for "The Streets of Paris" at the Chicago World's Fair. And still later, she took me to my first stage plays. All the worlds of art and imagination flowed to me through Neva, but especially she put me in touch with October Country, a year packed into a single month, a special climate which I still delight in. If I could have chosen my birthday, Halloween would be it.

Along with Neva's and Blackstone's influence, Buck Rogers arrived in my life when I was eight. I collected, and still have safely put away, every Buck Rogers comic strip from the year 1928 on up through 1940. With Buck Rogers came Tarzan and John Carter, Warlord of Mars, by Edgar Rice Burroughs. The

Burroughs books, borrowed from my uncle Bion, were soon read ten times over and memorized, chapter and verse. Simultaneously, I came upon my first copy of *Amazing Stories*, the October 1928 issue in which appeared "The World of Giant Ants" by A. Hyatt Verrill, and where I soon made acquaintance with Jules Verne and H. G. Wells.

I was exhilarated with their company. When I look back at my childhood I find I lived in a state of near hysteria waiting for Buck Rogers to slap onto my front porch each night in the evening paper. I exulted waiting to read the next Tom Swift book. I prowled the Waukegan Town Library for new volumes of Verne, Stevenson and Wells. The library was the greenhouse in which I, a very strange plant indeed, grew up, exploding with seeds. When I was twelve, I decided to become a writer. It was inevitable that my first "book" should be a sequel to a Mars volume by Burroughs.

Looking back now, if I were to point to one outstanding factor in my life, it would be my irrepressible vitality and hunger for great literary and artistic loves. I died a thousand deaths waiting over the years while Disney finished his *Fantasia*. The night after the premiere I saw the film with Neva. I still remember it as probably the greatest night in my life. I realize how silly this may sound to some, for I have seen much greater things since—[Lawrence] Olivier on the stage in London, for instance. But it must be remembered, I was twenty, and passionate, and the perfect age to devour, and keep on devouring and take strength from the feeding. I saw *Fantasia* twelve times in as many weeks.

This same hunger and drive has pervaded everything I have ever done. From the age of fifteen until I was twenty-eight I saw every movie that was released. I went to films at least four times a week, which means eight pictures a week! Out of this sublime madness has come the groundwork knowledge in film-making which has helped me an immense lot writing my screenplays.

Beyond Neva, there was the influence of my short story teacher, Jennet Johnson, at Los Angeles high school, a kindly, patient, warm and very human woman whose influence must weigh heavy on the scales. After her, my teachers were all established writers in the science-fiction field, Leigh Brackett, Henry Hasse, Ross Rocklynne, Jack Williamson, Edmond Hamilton, Robert Heinlein and Henry Kuttner. They read and criticized scores of my stories over a seven-year period and encouraged me to keep on. Without their friendship I could not have continued as I did in the face of constant rejections.

Show: Are you attracted to science-fiction literature because in a sense you are setting up your own standards, your own world peopled by creatures of your imagination?
RB: Perhaps. And yet, everything considered, and the evidence examined from the answers I gave to the previous question, I am undoubtedly a Child of My Time. We *all* are, of course. But I feel that I have rubbed my nose in machinery oil, rolled in the junkyards with the brute ruins of old car wrecks, sent in my Cocomalt tin-strip off the one-pound can to get my Solar Scouts button, lived, eaten and snorted forth the fine soot of our civilization. My body was born in Waukegan, but the chemistries of cities have infiltrated that body and influenced that mind in the years following. Science has raped as well as lovingly seeded our land. We are the natural children of that seeding and that ungentle rape. This is a science-fictional time. It would seem utter madness, and literary bankruptcy for me to ignore the moving sidewalk that electrically carries us pell-mell toward the future. We inhabit the very world I once saw behind glass at the Fair in Chicago in 1933 and again in New York in 1939. I am attracted, therefore, to my time, not to science fiction *per se*, but rather to the fantastic mechanistic elements that explode, implode and drive the machineries of our existence. Science fiction in these circumstances is simple exhalation after decades of breathing in.

Show: Was *Dandelion Wine* a nostalgic glimpse into the past, your past?
RB: Yes. It was a rummage through a fabled attic or basement storehouse. One of the unfortunate aspects of our new Age is that we no longer have attics or basements in which to put away the Past. I believe the Past is both bad and good, it can both wound and heal. If one goes to it to suffer, to self-lacerate, of course the junk must go out of the attic into the incinerator. But if it can be used to instruct so that a man, turning over the fabulous junk in his trunkroom, can feel like a centipede, I grew this leg that year, and this leg the next and the next leg the year after that, then a man extends himself in time, and becomes whole. It is good to see all the selves lined up, mirrored and re-mirrored in all the looking-glasses one can find put away with mothballs, with antimacassars and studio portraits. A man cannot possibly speak futures, unless he has a strong sense of the past. Especially a writer must have a place to stash all the trash of his various exciting lives. Each time he picks up a toy from the age of twelve, it becomes a three-dimensional Rorschach test by which to remember and know himself. I am not saying

those were happier days, they were not. But I *am* saying those days existed, look at them, know them, see them as well as you can. With amiable good will accept yourself as fool, dumbbell, clod, murderer, dreamer, dark shadow and lover of the sun. Man is Paradox. Attics and basements are good filing cabinets of the Paradox we are and always will be. We are hurricanes and calms, good friends and terrible enemies to the world.If I had my way I would insist that high schools teach courses in Paradox I, Paradox II, so that students, exulting in Idealism, would not so easily break their bones when colliding with the reality of their selves.

We in America suffer from a lack of knowledge in our arts of this Paradox. We leave the handling of what seems insufferable to men like [George] Bernard Shaw in England or [Jean] Anouilh in France. We prefer to paint all black or all white. The man who paints all black borrows tortures from the Past to destroy himself with. The man who paints all white ignores the Past at his own risk, and so risks destruction by others. Somewhere between sits Man and his Real Nature, multicolored, very fine and very dangerous.

When attics and cellars got crowded out of architecture by rising costs and inane builders, some of us, anyway, lost our chance to observe the Paradox in still-life.

So, in writing *Dandelion Wine*, I was doing more than time-traveling fueled by nostalgia. I was picking up and putting down objects which represented Noon and Midnight, good and evil, the vast cry of terror or the easeful sigh of relaxation on a summer evening early. My hope for the book is that people will wake in the night having heard a sound, themselves, making noise in their sleep remembering what I have written, and not know if it was a sound of laughing or a sound of crying which wakened them. Somewhere between, the unnameable thing, is what I wanted.

Show: Can you pinpoint any incidents in your life that have sharpened your sensitivity as a writer?
RB: Once I might have tried to nail down such incidents, but now I know that *all* of the incidents in my life sharpen my sensitivity and, in turn, I try to sharpen my sensitivity so as to be aware of all the incidents in my life. Not being able to point to a single event, I can only observe that once I really understood what a writer is up to or should be up to, my sensitivity increased. Once I really saw that writing and living were identical, that both must be passionate, immediate, I was well on my way. Life is First Thoughts and Second

Thoughts. Animal Man is brimful of First Thoughts and passions. In order to be human he has taught himself to have Second Thoughts, which we call Reason. These act upon our First Thoughts and move us toward the humane. We stifle our Prime Movements in order to survive in Cities and live by Laws. But these Primal Thoughts must go somewhere, must they not? They do not simply disappear? They are put away in our subconscious. There they may cause us severe upset, neuroticism, which may break out into violence or retreat into insanity. Our Arts, it seems to me, must be the immediate receptacle of our Prime Thoughts, our First Thinking. Then by reading about our First Moves instead of moving, we give ourselves time to make second motions. We do not have to act out the forbidden, we can dream it out in our sleep, or in our books.

This is where I argue with those who think there is a great difference between passionate emotion and thought. Actually, both First Thoughts, which are Passionate and move, and Second Thoughts, which are Reason and stand still, are thinking. But one electrifies while the other short-circuits. So we have come by some bad labeling and damning for the passions. All passion is considered non-thinking, when we know it is indeed immediate first thinking. All passion is considered bad but we can list millions of times in our lives when our passions served us well, preserved our skins and gave shelter, that is, love, to our family and friends. The trouble with the intellectual in our society is he suspects all emotion. So suspecting, he becomes infertile, incapable of creativity. For creativity can only occur in the reasonable man who has enough wit to be in motion, that is, be emotional in his art.

Living truth cannot be found by reason. Truth can only be caught in flight, when the passions detonate us and we surprise our true selves in the middle of the avalanche. After the uproar is over we can "think" about what we caught unaware rushing out of our subconscious onto paper.

So while I cannot pinpoint it, I would say that the days in the one year when I learned to trust my passion, my emotions, my hungers, my hates, my loves, my first needs, rather than the blind god reason, was the day I began to write good short stories. In truth, both gods are blind. Passion blinds itself to Futures by rushing ahead. Reason blinds itself to the Present and has no life, for self-consciousness destroys all spark, all *élan*, all chance to be natural. In the light of Reason, the subconscious shrinks snail-like back into its shell. Look away, pay no mind, give a shout, a yell, roar into your work and the subconscious on the instant opens out, changes from snail to lion and breaks down the last remaining bars.

In order to stay sane, we must live both ways, we cannot be all reason or all passion. Our arts can help us with our jungle needs and lead us around, by a suspenseful, delightful, strange and relaxing as well as enlivening road, to sweet Reason. But Reason, my God, cannot lead up to Passion. It does not know the road.

The horse is dead, but let me beat it one last time.

In sum, to Think one must first scare the Subconscious out in the open. By firing the emotions, by gunshoting the trees, by rifling the bushes and deep weeds, one shatters forth flights of discovery, of the lost, the hidden and shadowed. You cannot think them forth, they must be shaken, rattled and banged out into the air. There, perceived, you may capture the hummingbirds, net the rabbits, mesh the writhing snakes with observed Thought and filed data. But the night animals will not venture forth if Reason treads heavily. You will stay forever ignorant of yourself if you plod your oafish dumbweight foot through the underbrush hoping to find yourself by deep thinking alone. You will wind up a moron clobbered by mere fact and dumb detail.

Show: Were you a writer of early promise? Is writing an easy thing for you? Has it become simpler through the years to turn out a successful story?
RB: I started writing at the age of twelve. So I was a writer of early unpromise. All my stories from the age of twelve until I was at least twenty-two were pretty bad. But by writing every day of my life from the age of twelve on, I gave myself good habits, I learned my craft and when I had learned it well enough I began to relax and when I began to relax I began to write well. So, at the age of twenty-two I wrote my first excellent short stories, which, compared to other age groups for writers, I guess, makes me a writer of early promise after all. I knew the day I turned the corner and became a really good writer. I wrote a short story called "The Lake" in my twenty-second year. When I finished it my hair was standing on end and I was cold all over. I almost wept with joy. For I knew I had trusted my subconscious and allowed my emotions to write the story for me. "The Lake" is in my collection *The October Country*. You can read it now and decide whether, at twenty-two, I had indeed turned that corner into creativity.

Is writing easy for me? Yes, because it is a true joy. I am totally happy when I am plunged into the midst of adventures with my characters. I never interfere with my people. I let them live and in living write the story for me. So that means that in a single day of running with my characters I can write a complete first draft story. I believe first drafts, like life and living, must be immediate, quick, passionate. By writing a draft in a day I have a story with a skin around it.

If one waits overnight to finish a story, quite often the texture one gets the next day is different. You wind up with two kinds of flesh, one of which will not graft onto the other. Better to try for a swift and exciting first draft in one day, than to dawdle along the way and risk being intellectual about what should be a process as simple and basic as a heartbeat.

As for writing successful stories, I take the word successful to mean successful only in terms of the story itself: does it have its own life, does it move, does it have feelings, is it an entirety and a whole? If one can say yes to all these questions, the story is successful. Whether it sells or not is unimportant. One cannot for a moment think of selling. To do so would again be an interference. One does not write to make money. One writes to be truly alive.

Show: Are you an early starter or do thoughts and ideas come to you in the night? Do you struggle with rewriting?
RB: I start whenever my subconscious gives a helluva yell and tells me to get out of the way. Even so, I keep strict office hours, starting generally at nine every morning, five days a week. If I have had a good morning, by noon I let myself out for a walk or a workout at the gym. In the afternoons I rewrite and get out the mail. I am my own secretary, typing all of my manuscripts and letters. It is dangerous for a writer to have a secretary; he may fall into the bad habit of allowing her to type his final draft, which could be fatal. My final drafts are always nit-picking surveys of the manuscript. I look to change one word on each page. When I go through the story and find that every word is perfect, it goes into the mail. By typing the final draft myself, I make certain that those last small words get found and changed. The day I stop being this exact about perfection is the day I stop being a good writer.

So you see, after the emotion comes the calm analysis of what has been done.

If rewriting is necessary, I always rewrite from emotion. If a scene needs to be redone, I throw out the old one, refuse to look at it and do an entire new scene boldly and in high fever. If one tried to rewrite as coldly as one analyzed the problem, again one would wind up with two kinds of fish, one dead and one alive. So rewriting must be an identical process to the original one that got the story off in the first place.

So it follows I do not struggle with rewriting. I enjoy it as much as my first draft work. It is the cutting of a story that drives one mad. I usually go through and cut my manuscripts at least seven times. Cutting is the great art. Leaving out, finally, means as much as putting in. Often a fine story can be obscured by too many words. Learning how to bring the story to focus by cutting takes years of practice and careful restraint.

So, you see, I write whenever an idea looms up and knocks me down. If I happen on a line in a poem which suddenly opens up and becomes ten times life size, I run to my typewriter. A single line in a Robert Hillyer poem once caused me to write a story within the hour. An essay by Aldous Huxley mentioned "the little towns across the continental United States where nobody ever gets off." Immediately I thought, I wonder what would happen if I let a friendly character of mine get off a train in such a town?

Somebody says something in a conversation and I explode. Three hours later a first draft is finished.

I pick up a copy of *Harper's Bazaar*, which I think is the funniest magazine published in America, next to *Mad*, glance through the *Bazaar*, looking at the skinny-food-starved and sex-starved vultures which I take it are women, make a mental note never to go to bed with one, those cleaver shoulder blades look like guillotines and those elbows would pierce one's flesh immediately, throw down the magazine and go write a story about the invasion of a small Mexican town by a *Bazaar* photographer and some of his barracuda models. The result: "Sun and Shadow," in my book *Golden Apples of the Sun*. In it, I have a brave, wise old Mexican gentleman spoil all the *Bazaar* photography by stepping into each shot and serenely letting his pants drop. The photographer and his skeletons are put to rout. Bravo! say I, and the story is finished.

Show: Based on everything you've said so far, it would seem that the important literary decisions in your life have been made emotionally and not through what we call reasonable thought . . . is this true?
RB: Absolutely. When faced with alternative courses and choices about my future, I always ask my stomach, not my head, to decide. The head may rationalize a situation, throw up false fronts, convince one to take a job that is really wrong, but the stomach knows, feels, smells Sickness, if you are wise enough to pay attention to it.

As an example, a year ago, three groups of film people arrived the same week to bid on my novel *The Martian Chronicles*. I spent a day with each group, talking with them, finding out how they saw my novel as a picture. I then went home and stared not at the brain between my ears but the stomach beneath my navel. Of it I asked, which group is fairest of them all? Which will keep me happy, sane and creative, which will make me want to bound out of bed in the morning yelling to get to work?

My stomach gave its opinion—no, its firm conviction: go with Alan Pakula and Bob Mulligan, who produced and directed *To Kill a Mockingbird*. I went to them. I have never been sorry. It has been a wonderful and creative relationship.

Similarly, eleven years ago, when John Huston asked me if I would like to write the screenplay of *Moby Dick* for him, in Ireland, I replied: "I don't know. I haven't read the book yet." It would have been so simple to just grab the job and run. After all, it isn't every day one is offered a chance to work with John Huston and with Melville and with Melville's greatest work, *Moby Dick*, plus a free trip to Europe for the first time in one's life. Yet I knew I had to make a decision not on the reputations of the director or novelist, but on what the book had to say to me as a person. I went home that night, got out my copy of *Moby Dick* and did the best thing anyone can do with a book, opened it at just any page one third of the way, one half of the way, two thirds of the way through. This is what we do in libraries. This is how we find our friends-for-life on the bookshelves. We recognize our kinship almost immediately with this quick test. By sheer luck, I opened Melville at his chapter on the Spirit Spout, the great spout of the White Whale that fountained on the mysterious sea at night, a veritable Fountain of Versailles put forth upon the tides.

I opened the book again and this time found the poetic section of the seas of Brit through which whales swim slaking their immense thirsts.

Again I came upon the chapter which details the Whiteness of the Whale, the ghost color, the Arctic tints and hues of the Leviathan monster.

And finally I read Ahab's monologue on its being a mild day and a mild looking sky and the wind smelling as if it blew from the shadow of the Andes where the mowers lay down with their scythes among the cut harvest . . .

Very simply, then, I knew that Melville was, in that instant, a distant cousin. The right stuffs flowed in his veins and his work. I turned back to page one and read: "Call me Ishmael." The next day I accepted the job from Huston. In sum, I repeat the cliché: the heart has its reasons. Call it heart or call it stomach, it is the only way for any kind of artist to live.

Show: It appears from your answers so far that you are dead set against any sort of "slanting" on the part of a writer, that is "slanting" or "contriving" a story for a certain market or magazine.

RB: Right. There are two ways for a writer to be dishonest in this world. One is to write for the dollar, for the fast buck. That will insure him against ever knowing or discovering himself in any way. The second way is to slant one's stories toward an intellectual bias. For instance to cynically observe, this is the Color Year, so I will write a story about the Negro problem, or this is the year that [Franz] Kafka is A-OK, so I will write a Kafka-kind story. Or this is the year of [Eugene] Ionesco or [James] Baldwin or [Edward] Albee, so I will write me an Ionesco or Baldwin or Albee type play. This, too, is the work of liars and cheats, of frauds and mountebanks, to carve one's work in the likeness of others, to follow literary or intellectual tastes, to cross your political t's as others tell you. When you look to the taste of your time to tell your direction, you are already dead. You might as well quit then, for you will never be individual, never different, never exciting. Worst of all, you will come to the end of your life, with your well undug, your secret bones unrattled and your hidden tongue unspoken. What a shame, what a damned shame that would be.

Show: What are your suggestions to young people interested in writing? Are there rules for them to follow or should they break away and make their own rules?

RB: Write at least a thousand words a day for ten years. Write at least a short story every week of your life, or its equivalent in essay form, play form or in the novel. I dare any young writer to write fifty-two stories that are *all* bad. They may try to write fifty-two bad stories, but somewhere along the line, they will become passion's plaything. In the midst of their creative elation they will not notice until it is too late they are writing a good story. Habit is everything. Learning one's craft is locked into good habit. Once established, you will not want to break your fascinating schedule. Even the mistakes will become a kind of game, much fun, for they will be learning. Anyone who is learning and moving is not failing. No story is a total loss, if we look at it and know that it lost itself along the way.

As for rules, one must learn grammar and syntax and all the rest. One must imitate, of course, at the start of one's career, in order to learn. But always imitate the ones you truly love and who are like you in some way.

Soon enough, you will leave imitation behind, once you feel secure, and go your own way. Imitation is only bad if it dominates and continues as a mode of life for a writer.

Show: Do you intend to go on writing science fiction or are you attracted to other themes, other media?

RB: I do intend to write more science fiction, yes, for since I strongly believe this is the greatest age in the history of man to be alive in, I also believe that science fiction is the greatest literary form available to express the demands of our age.

Our huge step out into space, to the moon, to Mars and beyond, makes this the greatest time in all history. Why? Because it is commensurate with that unmarked time in prehistory when man, disguised, came out of the sea, built himself a spinal cord, reared himself up, swung in trees, lived in caves and finally named himself Man. The chrysalis time of Man was a great time. Now he has grown wings of fire to live in the air beyond the earth and in the alien airs of far worlds in a tremendous new era that will challenge and change, break and put back together every form of thought and all the ways of doing things as they are done this hour in this year. The writing must equal the age, or be lost forever. And it *is* the age of machines, which are Ideas locked into metal and powered with electricity. Man's philosophies run amuck or amble humming amiably in his devices. We must write of them. We must write of man fused to his contraptions and bemused or destroyed by same. At the same time, I hope to write, on occasion, more books about Ireland where I lived for almost a year, and about Illinois where I grew up. Whatever seizes me can have me. My mind speaks as it will. I have the good sense to stay dumb and listen and put down the words.

Show: Finally, if you were to label yourself for readers yet unborn, what sort of label would you like for yourself, science-fiction writer, fantasist, what?

RB: Let me answer that by sending myself on a journey back through the ages in a time machine. Arriving in Baghdad I would walk through the marketplace and turn down a street where sit the old men who are the tellers of tales. There, among the young who listen, and the old who say aloud, I would like to take my place and speak when it is my turn. It is an ancient tradition, a good one, a lovely one, a fine one. If some boy visits my tomb a hundred years from now and writes on the marble with a crayon: He Was a Teller of Tales, I will be happy. I ask no more name than that.

Ray Bradbury: Cassandra on a Bicycle
Pierre Berton / 1966

In *Voices from the Sixties: Twenty-Two Views of a Revolutionary Decade.* Garden City, New York: Doubleday & Company, Inc., 1967, pp. 1–10. Interview, Los Angeles, copyright © 1966, 1967 by Pierre Berton. Reprinted by permission.

"All of yesterday's blasphemy will be tomorrow's dicta."

Bradbury's fiction, often dark and macabre, deals with machines and speed, two aspects of the sixties that he personally detests. Though his tales are often studded with space ships that hurtle through the void at close to the speed of light, Bradbury himself, living in the world's most car-conscious city, has stubbornly refused to learn to drive. How does he get about? On a bicycle! Naturally, I began our conversation by asking him why.

Ray Bradbury: Well, it is a little late in the day to change my image. I'm sort of a romantic myth now, you see, so I'm locked into this thing. Even if I *wanted* to learn to drive tomorrow, I wouldn't dare; it would spoil everything. But, basically and honestly, I grew up during the depression when nobody could afford to buy a car. I think we had an old ten-dollar Buick. I think my Dad paid about ten dollars for it. We came west to Los Angeles in '34, and on the way, coming and going several times from Arizona to Illinois and L.A., I saw enough foolishness on the highway and enough destruction that by the time I was old enough to drive I didn't even think about it. And I haven't thought about it since. I rarely stop and think to myself: "Why don't you drive?" I took a bus here today.

Pierre: Isn't it very hard to get a bus in Los Angeles?
RB: No, I had good luck today. I went to a corner and there was a bus. I almost fell over! It was unbelievable! If I don't take the bus, I take my bicycle and I grab cabs. And then I'm picked up by strangers, which is a lot of fun. Several days ago I was outside the gymnasium in Beverly Hills waiting for

a bus, and a Mercedes-Benz pulled up with a woman in mink, and she said: "Would you like a ride?" I said, "Yes," even though I was rather amazed, and I got in and she drove me several miles to where I wanted to go, and I said: "Why did you pick me up?" And she said: "You looked very English and very safe."

Pierre: I don't know whether that is flattering or not.
RB: I know; I don't *want* to look safe.

Pierre: I would have thought in this enormous, sprawling city it would almost be impossible to get around if you didn't own an automobile. You don't find it awkward?
RB: No, I've learned how to take a book with me and relax. When you're waiting for a bus you can get a lot of reading done.

Pierre: Does the sort of thing you're doing represent a revolt against machines?
RB: No, but a revolt against the way we are building our city. I would like to see it replanned and done over, and the automobile eliminated as much as possible. Most of the major cities of this continent and all over the world are going to outlaw the automobile in the next forty years. They're going to have to. We can't make do with this thing. It's just destroying our cities. The time will come when we will go along and put a bullet in the carburetor of every second car, which will just be a great day for all of us. We'll all be free again.

Pierre: Suppose masked riders go out at night to kill machines?
RB: Yes, absolutely. I'd like to do a story on that. It would be great fun.

Pierre: Do you hate freeways too?
RB: Yes, I hate them for several reasons. They ruin conversation. Have you ever tried to hold a conversation on a freeway? You're braking the car! If you're not driving, you're steering for the guy who is steering. You're going eighty miles an hour, which is an outrageous speed, or ninety. Most people go ninety in forty-mile-an-hour zones. You can't converse and you can't see what you're passing. One of the reasons we had the Watts Area problem here last year—the riots—I believe, is the fact that nobody ever *saw* Watts. They were always passing it at eighty miles an hour. So if you're constantly passing

an area and never seeing it, you don't even know it's there. It used to be that you had to go through Watts to where you wanted to go. Maybe you might have found out that it wasn't a very nice area to live in if you had actually driven through it. It is actually a twenty-five-mile-an-hour zone.

Pierre: Funny to hear you say that eighty or ninety miles an hour is a terrible speed when you write about people who go much faster in rocket ships.
RB: Well, actually, all of my people travel very slowly. They may be on a rocket, but they are innate philosophers and blabbermouths. They like to talk about going slower in spite of all their speed. I use many of the machines of the present and the future, but you find that the heart of the machine is the man who is traveling very slow and looking around and saying: "This isn't good enough. We've got to do better." So it only appears that I'm traveling fast.

Pierre: You know, we've learned that science-fiction writers are the prophets of our time because so many of them have been right. Everything from the atomic bomb to satellites has been predicted in science-fiction magazines like *Astounding* and *Amazing Stories* for thirty years. As a science-fiction writer in 1966, what kind of a future do you prophesy?
RB: Oh, I prophesy a golden age as the result of the hydrogen bomb, in which this one science-fictional device will enable us to get along beautifully without war. We've been so busy being terrified by the Bomb, we haven't realized what a godsend it is. I predict there will be no more gigantic wars. The war we are carrying on now in Vietnam, which we don't call a war, is a very small exercise, which will soon be ended regardless of our rather stupid President [Lyndon B.] Johnson and the stupid people around him. The war will end. It will be no hydrogen-war explosion. We'll go on having these guerrilla excursions, here and there in the world. But we've stopped a lot of wars in the last twenty years because of this science-fictional device. People are always saying: "What do you predict?" I see the growth of the United Nations and the growth of understanding among nations—the result of all such science-fictional devices, including this one we are working with here, television. These are all empathy devices whereby these robots help us find out about one another. The more we can use them in these areas, the better world I think we're going to have.

Pierre: I wonder if the next war—I use the word loosely—won't be a psychological war between man and the machine to see who gets dominance.

RB: I doubt it. Let me use this example: I've been taken through the computer complexes out at the air force base in UCLA. And as we go through these computers, quite often a scientist will turn to me and say: "Isn't it wonderful?" And I always reply, "No! No! It isn't wonderful—*you're* wonderful. Let's put the emphasis where it belongs: *you* invented it; *you* built it; *you* put the information in; *you* take the information out. You're great and the machine is really of no importance whatsoever." So the battle will not occur between men and machines, but between men and men to build better machines. Because they are immoral. We have to look at an automobile, for instance, and say: "It's a lousy design!" All the automobiles in America right now are lousily built, lousily designed, and proceed to destroy hundreds of thousands of us every five years. We're killing off about three hundred thousand people every five years. That's a huge war, isn't it? So we've got to look at that machine and redesign it. And finally the government is going to have to step in and make General Motors and all the other people behave and put a bumper on a car. We have no bumpers on our cars any more! You touch them and they flake off! You touch any part of a car—you can reach up and rip off the lights, you can break the steering wheel very easily with one hand, a baby can go in and slam the door and it will fall off. All of our cars are tin: shoddy, inept. So we have to look at these things. And here's where the real war—the war between the mass of the people and the people who are selling us shoddy goods—that's where the wars are going to be occurring. Then, of course, we'll see the same thing corrupting Russia and Red China. They're going to be destroyed by automobiles, and we're all going to be in the same *meshugana* mess together. Then we'l fall weepingly in each other's arms in ten years and say: "Protect us from the machines!" We'll have to help the Communists against the automobiles.

Pierre: It's a curious kind of One World vision.
RB: Oh, it is going to happen, absolutely. The middle classes are taking over everywhere. Finally, we'll wake up in the midst of all our drivel and shoddiness. We'll turn to the philosophers, and then *they* will have to help us redesign the whole thing.

Pierre: Do you really think, Mr. Bradbury, the day will come when anybody will really turn to the philosophers and request help?

RB: Yes, I see it everywhere. I see it in the universities. I see it in this wonderful new generation coming up. We talk a lot about the beatniks, but they are a thin shell. We talk a lot about juvenile delinquency, but this is a thin shell. At the core of this fabulous generation there is great creativity, a great excitement, and a great desire to philosophize. They want someone to say: "Excellence is worth while. Quality counts. The job is worth getting done." This is one of the things about the Peace Corps in the last few years. These are the directions for governments to take all over the world. This generation *does* want to work; it *does* want to change the world. It *does* want to boot the old politicians in the behind to get them out of the way. If we can hold up new ideals, find the correct symbols to show ourselves in this rocket age, then they'll get in and they'll do the work. I've seen it happen, in universities where I've visited. The kids come up breathless after I talk about these very things, and they say: "Thank God someone's talking about it."

Pierre: Interesting to compare this new generation with the one just passed—the safe generation in the late forties and fifties.
RB: Yes, they got kind of lost along the way, and I don't know all the reasons. I blame the middle intellectual age there. Magazines like the *Nation* and the *New Republic*, the *American Scholar*, and many, many semipopular intellectual gazettes. They couldn't see the space age coming; and they left the work of dramatizing and being excited about the space age in the hands of a few people. But, suddenly, the space age is here with all of its ramifications, and we have to make do with it. All the religions of our world are changing rapidly; they are going way around back and coming up under the machines so that we are going through a vast age of blasphemy. Now the religions are going to have to come around underneath our blasphemy and reaffirm it. And all of yesterday's blasphemy will be tomorrow's dicta handed down by the Catholic Church and all the other churches of the world. In other words, we are refashioning God into a new image so that He will stay conveniently out of the way. So that we can get the work done of going into space, of landing on God's moon, of landing on God's Mars, and going places where, a hundred years ago if we had tried to go there, we would have been burned at the stake for doing the job. We're carrying on this kind of ardent mechanical blasphemy on many levels in the world today, and this is what excites the new generation: seeing how each machine, each development is changing our philosophy, changing our religion, changing the family structure, changing our arts.

Pierre: It *is* an exciting time, isn't it?
RB: It is. I think it's the greatest age in the history of the world that we're living in. We are privileged to be part of it.

Pierre: You know, I didn't get around to asking you about your predisposition for Halloween. You've said that you would have loved to have been born on Halloween. Why do you like Halloween so much?
RB: I suppose when you grow up in a small town rituals like Halloween and the Fourth of July mean a heck of a lot more to you. It is much more basic than in a large city. The whole image of Halloween has changed so fantastically in the last twenty-five years. It's not the same kind of fun. It's become a form of bribery where you go and get candy for not doing anything. Well, that to me is not what it's all about. I like the rawness and the nearness and the excitement of death, which went with the older vision of Halloween. In fact I've often wanted to do a one-hour special for TV in which I'd make a comparison between Halloween as it exists today and as it used to exist in America. And the way *Día de los Muertos* is celebrated in Mexico and South America, where they have the sugar skulls with your name on it, or the name of a dead loved one, and they give you a chance to symbolize and live close by death and try to understand this mystery. We've lost sight of it.

Pierre: The "excitement of death" is an odd phrase to use.
RB: Yes, it is. But children *are* fascinated by it.

Pierre: By death?
RB: Absolutely! They hunger for knowledge about it, and that's why horror films have been so successful over the years—not only with children but with older people too. We turn to our religions and our philosophers and our myth makers to explain the inexplicable to us. *Dracula* is a fabulous example of one way we have of looking at a realistic representation of a thing we can't really see. And a really good horror film helps us to make do with this fact for a little while. It is a very important part of existence.

Pierre: The presence of horror in our lives?
RB: Absolutely. We have to digest it and get rid of it to go on. We just can't face nothingness. We've got to make something of it. So we can hold death in

our hands for a little while, or on our tongues, or in our eyes, and make do with it. This is what we are all up to.

Pierre: I guess you would disagree with Dr. Frederic Wertham and those parent-teacher groups that are opposed to horror pictures for children.
RB: Oh yes, absolutely. I don't like the comic books that are sick; but there are some that deal with death in such a way that they leave the hair ball in your crop. The dynamic function of any art form is to build attention and then release it to you. The trouble with a lot of things on the American stage and the international stage—a play like *Who's Afraid of Virginia Woolf?*, let's say— is that they take an immense hair ball and cram it into your mouth and never give you the right to free yourself from this hair ball. Well, this to me is automatically uncreative, and some of these comic magazines we're talking about are non-creative and non-tension-relieving because they leave you with the hair ball. But the average comic magazine or adventure comic knows how to relieve the tension it has built. Then the child can go back to life again with no real illusion.

Pierre: What do you think is happening to horror? It's becoming a joke. When Abbott and Costello started meeting Dracula and Frankenstein, these horror figures became clowns. Why is this? Is it a good thing?
RB: No, I don't think it is a good thing. I think it is important to take death seriously and the symbols that we work with very seriously. Now when people get too pompous about it, then you go and prick the balloon with these little silly comics and with satire. I'm all in favor of that. But, if you have a continual bombardment of making fun of a serious attempt to make do with life, then you're in danger of winding up with nothing. And I'm afraid of this. I don't know what the answer is except to go out and make better horror films. I would like to make a really magnificent film that would scare the Jesus out of everybody, with a man like David Lean, who is one of the finest directors in the world.

Pierre: What produced you? What made you what you are—a writer of horror, fantasy, science-fiction—the best! Who are your heroes?
RB: My heroes are Buck Rogers, Flash Gordon, Alley Oop, Tarzan, Edgar Rice Burroughs, *The Warlord of Mars*, Edgar Allan Poe, H. G. Wells, Jules Verne, all the comic strips ever produced, all the films ever made, early radio, "Chandu

the Magician." I was a member of the Little Orphan Annie Secret Society. I sent away my Ovaltine can tops. I wrote "Chandu the Magician." Every night when the program went off the air, I would sit down and write it from memory, so I trained myself as a writer from the age of twelve by writing radio scripts. I got to know "[George] Burns and [Gracie] Allen" when I was fourteen. So I have been deeply involved in all the mass media, which has a wonderful mediocrity, and all the wonderful excellences that are buried in each of these mediocrities. I've taken from each and I've grown with each. And then I've introduced myself to people like Aldous Huxley and Robert Frost and Thomas Wolfe and John Steinbeck. And out of the cross-pollination of all these things I've made myself into a writer who I still feel is a great child of our times.

Pierre: I suppose all of this is what is now called "high camp." The intellectuals have taken over.
RB: Yeah, and I believe they're the *wrong* intellectuals—the campy intellectuals who couldn't care less about the things that we once loved. They've now picked it up as a dreadful kind of fad, and they're going to go to bed with it for a few months or a year. Then they'll throw it by the wayside. I say to them: "Go away! Go away! You're all frauds. You don't really care about our interests. I find you contemptible. You don't know how to love." I offer an example of the ridiculousness of these so-called wise people: seven or eight years ago I tried to get many producers in Hollywood to make a movie out of an obscure series of books about an obscure hero. The name of the author was Fleming, and the name of his hero was Bond, and they could have gotten these books—all five of them at the time—for five thousand dollars each. No one would touch them! I thought: "Well, my God, if someone makes a really fine adventure film out of this, it will make nothing but money." But nobody would listen. Of course, now, they're the biggest successes in the history of film making.

Pierre: Science-fiction writers are the Cassandras of their time, Mr. Bradbury.
RB: They are indeed.

An Interview with Ray Bradbury
William B. Allen / 1968

Phalanx, 2.1 (Winter 1968), pp. 11–19. Reprinted by permission.

(Editor's Note: The following interview of Ray Bradbury was conducted by four members of Phalanx staff, two students and two professors. The editor, William Barclay Allen, and the publisher, Peter W. Schramm, were accompanied by Professor George B. Tennyson, Editorial Advisor, and Professor Juan Vargas Duarte, Academic Advisory Board member. The interview was recorded electronically and then transcribed exactly. The discussion follows no particular theme or preconceived pattern.)

William Allen: This is not so much a question as a statement. You see, in my country, Chile, you are very popular; as a matter of fact there have been several lectures on you. A year ago a visiting professor from America and myself went to the Embassy to see about asking you to come to Chile and they seemed rather pleased with the idea. Have they contacted you about it?
Ray Bradbury: No, they haven't. You know, it's kind of incredible. I think I'm very fortunate, I haven't been taken up by the popular intellectual magazines of the United States in my lifetime, so far. I think that's all to the good. It's wonderful to be discovered outside your own country, and to be discovered by the children of your own country, and to let that gradually work up through the intellectuals so it's a slow process where you can conquer slowly. If it comes the other way it doesn't last. I think it is a kind of wonderful way to have things happen. So I am very pleased to hear about this reaction in Chile.

WA: You have said that Thomas Mann is one of your favorites. What do you think of *Death in Venice*?
RB: Well, I think the whole subject of homosexuality is coming more and more to the front in the literature of the world, and most of the people who are writing about the subject are not very good at it, are they? So they should all go read *Death in Venice* to find out how a master is able to, on many layers, lay back the soul of this man—this man who is dying, this man who has

a vision of beauty with a younger boy—and do it with great taste, with great sadness, with great concentration, with imagination. And it will involve them with sadness, involve them with the life of this man, involve them with a way of life and thinking which is not familiar to a lot of people, and make them sympathetic. A lot of people—like Leroi Jones, for example—do a disservice to the subject they're discussing. I think James Baldwin isn't good enough. I wish he were. I am always comparing writers to better writers. Now if James Baldwin could do something commensurate to, say, Thomas Mann with *Death in Venice*, I would say "bravo." I have no prejudices about subject matter. I have great prejudice when someone demeans any subject and makes more problems for himself than he should. I think when you compare something like *Giovanni's Room* to *Death in Venice*, you realize it really is pretty shallow.

I lived in Ireland for almost a year thirteen years ago, and I observed the Irish male in the bars. I've written a whole series of plays on my experiences in Irish pubs while I lived there working for John Huston on *Moby Dick*. So, the more I looked at the situation in Ireland, the more I realized that there was a great similarity between the Irish males and the inhabitants of Fire Island in New York. So, I wrote a short story in which I had a man show up in Dublin at the Royal Hybernion Hotel with five of his friends; he had sort of a canary quintet. They were going around the world following summer everywhere, and they hadn't seen autumn or winter in years. My Irishmen observe the arrival of this Fire Island sextet, chittering and singing and twirping together and all the Irishmen aghast, thinking there is going to be an orgy, their Island will be corrupted, or Dublin's going to be bombed or some awful thing—including the local priest. They begin to follow the sextet around town to see what they are up to, and find that they've only come to observe the changing of the leaves. They hadn't seen autumn for five or six years. They are there for one day before they fly on to the Bahamas or some of the islands in the Mediterranean. But there is a direct confrontation in the pubs between the Fire Island males and the Irish, who don't get married before they are forty. They can't afford to. They are unemployed half of the time; they have to wait for their mothers and fathers to die to get the property. And in the meantime, they are in the pubs; they are singing, drinking, reading poetry, admiring the drama. . . . Well, these are all things the Fire Island males also do you see. So the wonderful humor comes from making a one-to-one comparison of everything, all the way down the line to the final sexual thing, where, of course, there is a differential.

So I think mine is one of the few stories of high good humor and sympathy ever written on this subject. And I think the subject either requires the density of attack and imagination of a Thomas Mann or someone with a nice sense of humor, who can do the all-accepting thing of throwing back his head in the great, kind laugh, saying, "Look! Here are two separate groups of people, totally dissimilar in some ways, but totally identical in others." Then everyone can be involved in the fine joke, the warmth, and the good humor, instead of the bitter, the sarcastic, the cynical . . . really, the unaccepting humor which you find in some people. I'm really very pleased with this story, and I hope you'll look it up some time and read it.

WA: Where do you think [John Rechy's] *The City of Night* fits into all of this?
RB: Oh, I glanced at it in the book stores. I think that's the sort of book to be read by people who don't know anything about the world. I've lived here in L.A. since I was fourteen, and you know, if you just go out to the Pickwick bookstore once a week from the time you're fourteen until you're grown up—unless you lack eyes to see what is occurring in your society—you can't walk down Hollywood Boulevard and not be immediately perceptive of the situation, the various stratas of society there. You have to be totally blind. So I guess Rechy's book is for those people who have never opened their eyes in the world, and don't know that these sorts of things go on. It's a rather naive sort of thing. Of course, that's true for most of the Grove [Press] books and the pornographic press. They're for people, who, I guess, don't exist in the world, or have lived off in some area of the world where they have remained ignorant. Reading about that sort of thing has never intrigued me.

WA: Grove Press has a certain intellectual pretension, doesn't it? And doesn't it endeavor to appear intellectual?
RB: Have you noticed? It's kind of a wonderful joke, isn't it? How the advertising of many of the so-called intellectual presses in the last ten years has gotten to be more like Captain Billie's Whiz Bang and the old Ballyhoo Magazine of thirty years ago, or the Follies Burlesque. This is true in all the arts, and more and more in the presses and the movies. The art houses— what used to be art houses—are not art houses anymore, here in L.A. They started out showing [François] Truffaut films, but now they're girlie shows. And they open at ten in the morning. I don't know who in the hell goes to movies at ten in the morning. It's like drinking gin at breakfast, isn't it?

WA: Well, then, I assume you would put Andy Warhol and others in the same category?

RB: Yes, every age is a time of horse manure. And we are surrounded by two varieties of it constantly. One of them is commercial horse manure, and the other is intellectual horse manure. My main topic at universities and high schools is to try to help myself and help the students differentiate. The fact is, they can get just as much crud from the intellectuals surrounding them as they can from the commercial interests. There's no essential difference between the commercial interests. There's no essential difference between the commercial man and the intellectual. They all want power. They all want to tell you how to do things. But as soon as anyone tells me how to do something I say, "No, I have no time for you. I wish you could help me. I wish we could help each other more in our creativity, but there's no way for anyone to help anyone except to get out of the way, or to be a wailing wall on occasion. We can help each other if you want to be a writer or an actor or painter. I'm qualified in these various fields." So you can come to me and say, "Oh Lord, it's been a dreadful year. This has happened. That has happened." I can listen. I can say, "Yes, I know exactly what you're talking about. I've been through it and here's what I did." I help that way, but that's the only way. Anything beyond that, where I tell you to write *Valley of the Dolls*—that's selling big now—is ridiculous. Or, this is the year of Andy Warhol, so do psychedelic films. I wonder how many people Warhol's kidding? I wonder how many people are kidded by *Valley of the Dolls*? For they are identical. I see no difference. They are both frauds.

WA: What, then, is the role of education? What should students be getting from their educational experience?

RB: Well, in the arts—which is the only field in which I feel I'm qualified to speak—it is great gusto, zest, a sense of fun, and love. You, as a teacher, can reinforce love, and enable students to make choices out of love and fun and gusto. But not intellectual choices, because as soon as you begin to intellectualize you begin to lie. You begin to rationalize. Anytime I've ever made a decision, an intellectual decision, I've been invariably wrong. Anytime I make a decision out of my guts, out of wanting a thing, out of needing a thing, it's been right, because then you're working with your true self. Whatever intuitively in you needs to do something, go *with* it. But as soon as you step aside and say "Should I do this?" then you begin to make up reasons, and they sound fraudulently good. Our intellectual reasons for doing what we're doing in Vietnam sound so good, don't they? But our guts are upset because we know something's wrong. Why are we so uneasy with the Vietnam situation? Isn't it because we are intellectualizing when we should be emotionalizing, and our emotions tell us it's wrong? Our emotions tell us we should be helping the Negro, we should be rebuilding the cities. The whole country's going to hell because of the automobile which is destroying it. It's a bigger problem.

Actually, the automobile is destroying the cities into which, in turn, the Negro is being sucked by the automobile which has given him freedom. The fantastic thing about civil rights is the fact that a science-fictional device, the car, is what gave freedom to the Negro, gave him fluidity so he could move through our society. Suddenly the car has given one group of people freedom while, at the same time, it is destroying everyone's freedom, and we're not paying attention. So now, the reason we're uneasy is that we're seeing the whole country slowly being destroyed, inundated, smog bound. We're all suffering this at the same time. It's not just the Negro who is suffering. But in all the cities we don't like to go out in the streets anymore because it's no fun to drive anywhere. This city (Los Angeles) is dying and New York is already half dead. Ten years from now this city won't be worth living in, and we'll wonder why, because we weren't paying attention.

WA: What kind of thing can we do about the car, especially in a city like Los Angeles?
RB: Well, eventually you will have to outlaw it. It's easy to predict that within ten years, in New York City, the car will be outlawed from the whole city. And they'll build more ways of getting around, more subways—they're building one now which I think is finished. They will probably build some more. They will force people to use traveling sidewalks and a lot of things which we've known about for forty years but have never really tried. Disney has these "people-movers" out at Disneyland that he built last year. They would do a heck of a lot for vast areas in most cities. We need them out at the airport right now, where we have a real mess. We're in the hands of fools, the city governments of the United States and the national government, are all very foolish. Walt Disney was about the only bright guy around. He was the biggest, brightest, and most imaginative city planner in the world. Better than all the [Le] Corbusiers, the Frank Lloyd Wrights—all very enjoyable people— but the guy that, at a very practical level, began to solve the problems, and did

solve them, is a guy who was laughed at by people because he was a popular entertainer, not a great artist, but a very interesting thinker in terms of human beings and of moving people around and making sure their elbows don't bump too much. That's our problem. I'd like to have had Disney become mayor of L.A. I asked him about it at one time and his response was "Why should I become Mayor when I'm already King." Which I thought was a beautiful response. But anyway, let's get back to the educational thing.

The thing is, we think we can think our way to solutions when we must feel our way to solutions. The best thing that can happen in colleges and high schools is respect for intuition, and respect for love. When we meet loveless people, we must encourage them to move around until they fall in love. I'm going down to lecture at the school of architecture at U.S.C. for a day. I'll blow the place up and run fast.

How do I challenge them? I say "Look, I'm not fantastically qualified in architecture, but I have been interested in it because I grew up in the field of science fiction." That means you are interested in the total society from the time you're eight years old, on. You read about the total environment. So when I hit the school of architecture I'll say "Look, do you really know what you're studying, basically? At heart, is your love complete? When was the last time you walked around L.A.—I mean really walked? Do you do it every week? How much of L.A. do you really know? If this is the environment you're going to grow up in and change, is it because you love it as I love it and protect its good things and assault its bad things? How much do you really know? Are you on foot constantly, because if you're not, you really can't see this community. Drive by it and you miss it." Only by walking down all the side streets and taking in the texture do you see the individual life of a person who lives in a house, how he plants his garden, how he decorates his roof, or porch, how many people sit out at night, how many people have furniture on the porches to sit in, how open is the house, can you look inside and see what's there? Is it a closed house, what kind of flowers do they plant? . . . This is all fascinating, but who sees it? We're all so speed-oriented and the people in the school of architecture are too. So then I say, "Have you ever been to a cement mixing plant? Because you're going to be working with these materials. What do you know about cement? Have you ever been to a quarry? Have you ever watched stone being taken out of the quarries? *Shouldn't* you look into this? This is material you're going to be working with. Your love should start in the earth and grow out of the earth, so that you look totally at everything you're going to be working with. The entire history of architecture, of course, you must have been involved with—including such fantastic visions as Piranesi's [Imaginary] Prisons. You're never going to build anything like this, but it's very necessary that the imagination be drawn to the outlandish." I'd much rather have them design something ugly which can become beautiful. See, if it's really ugly, it can become beautiful after awhile because it is so outstandingly bad. But everything is so safe nowadays. I'd rather have somebody be brave and do something dreadful. And you'd stare at it and say, "My God, ick, that's awful . . . ," you know. Like the Prince Albert Memorial in London—that's fantastic. You mention it to a Londoner and he says, "Oh, that dreadful thing." But if you kidnapped that monument tomorrow, if you could move it with a machine, my God! what an uproar there would be. They'd suddenly realize that that beautiful ugly thing was gone. Same thing with the Eiffel Tower. But from one end of Wilshire to the other, here, there's hardly a building that is ugly. And there are very few buildings that are beautiful. There's neither. There are just nice square boxes—all very safe.

So, I'd much rather, as I say, overdo a thing whenever I write a story. I always give myself more material than I need. Whenever I write a novel I write three times as much as I need, and I tear it back down. When I wrote the screenplay *Moby Dick*, I wrote twelve hundred pages and ended up with a hundred and fifty. But you've got to do more in order to end up with less. . . . If you start with less you'll never have the more.

And then, gradually, you cut back, refine, so you get the things you want. This is true with everything. This is true in education; the helluva yell is the thing you start with. And if you can find someone with enthusiasm they're on their way to a goal. That's half the fight. Most of the people you run into are not enthused about anything. There's your problem. I never worry about the guy with enthusiasm. He's going to make it. If he wants to make shoes, he'll make the best shoes in the world. It's the guys that haven't selected a love yet that I worry about. The best things schools can do is to offer a huge seedbed of selection or enthusiasms, and then teach, somehow, enduring love of subject so much that students catch fire from it. That's really what you're there for.

WA: Is this really happening? Aren't the teachers better at stifling?
RB: I see variations on it, but I also see many teachers who also love what they're doing. It's pretty evenly distributed. Sometimes you see more teachers

on a new campus that hasn't stratified itself yet. I went down to Palomar College a year ago. It's still so new that there hasn't been an edifice of people built yet. It's a little more relaxed; there's not as much status-grouping and what have you. I think more colleges should shake themselves up. It might be good for everyone to be shaken free of a given university or high school every four or five years and be kicked out and sent somewhere else.

WA: Faculty too?
RB: Everyone! It's a wild thought. I've never said it out loud before. It just occurred to me it might be a good idea. After a while it's the same old lunch with the same old people, isn't it? We all get bored. I have to watch it in my own profession, too, even though I work for myself most of the time.

WA: You don't think it follows the popular notion, then, that the Ivy League Schools are good and other schools are not as good in terms of giving an education? By your description, for example, a highly stratified school like Harvard is not necessarily the best atmosphere.
RB: It wouldn't be good for a writer. I think any school is bad for any writer. In fact I encourage students, if they come to me, (and) if they're in college already and say they want to be a writer, to get the hell out of there. Because what you've got to be doing is spending eight hours a day on this machine (typewriter). And then, anything you need besides that you can pick up. You can go (to school) at night nowadays. They have fabulous classes at night if you want them. But the only things I would suggest studying at night—that would be good for a writer—would be, say, the history of the Renaissance, art, some sort of primeval psychology—anything that strikes them as exciting. What the hell! Take it.

WA: Not necessarily creative writing?
RB: Not creative writing! I don't think there are that many exciting teachers around. If you need the company, if you need some of the crowd too, on occasion, you can take those at night. In high school, I had one year of short story writing, but that was it. Then when I began to find friends in the writing field whom I could go to, who would encourage me, I formed little groups the last year in high school where prospective writers and artists got together and met at each other's homes. We need a lot of *ad hoc* personal groups. Lots of little *ad hoc* churches. People with similar miseries and

delights who could meet once a week to say, "God dammit, isn't it awful. But we're going to get through it somehow." I joined an acting group when I was nineteen and got a lot of acceptance there. I was in various science-fiction fan groups here in town, published my own magazine when I was seventeen.

It's this type of activity you need when you're growing as an artist, an actor, a writer—much more than the college atmosphere. It's the personal ground around you.

Maybe, eventually, the universities, recognizing this situation, will begin to form these more loosely organized groups of writers who will meet, not in classrooms, but in the professor's home one night a week. I think the conviviality of the home, the relaxation of sitting around in the easy chairs and reading stories to one another is what most of us need. Sometimes when you read a story aloud you can discover its flaws much more quickly. You're much more embarrassed by your own mistakes. It's happened to me and *it still happens* occasionally.

WA: Universities have a tendency to bureaucratize everything, so if they started that, you see, it would start with something in the home, and next, they would build a home in the middle of the campus which would be the home, then it would become the institute and so forth.

RB: Yes. I hate this term "writer-in-residence." That makes me feel very uneasy.

RB: Well, it seems that the teacher is bored by what he's saying; the students, too, are bored. If you want to get any kick out of the subject, then you read something outside your classes. Right. The thing is . . . the one all-around good local teacher is Bob Kirsch, who writes for the *L.A. Times* here, because Bob is very relaxed, and his tastes move in every field. He reads a mystery, a science-fiction novel, a James Bond book or a Sax Rohmer book and takes it for what it is. He'll say this is good of its kind and be very relaxed. But so many of these teachers of literature. . . . Well, look at the New York School. They scare the hell out of me. Every time I pick up the *New York Review of Books* . . . snobs! One week you have Susan Sontag writing on Norman Podhoretz and then you have Podhoretz writing on Susan Sontag. Then the following week there'll be a review on their latest novels and . . . the whole thing is so incestuous that it can't help but kill itself. Most intellectuals will not accept the fact that you can sit down and read Gerard Manley Hopkins one minute and the next minute pick up [Thomas Love] Peacock, [George Bernard] Shaw, Ayn Rand, [William Somerset] Maugham, Christopher Morley, Thomas Wolfe, Buck Rogers, Aldous Huxley, Jules Verne . . . and read them all and love them equally. This is what life says: Why do we have to stop our pleasures? Why can't we pick up James Bond and not have to apologize?

It's the ability to immediately go with a new kind of love and not just stick with the safe love, the "in" thing.

WA: Would you say this is what the intellectuals can't understand, this taking on many things at once? And what do you think is the reason for this? Obviously we live in a world of specialization that lends itself to this, but precisely why are intellectuals this way?
RB: Yes, they think something's wrong with you, and I think it's because . . . you've begun to put your finger on it. Any single critic or teacher who is specializing in a certain area is going to feel threatened if he doesn't stick with that. So they get established in the field and instead of broadening themselves, they think they're safe by specializing. But they're vulnerable because new theories may come along in literature in a few years that may knock them right out of their position, and they may not be ready for it.

WA: Do you think this specialization tends to deaden their sensitivity to the rest of the world about them?
RB: Well, yes. That's why science fiction is *the* literature. Of course, I'm prejudiced. I've worked in the field for years. But my prejudice is based on some easily verifiable facts. Look at the totality of science fiction. As I said earlier, there isn't any area of life that it doesn't move into. It's the literature of our time. Any literature that is written in our time that *isn't* science fiction is ignoring our problems.

The New York novel, the New York intellectual—Jewish, forty-nine, semi-homosexual—novel is not awake. Here's the theme of the average New Yorker's novel today: A guy hits forty-five; he's an intellectual who looks well upon himself and his IQ. His problem is: Is he going to divorce his wife; is he going to move in with his mistress, or the boy down the hall? He's Jewish on top of this, which gives him problems; or he's colored, which gives him super problems. So he may have three problems lined up and he's living in New York City, which is impossible. You *can't* live there. It doesn't really exist.

William B. Allen / 1968

It's a very narrow world which ignores all the science-fictional things which are changing our society. TV is a science-fictional fact. I use this label because twenty years ago this machine didn't exist. It was just beginning to appear in the store windows of America and we all collected and looked in at the window of the local TV repair shop, and we didn't own a set at the time. Most of us didn't. So suddenly this one device has changed the American family totally. Motion pictures are another science-fictional device. When I use this term "science-fictional," I mean a device which didn't exist a few years ago which suddenly comes along and revises a whole way of life. We have to weigh, then, the effect of these machines on our society. The incredible combination of TV, motion pictures, radio, and the automobile freed the Negro. They're all recent accumulations as the result of one science-fictional device, the car, which was utterly impossible.

If I had written a hundred years ago about any of these devices in the future doing what they have done, people would have said, "You're out of your skull. You're writing things that'll never happen." I know this intimately because I have been laughed at by people who said the space age would never come. Now, in the midst of the space age, I say to those people, "Not only did you ignore the rocket ship, you foolish people, but now you're ignoring the car, the TV, radio, and the H-bomb (which has totally changed politics in the world)." One science-fictional device, the hydrogen bomb, is making peace in the world, giving us a chance to build toward the United Nations. It's slow. I despair as much as anyone. But the war in Vietnam is not as big as it could be because of the hydrogen bomb, a science-fictional surprise which holds us unwilling murderers in check.

Well now, any fiction that ignores all of this is not a fiction of our time, and the only way you can write about our time is by saying, "For Christ's sake, look what's happening to our thinking." How many jobs have been lost because of the telephone? And how many have been created? How many opportunities have been lost by people foolish enough to pick up the phone, trying to do something with it that can't be done, lacking the human touch? So, they lost out on a good part of life because they use this device as a substitute for personal contact. How many friendships have been destroyed? We can't weigh these things; they're subtle, but that is the excitement of working in this field and saying, "Hey, let's watch the family." In the field of education, a lot of people criticize TV without realizing that it's a "cliché-teaching" device. It gives the students who come into the colleges today, on a certain level, a knowledge of cliché that we didn't have for five years later when I was growing up. So TV is an invaluable teacher—of mediocrities. But that's very necessary, because unless you know what's mediocre, you are forever assigned to mediocrity. It's like the old saying about history: He who doesn't know history must repeat history. It *all* must be learned. In order to be a good writer you must learn everything that's bad, which settles in the subconscious, so whenever you sit at the typewriter you don't have to think, "This is a cliché coming up!" Your subconscious eliminates the cliché. You don't have to think about it. Most of the people who are locked into repeating clichés and having to think about clichés have refused the chance to learn them. I believe in letting my children have all the TV they want. I'm not one of those intellectuals who say you can only watch this or that. No, no—just go *at* it! Because the sooner you do, the sooner you're going to get bored, walk away and look for that special book. I'm one of those who believes in IQ. I believe in intelligence. I don't believe it can be destroyed, if you relax and yell and run and yell and are excited. It can be crushed with criticism. "You *really* read the Bond books? Hmmmmm, well, well. You poor thing! Do you actually *like* them?" Do that often enough to your kids, your friends, and the element of fear enters. So my kids, anything they want to read, I let them read, or see. An example: I went into the living room, fourteen years ago. A Dylan Thomas record was on, "A Child's Christmas in Wales." I thought my wife had put it on. I walked in and my four-year-old daughter was listening to it and she said to me, "He knows what he's doing."

A couple of years later she was reading *Moby Dick*, at age eight. My first reaction was to take the book away. Then I said, "How're you liking the book? Enjoying it?" She said, "Yeah, but I skipped a little." I said, "I do, too." Learning how to skip, to come back later. . . .

Everything is relaxation. Hang free. Go with it, you know, because you keep growing. Boredom is mixed at the center of all art. Boredom is the center of growth and education. Learn how to respect being bored, teaching people creatively how to become bored, which means growing up so you want to move on. But see, the intellectuals don't really believe in their own intellectuality— in IQ, the supremacy of quality in thought. They really believe people can be corrupted. And I believe only fear corrupts. Only attacking people can corrupt them. I've watched when my oldest daughter was nine, and we were watching *Sunset Strip* one night. A dreadful show. I sat there because I wanted to be convivial with my kids. My oldest daughter got up and walked out of the room. I said, "Where are you going?" She said, "I know what's going to happen next." You see, I am not the teacher; she taught herself.

There's nothing you can do with the morons of the world. Let's not kid ourselves. This is one of the great problems of education. We do what we can to prepare them for a world in which they aren't going to be interested in many areas. As far as the bright people are concerned, just get out of the way. Let them follow their happy heads, take the joyous way they want to go.

WA: I read your last article in *Playboy* on death and horror movies. Tell us now, just what is this unreality about death that you seem to say we have?
RB: Well, it's always been true. In other words, Man, when he first began to think, when he lived in a cave, drew pictures to illustrate some idea about death, and gradually all these symbols grew up in the various mythologies so that we could draw a picture of a thing that couldn't be thought about. We really kid ourselves about it. The death of others is an impossibility because suddenly they cease, that's all. Everything's mystery from that point on. My mother died a year ago. Suddenly, "Bang!" you know, she was gone. That's all you can say about it. She's gone. Everything stops. You *can't* draw a picture of that. You must touch the thing that's not going to be touched. So, really, the age-old problem is still with us and we can't give up finding ways to think of it. Every time we think we've gotten away from those problems we're kidding ourselves.

We think we've gotten rid of God. How stupid. It reminds me of that old saying, "Shut the door, he's coming in the window; shut the window, he's coming through the floor." God takes on new disguises; death takes on new disguises. So we need new mythologies; we can't give up mythologies. We kid ourselves we're sophisticated enough, but what a mistake sophistication is. It's better to nail down a thing in some picture form where we can make do with it for awhile. You have more important things to do than think about death all the time. That's the reason for symbologies. Why go around ruining a life every day by saying, "Gee, I have to die." It's better to see it in some form like Dracula, then kill Dracula at the end with a stake and gain a little life for yourself. It gives you time to think of something else. Otherwise you're faced with your eventual death, which is unthinkable. As for God, my own conceptualization of Him is ancient and convenient—that we are God and are responsible to ourselves, which is great. A lot of people don't want to be responsible; they want to be irresponsible. So it's easier to create a God who

can be filed in a box off there. If God is out there you can blame him. But if God is here, there's nobody else to blame but yourself. If you are a piece of the moving flesh of God, you're responsible for your part of the universe. That means anything I do hurts me and other people. So it's an immediate. . . .
It is what [Jiddu] Krishnamurti was speaking of when he said "In the moment of thinking evil, think good. In a moment of doing evil, do good." Instantaneous Golden Rule—Instant Golden Rule. That's great. That way I know all the rules and don't have to blame anybody but myself. And if all the people believed this way, I think we could have a good world. It's the old story of lighting a candle in the corner where you are. Very primitive, very naive, but a very healthy, very real way of looking at the world.

WA: Would it be unfair or wrong to say that one finds much of [Walt] Whitman or [Ralph Waldo] Emerson in Bradbury?
RB: Not too much. I read Emerson so many years ago that I can't really say that he rubbed off that much. Little of Whitman, and I was very young. But Whitman could have come to me through other people, people like Norman Corwin or Thomas Wolfe. I'm not sure how much Whitman Thomas Wolfe read, but there are echoes. Emerson could have come to me through other people too. But if I really listed influences, I don't think I would put them on the list anywhere. Consciously, I only remember those people who I knew I couldn't live without. Edgar Rice Burroughs—if you had taken his books away from me when I was ten, I would have died. He was just the greatest writer. And then Jules Verne. My really greatest influences have been the writers of children's books—like Robert Louis Stevenson, Mark Twain, H. G. Wells. Those are my primary influences. In fact, the reason why a book like *Something Wicked This Way Comes* exists is because I went into the library one day and looked around and said, "Oh God, I want to wind up there on the shelf one day, between Mark Twain and Robert Louis Stevenson." These are my heroes, and I don't really have heroes among the popular American novelists. Sure, I admire them, but it's not the same kind of love. You never get over the original love. I can go back to *Huck Finn* or *Treasure Island* or even something like [Oscar Wilde's] *Dorian Gray*—another level that I consider a children's book in many ways, at least a late childhood book—and have the hell scared out of me. Or *Jekyll and Hyde*. These are primal influences and they're great fun. So I said to myself, "I want to write a book that will scare the hell out of me." That's the first thing it *had* to do. It must be a secret book; a book about boys and

their secret worlds, away from their parents and sneaking around behind the scenes of life from house to house. And they've got a pole that they shove across from one window to another between one boy's house and another boy's house. . . . Then they do all the great wild things boys relish and want and do in their heads and hope to do in the world. Night things. Middle of the night things. Adventures. Revelations. Running on midnight grass. Being pursued. Having death near. Surviving. And running together again, laughing at all the great times. And, exhausted, bedding down with new dreams about fine tomorrows.

In sum, I wish to belong to new children as they come into the world who may then grow up, read me again, and still be scared by me and relish things with me and like me.

For finally, one doesn't wish respect from one's peers, but that special regard which we call love, which gathers about honest and excited children and which hopefully waits to be reactivated when we, as adults, pick up old books and pray that they scare, stimulate, and delight us all over again.

The shelves of the libraries are small and uncrowded, really. God grant room for such as me to be trapped between the kind shoulders of Verne and the sharp ribs of [Rudyard] Kipling.

Ray Bradbury: On Hitchcock and Other Magic of the Screen
Arnold R. Kunert / 1972

Interview by Arnold R. Kunert, Spring 1972. Reprinted by permission. A similar version of this interview was first published in *Take One*, 26 September 1973.

Kunert: Ray, what I'd like to do is trace your writing career in film from its earliest point, 1953, with *The Beast from 20,000 Fathoms*, and ask you to react to the treatments done with your works, what suggestions you would have made, given the power to do so, and so on.
Bradbury: Very good.

K: How did you happen to become involved with the film version of *The Beast from 20,000 Fathoms*?
B: The first recollection I have of that film is early 1952, when the producer of the film, Hal Chester, called me to Warner Brothers studio and said "I have a screenplay here I want you to read. Your friend, Ray Harryhausen (one of Hollywood's most respected visual effects technicians) is going to be working on this film. We know that you've known each other for many years. Would you like to work with him?" I said, "God, of course! We've always wanted to do something together." Then he said, "Well, read the script, and, if you like it, maybe you can revise it or redo it or maybe even re-write the whole thing. Do you have time right now to go into the next room and give us an instant report?" I thought he was rushing things a little, but what the heck. I wanted to work with Ray, so I went into the next room and read the script, which was not very good. After I'd finished, Chester asked me what I thought of it. I told him I thought it was all right, but that it was very much like an idea of mine, a short story that had been in the *Saturday Evening Post* about a year before. Well, his jaw dropped, his eyes bugged, his wig turned around three times, and then I realized that someone in the studio had "borrowed" my idea and written the script. Then they had called me in, forgetting where they had borrowed the idea, and asked me to re-write it. An incredible, ironic situation. I played it very cool and said nothing. I went away from there and the next

day I received a telegram saying "We wish to buy the rights to *The Beast from 20,000 Fathoms* for X number of dollars." So, that's how the film got under way, under these very strange circumstances. I really had nothing to do with the film. I didn't write the script. I think the studio was a little embarrassed by the whole situation. It was one of those flukey things. One hesitates to say the "borrowing" was deliberate. It's often on a subliminal level. You try to give people the benefit of the doubt and there are legitimate times when we write things that we don't realize are based on ideas we've seen in the past. I certainly have caught myself on one or two occasions, promptly dropped the story and tried to forget about it—not to repeat the mistake. Anyway, they went on and made the film.

K: Do you think you would feel differently about the whole situation had they come to you and asked you to write the script fresh?
B: I honestly don't know. You try to remember what you were doing at certain ages and how you reacted to people. People are always asking me why I make the kinds of decisions I make about films. A lot of it is loneliness, neglect, and a love for the medium. Sometimes you make decisions for strange reasons. You have to be honest about it and not make up reasons and kid people into thinking that you think certain directors were best for your films. I'll discuss it at greater length when we get to *The Illustrated Man*. In the case of *The Beast from 20,000 Fathoms*, that was merely an accident. I wanted to be affiliated with Ray Harryhausen. My God, we've known each other since we were both teenagers. He was the best man at my wedding. We're still extremely close friends. So the decision to sell *The Beast* was a combination of accident plus a love for Ray Harryhausen and his work. They didn't use my story very much in the finished film, and that's their fault, isn't it? I wasn't there to supervise. They didn't ask me.

K: Why hadn't you become involved in films before this time?
B: Well, I suppose I was afraid. I was afraid of getting involved with the studios. Afraid of giving up my loneliness. I'm a loner by instinct, and I think it's been the correct thing to do. Every time I get out in huge crowds of so-called "creative" people I am really not happy. I have no respect for other people's opinions. I wish I could say otherwise, but that's the way I am. I detest fake humble people or even half-humble people. I don't believe their humbleness. I think that we're all in the arts and crafts and that you simply cannot be

humble. You must believe in creativity in order to survive and the more you do of it the more certain you are of what you can do, and the less you want to listen to other people. So, I held away from the studios for many years, even though I love motion pictures, knowing that some day I would go into filmmaking, and wanting to with all my heart, part of me wanting to because I loved films. I have seen just about every film ever made and many of them dozens of times. So, when friends used to write me in my late twenties and early thirties and ask, "Hey, Ray, when are you going to write your first screenplay?", I always wrote back, half-seriously, half-humorously, "When John Huston offers me a job." Huston was my big hero. There were very few American directors of that period (late 1940s and early 1950s) I wanted to work for. Later on, there were many foreign directors that I fell in love with. David Lean was just beginning to come on the scene in London at that time.

K: When did you first see John Huston?
B: In 1949, Norman Corwin, a very dear friend for many years, invited me over to hear one of his United Nations broadcasts. Seated right behind me was John Huston and his wife. I looked up and saw him and my heart sank, and I thought, "Oh, my God, here's my hero. I want to grab his hand. I want to run up to him and say 'I love you! I love your films. And oh, my God, employ me!'" But, I held off.

K: Why?
B: I knew that I wasn't ready. This is a hard thing to get over to younger people. You've got to prove yourself, and they're always saying, "Yeah, but how do you prove yourself if someone doesn't give you a chance?" Well, you make your own chances in other fields. You print something in a book, you put it in magazines, you write poetry, you paint. You've got to have proof of your ability to show someone. I simply did not feel that I had enough to show Huston, enough to prove my ability. What's the use in going up to a man and saying, "I love you," if you can't also prove you love your craft well enough? So, I sat in my seat that night at the theater. I didn't allow myself to be introduced to Huston. I didn't want to gush, because I knew I would, and as I sat there I thought, "No, I'll write two more books, and when they are published, then I'll call my agent and tell him I'm ready to meet John Huston." All of this happened in the spring of 1949, because I hadn't gone to New York yet to sell *Martian Chronicles*. Norman Corwin persuaded me to go to New York, where

I sold two collections, the *Chronicles* and *The Illustrated Man*. They were published in the next two years, and then, on the day of publication of *The Illustrated Man*, when I had three books, *Dark Carnival*, *The Martian Chronicles*, and *The Illustrated Man*, I was ready. Forgive my braggadocio, but goddam it, it all makes sense. I knew exactly when I was ready. We all know this. You know when you go off half-cocked, when you're an ass, and when you do something you shouldn't do, that you haven't prepared yourself for. I *knew* I was prepared. I was turning thirty-one, and I said to my agent, "Now call John Huston, find out where he is; I want to meet him." He put in a call, and we made one date and I went over to a small studio in Hollywood, but Huston wasn't there. He'd been called away. Something had come up on the film he was making—final cuts or something of the sort, and he left his apologies. Well, my heart sank, and I thought, "My God, I'm going to miss him." I'd heard he was leaving town soon. Well, the next day he called back and we met on February 14th, Valentine's Day. We had dinner and I said my little speech. I put my three books on the table and said, "Here they are, all signed to you. I think you're wonderful and I want to work for you someday if you like my books. If you find in them what I find in *The Maltese Falcon*, *Treasure of the Sierra Madre*, and so on." It was a very brief meeting. We had dinner, a few drinks, and the next night, the fifteenth, a preview of *Red Badge of Courage* was being held and John invited me over to see it. There was a very mixed reaction from the audience. Some people got up and walked out, but I found it to be a remarkable film, and I think that every time I've seen it since, even in the cut version, I like it very much. Well, after that I didn't see John for two years. He wrote back two months later from Africa, where he was shooting *The African Queen*, and said, "Yes, I like your books. Someday we're going to work together." We wrote back and forth about twice a year for two years and then on August 15, 1953, upon returning from a book-hunting expedition in Long Beach with Ray Harryhausen, I discovered a message from John asking me to call him. I called his hotel and he asked me to come over for a drink. He put a drink in my hand and asked me what I was up to. I said nothing. I had just finished *Fahrenheit 451* . He said, "Do you have any free time?" I replied that I did. Then he said, "Well, how would you like to go to Ireland with me and write the screenplay for *Moby Dick*?" I said, "My God, I don't know! I don't know!" He said, "What do you mean you don't know?" I said, "Well, I've never been able to read the book. I've had it around the house for years and just eight weeks ago, I picked it up, not knowing that

you'd be asking me to read it. I'll go home tonight and read it, then tell you tomorrow at lunch what I decide. I don't want you to hire me and have me do a bad job." So I went to the copy of *Moby Dick* I had at home, a big, heavy, limited edition which is very hard to read. I couldn't manage with it, so I went to a local book store, bought a smaller edition, and took it home, walked in and said to my wife, "Hey, see this book! Well, depending upon what I find in it tonight, we either do or do not go to Ireland in two weeks."
A dreadful thing to say, but I felt so responsible and so pulled. In a moment like that the tendency might be to lie. You don't know what's going on in your heart, because you want to work for the man you admire, and working on something of Herman Melville's, the great American novelist, makes it even more difficult. So, I sat down and tested myself the best way any writer can test himself, not by opening to the first page, but by diving into the middle. I just opened the book at random and dived in. And, of course, *Moby Dick* makes for grand diving. It's an ocean of fantastic bits and pieces. It's a Shakespearean pageant with flags and pennants and fleets of ships and whales. One moment you're examining the various colours of nightmare, panics, terrors, and the next you're studying whiteness. The whiteness of the Arctic and the Antarctic, the things born beneath the sea that surface without eyes, and on and on. I finally got back to the scene where Ahab is at the rail, saying, "It's a mild-looking day and a mild-looking sky and the wind smells as if it blew from the shadow of the Andes where the mowers have lain down with their scythes," and I turned back to the beginning and read, "Call me Ishmael," and I was hooked! I didn't know why I was hooked. But, there was something vaguely familiar about the whole book. Later, I realized that I was reading [William] Shakespeare all over again, and then, much later I discovered, in fact, only in recent years, after I had finished the screenplay, that Melville had completely written *Moby Dick*, and then had thrown out the original version that he had finished sometime in the 1850s when Shakespeare had fallen into his life. A neighbour had given him an edition of Shakespeare with large type, which was very rare in those days. Most of the books then had very small type which he could not read. So he had never read Shakespeare before. All of a sudden, here is this grand poet and rhetorician impinging upon his life. So he rewrote *Moby Dick* entirely. Shakespeare has been one of my loves since I was fourteen years old. Suddenly, as I read *Moby Dick*, I found myself in familiar territory. I sensed that I was reading a poet, but I didn't sense that it was the bastard son of Shakespeare, and since I had always considered myself, rightly

or wrongly, to be the bastard son of Shakespeare, I think you can understand why, at two in the morning, I found myself totally absorbed in the novel. I went to John Huston the next day and said, "Yes, I think I'm old enough. I'll be turning thirty-three next week. I want to write the screenplay." And so John and I went to Ireland where I was to do my first screenplay. It seems to me that I'm jumping all over, but I had to explain how I got into films through Huston who, at that time, was my idol.

K: Ray, let's backtrack for a few moments. The press book for *It Came from Outer Space*, released in 1953, states that the screenplay was based on a "treatment" by you. How extensive was that treatment?
B: Well, it was huge. I did a screenplay, really. I was so naive. They paid me $2500 and I did the whole screenplay. I earned around $300 dollars a week for the script.

K: Did the studio production head feel that the script was not commercial enough?
B: No. They liked it. But they didn't want to trust me with doing the screenplay because of my lack of experience, even though I had already done it in treatment form. It's written like a short novel, 120 pages. I think I could have done the script, but they had a screenwriter at the studio who was a professional and they wanted him to do it. Apparently, it was very easy for him.

K: How extensively did the screenwriter borrow from your treatment?
B: Very heavily. I haven't gone through to see how many scenes, pages, or paragraphs. I may have done so eighteen years ago, but I've forgotten and I don't want to be unfair to the screenwriter. I do remember, however, that it very heavily leans on what I provided in my naiveté. That's O.K. Fine. It's a way of learning. It's a way of growing. *It Came from Outer Space* was, I suppose, my first *real* screenplay, even though I didn't know what I was doing.

K: Was the treatment for that film based upon any of your published or unpublished stories?
B: No. It was essentially original, even though the theme was by no means fresh. It had been done as far back as the days of Jules Verne. Probably even before that. It's a variation on ancient themes.

K: Do you feel any bitterness at not having been chosen to write the screenplay from your own treatment?

B: I was a beginning writer. Especially in films. I couldn't demand to do the screenplay. Now that I'm older, I can ask for that sort of thing and quite often get it. The final version of *It Came from Outer Space* is a good film. Some parts of it are quite nice. It was one of the first films to use helicopter shots at all well. I had more of that in *my* version. I had more to do with the telephone line operators and the wires. What little was there in the film was quite evocative, though, and a bit chilling.

K: Many of the scenes appear to have a Hitchcock feeling to them.

B: That's right. Yet, there were some things in my treatment which were overdone in the film and which I simply don't believe. They're just bad. Also, I hope I didn't have in my treatment the scene where the little boy comes to the door in a Halloween outfit and the girl screams so unbelievably. No one would scream that way at a kid at the door with a ray-gun outfit. So, that's bad direction. Jack Arnold is responsible for that. He should be paddled. I'm sure he's embarrassed whenever he recalls that scene. There are also all sorts of fake dangers in the film. I told the studio in my treatment that the *suggestion* of terror would be better than *showing* the monsters. But, they insisted on showing the monster and, sure enough, there it is. If trimming in the film were possible, having the monster on screen for just half a second would probably help immensely, because you couldn't really see what it is but, with the film now the camera is held on it for three, four, five seconds and that's plenty of time to see all the make-up dripping off. So, well, what the heck, it's a good film. I have nothing to be very proud of—or ashamed of.

K: From there you went into *Moby Dick*?

B: Yes. Now *there* is a film of which I am *immensely* proud. I am sure it has many flaws that I can't see. I'm too close to it. Its basic flaw, I suppose, is in the casting of Greg Peck as Ahab. But that's interesting, too, because when I got to Ireland, and I sat down with Huston the first few weeks and he told me somewhere along the line that they had hired Greg Peck some little doubt must have shattered my face. I have always admired Mr. Peck. In certain kinds of films I thought he was terrific. But I couldn't imagine him as Ahab, and I suppose I mentioned that to John. I told him that I had wanted Lawrence Olivier as Ahab. John told me that the studio told him, rightfully, that if you hired Olivier you'd lose all your money. And of course you would. You see, you and I can sit here and pontificate all day about Lawrence Olivier and how much we love him. He's the greatest actor around and has been for the past twenty-five years. But that doesn't solve the problem of casting a film, because you could put Olivier in a film, put out four million dollars, and lose every penny. No one ever goes to see Olivier in films. I don't think he has ever had a financial success over the years which would make a producer feel confident enough to cast him in an expensive film.

Films like *Henry V* and *Richard III* made their money back over long periods of time and in special situations, like putting them in schools, herding classes to them, forcing them. Every English teacher and drama teacher in America whipped their kids into going to see these films. After they got there they enjoyed them and discovered Olivier and said, "My God, what a man. What an actor!" But put Olivier in an ad and release it in the theatres? Forget it! When both of the films I just mentioned had their early runs in Los Angeles, the theatres were filled with classes from the nearby schools. The ordinary public wouldn't go. I want to make this point clear. People need to understand what the economics of film-making really are. We shouldn't kid ourselves that the average film producer is in it for aesthetic reasons. That's not why he's there. He shouldn't be. He has too much money invested. If you're financing your own film, then it probably doesn't make much difference, but when someone else is financing you it does indeed make a difference. Today, there is more than ever a feeling that if you don't like what someone does, find someone else to do it. Nobody is making you do anything. Any time you don't like the world, you can leave it or get another job or you can travel. This is a free society and most societies are fairly free. There are certain restrictions in every society.

K: Did Huston approach the Warner Brothers people about doing a film version of *Moby Dick* or was it the other way around?
B: I think John initiated the decision to do the film. He had worked on a screenplay with Anthony Veiller, who has been around Hollywood for some time. After we got to Ireland I told John I didn't want to see the script because I didn't want anybody saying that I had lifted anything from somebody else's script. Anyway, you're going to be following Melville, so there will be some duplication automatically. I was very careful never to let that other script near me until after I had come home from overseas and had finished

my job. Then I was curious to see what Veiller had done, and as it turned out he had only done the first sixty pages or so and they weren't happy with that. I was happy to see that I had done an excellent job by comparison.

K: Did you receive any of the traditional studio interference while you were preparing the script?
B: The great thing about this is that the studio stayed absolutely away. It was the Mirisch brothers who financed the film with Warner Brothers. I only met them once while I was writing the screenplay in Dublin and then again in London when I was finishing. There was no interference of any sort. Huston simply said, "Now, look, *I've* hired Bradbury. I trust him." When I asked him, upon arriving in Ireland, whether he wanted the Freudian version or the Jungian version of Melville's white whale or the Melville Society's version, he simply said, "Ray, I want the Bradbury version. That's why I hired you. You're going to do the script any way you want it. And get it done." That was great! There is a wonderfully amusing little sidelight to tie in with this, however. I had been working, oh God, I guess three months. I had about ninety or a hundred pages done when a cablegram came from Warner Brothers. Huston's secretary brought it in. John read it, sat down, and put his head in his hands. I read it. It said: "Insist that strong woman's part be written into *Moby Dick* script or refuse to proceed. Signed, Jack L. Warner." Well, I threw the cablegram on the floor and jumped on it with both feet and I swore—I rarely used such words. I must have burned the secretary's ears off. And in the middle of swearing and cursing at the Warner Brothers people and Jack Warner, I looked up and saw Huston rolling on the floor, laughing, and I realized the son-of-a-bitch had sent the cablegram himself as a joke. So then I called *him* some names! And then we all broke apart and laughed. It was a wonderful day!

K: Huston had probably had something that ridiculous actually happen on more than one of his films.
B: Oh, sure. And that's why he knew I'd believe it and be sucked right in. That was the first of a series of practical jokes John would pull on me. They got a little worse later. Let's get back to the casting for a moment. I said I'd wanted Olivier and John said there was no way to make back the investment, but then he said, "Now, look, I really think I can get a performance out of Peck. Did you see *Red Badge of Courage*?" I said I had. "What did you think of

Audie Murphy?" I said it was a new Audie Murphy. He said, "Now, what about *The African Queen*?" I said I thought it was a new Bogart. In fact, many of the Bogart fans don't like that film because it's not Bogart to them, but I think it's just delicious. It's so good! I've seen it at least six times. So, on the strength of what John had said to me, I said O.K. He said, "Ray, if I have to put strings on Greg, I'll get the performance I want." I really believed John could do it. Anyway, when you're with a director you love and admire you fall under his spell. Anything he says is right. It's like being with God. And this is true for every director I've ever been with. That can be good and bad. It must be a terrible burden on them. They must be perfect human beings. They can't truly be themselves. Human beings. They are on a pedestal and cannot let down their guards. Anyway, here I was with John. He cast Peck and now when I look at the film that seems to be the film's major failing.

K: When did you first see the completed film?
B: I first saw it at the studio about two years after I finished the script. I finished in April of 1954 and came back to the United States almost immediately afterward.

K: Why didn't you stay on to see how the film was done?
B: Primarily because by the time I had finished the script I was exhausted. I had been working twelve hours a day, seven days a week, for six or seven months and I was going mad to see my family. My family was down in Sicily. The weather had been so bad up in Dublin. The snow, the cold, and the fog and the poverty. Ireland really is a dreadful place. It's just beautiful and the people are wonderful, but the weather is horrible. And the rain comes down day after day for thirty or forty days, no sun for weeks. You get suicidal. That time in my life I can point to and say I honestly had suicidal feelings—which I can look back upon now and realize were a combination of many different things: the weather, being away from home for the first time in my life, all the people I knew and loved. We knew no one in Ireland. Working on Herman Melville was a huge burden. I didn't know it was going to be such a burden. I didn't know that all these things were the result of carrying the weight of the albatross and THE WHALE on my shoulders, plus John Huston. Here I was, working for my hero and, God, how I wanted to do well. I wanted to show off and write brilliantly all the time. But you can't do that. That's not the way writing happens. You hope it happens every day, but it's a matter of luck.

You just go to the typewriter and get to work—hoping for the best. About sixty days into writing the script, right around Thanksgiving of 1953, I had finished about fifty-five pages and John had seen none of it yet. He had been so wonderfully patient. We had had lots of dinners together, gone on a few fox hunts, and met a few of John's friends, but I had had these terrible depressions day after day and never had anything like it before. A few when I was younger, but I had always known, or had enough sense, when I was in my teens and twenties, to shift gears and go do something else and the depressions went right away. It's a great secret that many people are unaware of: just go jump in a pool, swim, hike, ride, do something different. Write poetry instead of short stories, write a novel instead of a play. Do something different. Change your mood. Don't put up with it. It's nonsense. But in Ireland I couldn't change my mood. I was stuck with Melville. I was stuck with The Whale. I was stuck with Huston. I was stuck with Ireland. So, I went to John and turned in the first fifty-five pages and said, "Now, look, I have a twenty-six-week contract, but I don't want to honor that contract if I'm not doing good work. I could stay on and take your money and do a bad job, but I don't work that way. I couldn't live with myself. Read the script, and if you don't like what you read, fire me. I don't want to go on with this if I'm not doing well." John went into the big room of his big house in Killcock to read the script and I went upstairs to wait for two hours. Then one of the most beautiful things I've ever heard in my life came about when John came to the foot of the stairs and called up, "Ray, come down and finish the script." Isn't that a great way of saying "You're hired permanently"? I was practically in tears. I came down and I was so relieved that the depressions went away. And I realized then that I'd been living under the shadow of Huston and Melville and all of these things had gotten through to me. This huge weight came off my soul and I was able to work even better from then on.

K: Did Huston collaborate with you on any part of the script?
B: No, there was never any collaboration, in spite of the fact that his name appears on the credits.

K: How did he manage to get his name on the credits?
B: That's a long story. John wrote a few scenes to show me ways of going. Certain kinds of things. But he's not a screenwriter. He's always been a collaborator in the past, supposedly, but I don't know, since I wasn't there, how or

what the collaboration consisted of. But on this film there was a very clear definition of our respective roles. He was producer and director and I was the screenwriter. I worked six or seven months on the screenplay. I did eighteen or twenty outlines and thousands of pages of materials, as I recall, to wind up with a script which was 150 pages long. And all of this was typed up by Huston's secretary and by Huston's office staff, with Huston's mimeograph material. All the copies of the script you will find anywhere in the world say "Screenplay by Ray Bradbury." There's no mention of anyone else there. Why would Huston's secretary type my name on there if I hadn't done the script alone? If it were my secretary it would have been suspicious. So I finished up and the last day before I left London I went to John and said, "Hey, this has been a great experience in my life. I know it's going to change my life forever and I'm deeply grateful. To show my gratitude for your help along the way, I would like you to share the screen credit." He said, "Oh, Ray, cut it out. No, you did the screenplay. You deserve the credit alone." But, I offered out of my love and overwhelming gratitude, even though he did nothing on the screenplay. I wanted to share screen credit, but he refused. So that's nice and clean cut, O.K.? A year later, I received a special delivery letter from Warner Brothers: "If you do not contest this in twenty-four hours, the screenplay credit will read as follows 'Screenplay by John Huston and Ray Bradbury.'" Well, I fell right over, and I got mad and thought, "My God, why would he pull this sort of thing?"

K: Did Huston put in for the equal billing?
B: Yes. And the studio went along with it because they believed John. I went over to the Screen Writers' Guild immediately. I said he didn't write the screenplay and couldn't ask for it. I was furious. I was murderous at that point. If he had accepted the day I had offered it to him I would not have objected. But this way was different. It was going the other way and it was thievery. So I filed through the Screen Writers' Guild. We had readings of the scripts by three people, who then judged and I won. I got sole credit on all the early ads for *Moby Dick*. Then John came back from Europe, went to the Screen Writers' Guild, and said he wanted the case reopened because he wasn't there when the decision had been reached and he had new evidence. And they reopened the case. Now that's not allowed! It's against the rules of the Screen Writers' Guild. Once the case is settled, and one of the parties isn't there, that's his hard cheese. But they did reopen, and John submitted, as his

evidence of what he had done, a copy of my screenplay with my name on it, in which he had gone through with a red pencil and indicated sections that he had *supposedly* written. What kind of evidence is that? Against my two thousand pages of corrected script that I have put away. I have them all in my basement at home. Plus all my notes and outlines. But I lost. I saw the letters from the second group of judges, which said: "If judged on the material alone we would have to give the credit to Bradbury. But the fact that Huston is such a famous director makes us lean over backward."

K: You eventually got top billing even though it was a split credit.
B: That's right.

K: Was this typical of Huston's behavior?
B: He has done this on more than one occasion and I don't know what all the motives are. I don't know the circumstances. One cannot judge all the other things. But in case after case he has shared screen credit, which makes me wonder how much he has contributed. I really don't know. The best way to find out if there was a real 50-50 thing there is to contact all the other screenwriters. The credit on *The Maltese Falcon* is very mysterious. I've heard all kinds of things about it, but I hesitate to gossip. It's ridiculous. I *know* about *this* case. I was there.

K: Were you able to write anything immediately following your completion of the *Moby Dick* script?
B: No. When you get to the end of a project as big as that you're exhausted. I just wanted to go somewhere and lie down. It was the first time I had ever had a day off from writing in twenty-one years. I had been writing since I was twelve, and for the first time I really felt the need of a vacation. So I took two or three weeks off. My family and I toured through Sicily, and up through France. By the time I got back to New York I was well again. I was recovered from Melville.

K: It took you several years to put your Irish experiences on paper with "The Anthem Sprinters" and other stories. Was this because of your overinvolvement with Ireland during the *Moby Dick* period?
B: Yes. All of that came out much later than it ordinarily would have. The experience with *Moby Dick* is a very mixed one. It did indeed change my life.

I'm still immensely grateful. I think it was brave and wonderful of John to hire me. He liked to tell people he had hired me for the shock value. That was part of it. People would say, "The science-fiction writer is going to write *Moby Dick*?" and John would laugh and they would think it was a joke. Then they found out I really was working on the script. I'm sure that must have been about one per cent of the reason for John's hiring me. The extra joke element. As I've said, John enjoyed joking around. But I am quite sure that the greatest part of his decision to hire me was based on his reading of some of my work and seeing that I did have something poetic to say. At least, people tell me I'm poetic. Over the years such people as Aldous Huxley have come to me and said, "You're a poet. It's right there in the *Martian Chronicles* stories. Let me read this to you." I was quite surprised by that. My life has been a surprise to me. And I guess that's a great way to live. To surprise yourself and have others surprise you.

K: Do you feel any resentment toward those who regard science-fiction literature as *less* than poetic?
B: No. But many fine writers have been sorely neglected over the years because they have *chosen* to write science fiction or imaginative literature.

K: Do you see a change in that attitude today?
B: Well, we are still fighting the fight. It's amazing how many people still come up to me and say, "Hey, I've put off reading you because I thought that you were a science-fiction writer and science fiction wasn't good." I've actually heard this from librarians *and* English teachers.

K: How many years passed after you finished *Moby Dick* before you did another script or treatment for television or motion pictures?
B: My first work in script writing after *Moby Dick* was in television. I didn't get into television until after about ten years from its beginnings in the late 1940s. I recall first doing a story for *The Jane Wyman Theatre*, a fantasy about a carnival man and his wife, called "The Bullet Trick." The wife was having an affair and they have to go through a bullet trick routine in which the husband forces the lover through some means to fire a bullet at the end of the act, which the wife is supposed to catch in her teeth. We have a feeling at the fade out that maybe the husband substituted a real bullet for the blank so that when the lover fires the wife will be killed. Joseph Wiseman played the husband, who was

quite good. It was fair. That was my first television show. I was afraid of television, and for good reason. Quality has rarely been there. At least when you make films, even if they're magnificent failures, there's a helluva lot more quality. *The Illustrated Man*, for example, is not a good film, but it has a lot of good stuff in it. It's beautifully photographed, the set design is quite interesting, and so on. Everything is there except the film. It's beautiful to look at, and the music by Jerry Goldsmith is gorgeous. The performances are mixed, but occasionally just right. It should have worked, but it didn't have either a screenplay or a director who knew how to direct. With TV, my God, your chances are even smaller. When the Hitchcock television people came along, however, I began to work once or twice a year on television. We had a beautiful relationship. In fact I still do, with Joan Harrison, Norman Lloyd, and Mr. Hitchcock himself. I didn't get to know Mr. Hitchcock too well until quite recently, actually. In fact, I've spent more time with him recently because I was helping Arthur Knight interview Mr. Hitchcock at the studio. That was glorious. He is a super-enthusiast.

K: How many shows did you do for Hitchcock over the years?
B: I would say at least twelve.

K: That many?
B: Yes. Around eight or nine half-hour stories and three hour shows. One of the three hour shows was for *Alcoa Premiere* on a segment produced by the Hitchcock people.

K: That would have been "The Jail," in 1961.
B: That's right. And that show has never been repeated since it was first shown. There were one or two letters from religious groups around the country because I transferred souls. Isn't that ridiculous? And the most ridiculous thing is not that the letters were written—I respect anyone's writing a letter, what the hell—but that anyone at the network would listen to them seems absurd. I don't think you'd have that sort of thing today, but eleven years ago, when the show first came on, there was static and they canceled any further showings of it.

K: How did you happen to hit upon the idea of "The Jail"?
B: It goes back about twenty years. A friend of mine brought a tape recorder to a writer's meeting. I asked him if I could play around with it. I hadn't seen

that many at the time. I wanted to see if I could dictate a story and I had this idea about a society jailing people in other people's bodies, which I thought was fascinating. I guess the idea originally came from going to a hospital. When you go to a hospital you're so glad to be out. The people there are trapped. Their bodies are where they don't want them to be. They are incarcerated in an environment where they don't want to be. From the hospital I got the idea of the personal jail and then I got the idea of the society that says, "OK, we've got news for you. We're going to take your nice, fresh body and give it to someone else more deserving and then we're going to trade souls and you're going to wind up with that fellow's soul. This way we don't need executions." And it had a kind of a wonderful justice about it. What worse punishment could there be than being jailed in someone else's sick body and they, in turn, if they're worthy, having a different body. No execution. No electric chairs. No switches pulled. I think it's a fascinating idea. I did a tape of this idea which I still have somewhere, and then I had it put on a record later, and didn't think about it for eight years. The Hitchcock people called me and told me they were going to do a show for the *Alcoa Premiere* series. I went to lunch with them and, as usual, I described two or three ideas, and asked them to pick the one they liked. They liked "The Jail," I wrote the script, and it went on just as we had discussed it. This was the best part about working with the Hitchcock people. They respected my opinions and I respected theirs. No one slighted anyone. You must have this when you are writing.

K: How many of the twelve or so Hitchcock scripts were written by you and how many were adapted by other writers from your work?
B: I did most of the half-hour scripts myself.

K: What were some of those shows?
B: Oh, we did "And So Died Riabouchinska," the story of a man and his puppet. The man murders and the puppet, inside his mind, makes him give himself up. At the end, the puppet turns against him and won't speak. The lead was played by Claude Rains. It was not a *great* half hour, but it was such a pleasure to see Claude Rains in something I had done. And then they did "Marionettes Inc." and Norman Lloyd acted in that and played the two parts of the robot and the husband. I think Robert Stevens directed that. Then we did "Looking for Death," about two old insurance salesmen who theorize that

when the temperature hits Fahrenheit 92 more murders are supposed to occur than at any other time. There was a Mrs. Shrike who lived upstairs, who screams at everyone because she knows she's going to get killed that day. The husband comes home at the end of the day with a longshoreman's hook dangling from his pocket and we know that he's going to kill her. The two insurance men are murder preventers. Jo Van Fleet played Mrs. Shrike, and she did quite well with it. One of my favorite shows from the hour-long Hitchcock series was "The Life Work of Juan Diaz," along with "The Jar," adapted by James Bridges, who recently adapted the script for "The Forbin Project." I should have done the adaptation of "The Jar" myself. I don't recall now why I allowed anyone else to do it. I suppose I was busy on something else at the time.

K: The script for "The Jar" worked very well, in spite of the fact that you didn't write it. It has some fine scenes in it.
B: Oh, it was a fine adaptation. Pat Buttram was very good. I just played it again the other night at home. After "The Jar" came "The Jail," with John Gavin and Bettye Ackerman and James Barton as the old man whose soul is transferred to Gavin's body. It was one of the last things Barton did before he died. I still hear from his widow, God bless her. She writes me every Christmas "from Jim in Heaven and Mrs. Barton." Isn't that nice? She's a darling, sweet lady. I was lucky in television and as soon as Hitchcock quit, I quit. I had some bad luck with Rod Serling on the one script I had written for *The Twilight Zone*.

K: "I Sing the Body Electric".
B: Yes.

K: What happened to that script?
B: Well, I adapted it for the half-hour show and I was very excited about it. I asked Mr. Serling if I could count on it being filmed exactly as I had written it, as had always been the case with Hitchcock, and he assured me that it would be. So, the night the show aired I had all my friends tune in. We discovered that the most important part of the script had been cut. The speech where the grandmother explains what she is—a robot. The moment of truth. That's the time that I realized that all major studios working in television have a man they call "The Truth Dentist," who extracts all the good stuff

from every script—just pulls it out by the bloody roots and throws it away. Every studio has a dentist, a dummy who says "Oh, this is slow. Let's rip that page out." In my particular case, that was the page that explained the whole story. Without it, the story has no meaning. Who cares about a robot grandmother if she doesn't have meaning? You want to go to someone, anyone, and ask "Who are you? What are you? What are you doing here? Where have you been? Where are you going?" And they answer, and that gives meaning to them. Friendships are based on an accumulation of data about one another. We get to know each other and then, based on what we learn, usually in a few hours, we make new friends. So, here in "I Sing the Body Electric" I had the robot grandmother explaining the dream of Fantoccini, Inc., what makes these fabulous electric marionettes so beautiful, what their common humanity is. Machines are not inhuman if they embody humanity. If you put a dream into a machine, it becomes more than a machine. It becomes part of the dream. We can create good machines and bad machines and that's the whole idea of the story. But the truth dentist extracted that. So much for Mr. Serling. Motion pictures are not machines—they're dreams. Mechanical dreams that are fabulous and change our lives and make us better. Make us behave better. Good God, this is a Christian device then, isn't it? It does more, in many cases, than all the preachers in history have been able to do. Since they came into widespread use sixty or seventy years ago, motion pictures have been able to do more good than almost any other device or human being that ever lived, by showing us examples of other ways of living so that we say, "Hey, that Russian is a human being, that Jew is a human being, that Catholic is a human being, that woman is a human being, that man is a human being." And so we get away from labels and we relax and say, "Jesus God, let's forgive each other." The data collecting that goes into hating is simple and direct, the data collecting that goes into loving takes more time and energy. Staying in love takes effort. We are tempted to throw up our arms and scream, "This is madness!" But most of us don't. We do make it to the end. We do stay sane. We *do* forgive one another and we *do* keep trying.

K: Then, of course, you forgive Jack Smight for what he did to "The Illustrated Man."
B: Oh, certainly. Let me tell you about that film. The reason I sold *The Illustrated Man* to Smight and the Warner Brothers is because no one else wanted it. That project was around for 16 years or more. I first conceived of

using *The Illustrated Man* as a radio series even before television. I wrote some preliminary radio ideas about *The Illustrated Man*. It is kind of crazy using *The Illustrated Man* on radio because, of course, it isn't a visual medium. But he could be described anyway. I think it could have worked. But it is *really* made for television. Producer Jerry Wald was interested in making a film version about fifteen years ago. Jerry and I got along fine. He was a vulgar, nice man. He was what we used to think of as the typical Hollywood producer. Now that I look back, he's Jesus Christ by comparison to some of the people I see today at the studios. The barracudas have taken over. He was a saint. And he was a smart cookie, too. He did something which most other producers had never thought to do. He wrote all the libraries in America and asked them to tell him which books were being borrowed. He didn't want to know the best sellers. He could have got best seller lists from publishers. No. He wanted to know what the people in Waukegan, Podunk, and so on were reading. He got twenty thousand lists back. He added them all up, got the twenty most-often-borrowed books, which had nothing to do with best seller lists—some of them were fifty years old, some twenty years old, some by Willa Cather, some by Thomas Wolfe. Then he went out and bought up all the books he could from his list of the most borrowed. Some couldn't be purchased for legal reasons, others had already been sold. Now that is a brilliant man. Nobody had ever thought to do this before. So my meeting with Jerry Wald was very convivial. He wanted to do *The Illustrated Man*, so I did an outline and a screen treatment, but nothing ever came of it because he couldn't sell the studio on the idea. Ten years went by. Nobody in the whole damned country approached me again about doing *The Illustrated Man*. You get tired of waiting. You get tired of no one loving you or paying attention to you. So finally, when Jack Smight showed up, even though he didn't have a huge reputation as a director, he had to be the greatest man in the world to me. He had done some good things in television.

K: *Harper* is quite good.
B: Yes. It was fine. Not a great film. I like it less now than when I first saw it. It had some nice things in it, but it needed a little better script. Well, anyway. Think of how I felt after ten years of neglect. I knew the property was important and good, but no one else did.

K: Were any conditions, such as script approval, attached to the sale of the book to the studio?

B: No, the book was sold with only one condition—that I be allowed to choose the lead. So Smight said, "Sure, make up a list." I sat down and wrote Burt Lancaster, Jack Palance, Kirk Douglas, Rod Steiger, and two others. All good people. All fine actors. A couple of months later, Rod Steiger called and said, "Hey, I'm in your film!" I was very happy. But no one said anything about the script. I wasn't asked to do it. The script was very bad and the film, as a result, couldn't be much better than the script. Steiger tried to revise as he went along. No one asked me to read the script. They knew I would jump all over it. I had no intention of interfering unless I was asked. I had sold the book and I had no business with it. I could have revised the script and it would have turned out much better, I think. It's too long. It's filled with clichés. It gives away climaxes too soon. One of the stories, "The Veldt," starts in the middle. You shouldn't go into the veldt for at least half an hour. You need to prepare the house, the characters, and then go in. You must milk the material. Milk it! Let it out point by point. Instant by instant. Keep us on that hook! This is all good and honorable and right and beautiful. God, you can see this perfectly in a film like Hitchcock's *Rebecca*, where the information is paid out and you are made to wait and build and build and build. It's a long film. It gives you a lot of information and not much *seems* to happen, except that it does! It's magical the way the character of Rebecca, this ghost, comes before you and you really know her by the end of the film. When she's halfway through she turns into a monster. You *were* admiring a lovely woman. All of a sudden you realize this is a monster, *hated* by her husband, who reveals this in the course of the film. God, how I admire Hitchcock and his screenwriters for what they do!

K: You had better luck with *Fahrenheit 451* three years before *The Illustrated Man*.
B: Yes. I thought François Truffaut did a fine job with *Fahrenheit 451*. I loved the adventure, the chase, the way he handled his actors.

K: You have said in another interview that you thought the film could have contained a few more minutes of chase sequence.
B: Yes. Montag gets out of the city too easily. You can't get out of any city that easily.

K: Did you envision Truffaut's doing the film with as little background action as it has? The critics who complained about the film cited this as one of its major faults.

B: No, I respect Truffaut's aesthetics and way of doing things. Now this is a different case from the one with Jack Smight and *The Illustrated Man*. I had given it to Jack because no one else would pay any attention. My motives for selling *Fahrenheit 451* were much more complex. Number one, Truffaut was an established, new, young director with a very huge reputation and everyone in the world was talking about him, so I was very flattered when he showed up and wanted to do the film. It took quite a long time to set up the agreement and get backing. Finally he asked me if I wanted to do the screenplay. I told him I didn't because I had done the stage version in Los Angeles five years earlier, and I was tired of it. I told him I thought I would be a danger to him and that he should not let me near the script. I found out later that Oskar Werner turned down Truffaut's script at first because he didn't feel it was close enough to the original text, but after Truffaut couldn't get Jean-Paul Belmondo and one or two others, he came back to Werner and Werner insisted that he rewrite the script closer to the original novel. Truffaut agreed, but even along the way they began to fight because Werner wanted even more from my book. I can't very well criticize Werner, can I? I'm glad I didn't fly over to see the filming. I was invited by Truffaut, but thought better of it. Additionally, it was the middle of winter and I could not see myself flying to Europe in the middle of winter. The studio was upset with me because they wanted me to make a promotion film. When the film came out there were very mixed reactions. It did very well in all of its initial openings, in college towns. In fact, were the film coming out today it would probably go into all the college towns and do extremely well. I've seen this coming for thirteen or fourteen years, and I've tried to tell the studios, but of course they haven't listened much. Wherever they played this film in college towns it did well. Wherever they didn't, it failed.

K: The film seems to me to improve with age. Do you find this to be the case for you as well?

B: Yes. There are many fine little throwaway items that one often misses on the first viewing. Truffaut probably didn't have the city congested with people, for example, because he wanted to suggest that everyone was inside—watching television. The only part of the film that I really object to is in the center of the film when it gets a little too explanatory. The school environment and the conversations between Montag and the girl don't work well for me. Many of the scenes, however, are very poignant. The little scenes. For example, the first night that Montag reads a book, sitting by the television set, and using the light from the set to read is a great touch. That isn't even in my book. And the careful articulation of the words from [Charles] Dickens, running his finger over every word, stumbling. This is a *great* scene.

K: You have said that the conclusion of the film is among the most beautiful in the history of film.
B: Yes. I've gone around and around with people about that. People have told me, "Oh, well, you wouldn't go around like that reciting books." That's not the point! They're a living metaphor. Anyway, people don't do a lot of things we see in films. But you wish they could do them and you help what you see take that extra step. That's what art is all about. It's the dreams we wish we'd had. It's the lives we would like to lead. It's knowing that we go around with books in our heads. So these people at the ending of the film only articulate as walking metaphors what *we* are as people. Each of us has some part of some book in our heads. Some of us have good memories. Some of us have poor memories. But we all have memories of a book and how it changed our lives. So to me, that ending is beautiful. It's a lovely movie. It's a haunting movie. And the great thing he does when he burns the books is that he traps each of us with our own prejudices. There must be at least one book for each of us which, when we see it burning, we say, "Yeah, that's O.K., burn *that* one." Then we catch ourselves and say "Wait a minute. Stop!"

K: The specific scene where Truffaut actually shows specific books being eaten by the flames draws a strong reaction from my students. Even if it is intended merely as a part of the film, many of them are outraged that books are being burned at all.
B: I can believe it. But that was precisely the reaction Truffaut was hoping to achieve, wasn't it? What's worse, there are probably certain elements in today's society who would gladly burn books, given the opportunity.

K: In 1968 and 1969, in addition to having *The Illustrated Man* adapted, one of your short stories, "The Picasso Summer," was sold to Warner Brothers. What happened to that film? I recently saw it on network television.

B: That project began as a half-hour television show. It would have been beautiful. Just the right length, with some animation to illustrate Picasso's work. But we couldn't get anyone to finance it. Eventually it evolved into a feature film. I fought the idea. I didn't know how it could possibly be done as an hour and a half film. But they told me I could do the screenplay, so I thought maybe it could work. They hired Albert Finney, a fine actor, and we went to work on the film. When I had finished the script, the studio people said they loved it. The director jumped up and down. Fantastic! Brilliant! All the superlatives. Just before the crew left for Europe to shoot the film, I asked the director if he wanted me to change any parts of the script. He told me that they would shoot it as it was written. I believed him. As it turned out, the director threw out many key scenes in the script as he shot, and when he returned to the studio he had nothing to edit. It was a total disaster. Eventually I got him fired, and we tried to piece the film together. I even offered my time free to try to salvage the film with a new director. It didn't work. The studio didn't even release the film to the theatres. Finally, last year, it was sold to television. When I heard it had been sold to television I asked for the privilege of editing it. I was turned down and the print that eventually aired was absolutely horrible. Some of the scenes that had originally worked were missing—they'd been cut—and the rest of the film just fell into a heap.

K: The screenplay credit lists Douglas Spaulding, your alter ego in *Dandelion Wine*, and another writer. Who was he?
B: A gag writer from television who was brought in by the studio to inject what the studio called "humor" into the film. I don't even remember his name. He couldn't have made much of an impression on me.

K: What was your primary reason for keeping your name attached to the film, albeit in a pseudonym?
B: It's always a good idea to keep the rights to anything if you can. Even if it's bad. At least you know you own it and no one can tamper with it.

K: Your most recent work to be done on film was Jack Smight's *The Screaming Woman*, last season on ABC's Movie of the Weekend. How did you like it?
B: It's a much nicer film than what Jack had done with *The Illustrated Man*. It had a much better script and that really shows on the screen.

K: Merwin Gerard, the scriptwriter, has done some fine work over the years, hasn't he?
B: Yes, he has. Particularly in a series called *One Step Beyond*. I made a point of seeking him out the night of the preview of *Screaming Woman* and shaking his hand and thanking him for the fine things he had done with my story.

K: Do you object to the use of an older woman in the role of the youngster from the original story?
B: No, because Smight's and Gerard's reasons for the change were valid. They told me it was difficult to cast the part of a child who could sustain interest throughout the entire story, which ran about seventy-five minutes.

K: It probably would have made a marvelous half-hour show with Hitchcock, or someone with his imagination.
B: Oh, yes. But, I like what has been done, anyway. I loved watching Olivia de Havilland. And the ending really works! Especially when you see it in a projection room. When that hand came up and grabbed Olivia's hand, everyone jumped! I did, too. It scared the hell out of me! Even though I should have expected it.

K: Ray, I'd like to conclude this interview by having you discuss some of your unrealized or upcoming projects. You've written at least one script for *The Martian Chronicles*. What has happened to it?
B: Actually, I've done two scripts for *Chronicles*. One for MGM and one for Pakula-Mulligan Productions. Apparently it's just too expensive. The budget we got on it was between eight and fourteen million. People are very chary of Mars these days, too, since the Mariner rocket program began and the planet has been photographed. I like the script pretty well, though. I doubt whether we'll ever get it made.

K: Was your long short story "Lost City of Mars" a part of your script?
B: Actually, it was originally only a story insert and Bill Nolan, a good friend, told me that I had a great short story, so I wrote the short story from that and had it published.

K: How does *Something Wicked This Way Comes* look as a future project? You mentioned a few months ago that you were negotiating with Sam Peckinpah to do it with you.

B: I've been trying to get that book filmed for the past eight or nine years. The latest dealing is with Sam Peckinpah. He told me he will shoot the book, but it isn't going to be quite that easy. I'm in the middle of doing the screenplay now. He and I get on beautifully.

K: Peckinpah has been severely criticized for the violence in his films and yet he has made some extremely sensitive and beautiful films over the years.
B: Yes, he is constantly being misinterpreted. For example, in *Straw Dogs*, everyone has screamed about the fascists *inside* the house, when it is the fascists *outside* that Peckinpah is concerned with. There are no Fascists inside. They're outside trying to get in. Past a certain point you'd better not let them. They'll rape your wife and kill you. This is the message Hitler taught the world. We took it too long. We finally had to stand up.

K: How complete is the contract on *Something Wicked This Way Comes*?
B: Oh, it's really just a matter of finding a studio to release and finance. I feel very good about it.

K: "And the Rock Cried Out" was to have been done several years ago. What happened to that project?
B: Much of that story says things which are still pertinent, but I think it reached its prime some time back. I doubt whether it will ever be filmed.

K: You and Chuck Jones have discussed doing an animated version of your new novel, *The Halloween Tree*. Do you still plan to do it?
B: Yes. I've written the screenplay already. The problem now seems to be getting the animation for it. Most of the studios have closed down their animation departments to save money—Chuck was the head of his department at one of the studios, as you know—and it will probably take some time before we can work something out.

K: You recently did a musical version of *Dandelion Wine* at Cal State, Fullerton. Do you plan to go into film with it?
B: I haven't really thought about it. It might be nice. I'm very close to the play. It has some flaws. Everything I've done is flawed. Most of what is written or has been written over the years is flawed in some way. *Moby Dick* is flawed. Shakespeare's plays are flawed, full of carbuncles, acne, and pimples.

They just happen to be brilliant and eternal. So what the hell! You go with your own flaws. It's part of growing. Getting accustomed to the way you look is growing. We would all like to be Steve Reeves and lift 400 pounds, I suppose, but that's not our destiny. Some of my literary children are very common and plain. Some are quite beautiful with moles on their cheeks. I really have a very relaxed attitude toward my screenplays, my plays, my novels, and so on.

K: Do you think you've been treated fairly over the years by those who have been involved with your works?
B: Oh, I think so. Sure. People do the best they can. There are the rare villains, but I honestly think Smight, Huston, and the others thought they were doing the best they could do. It's very difficult for me to hate anybody. Except outright villains.

K: What do you see as the future of science fiction and fantasy in the film medium?
B: Oh, we're just beginning to make progress. The area is becoming more accepted all the time. I'm very optimistic about everything. I intend to keep working in film as long as I am wanted.

K: Thank you very much, Ray. You've been more than generous with your time.
B: You're quite welcome. I hope I've been of some assistance.

Ray Bradbury: Space Age Moralist
William F. Nolan / 1972

Unity, April 1972, pp. 44–47. Reprinted with the permission of William F. Nolan, copyright © 1972.

The world knows his work. Ray Bradbury is one of the major international names in the genre of science fiction. His words are translated into nearly every language; his books have become important films (such as *Fahrenheit 451* and *The Illustrated Man*); his stories are dramatized on the BBC in London, on radio in Canada, on the stage in New York; he is an in-demand speaker on university campuses. A master of the short story, poet, playwright, essayist and philosopher, Bradbury is a space-age prophet who is not afraid to speak out boldly regarding man's destiny in the universe. The body of his work represents a study of morality set against the backdrop of the future.

"We are now into the greatest age in human history," he says, "and, sooner than any of us suspect, man will be leaving his home-planet Earth and voyaging into space on a tremendous new wilderness trek."

How will man react to this ultimate challenge? What values will he bring into space with him? How will he deal with what he finds in the vastness of our universe?

Since 1941, over the course of three busy decades, Ray Bradbury has been examining such fascinating questions within the commercial framework of science fiction. He has confronted his fictional heroes with tomorrow's unique conflicts, then has resolved these conflicts in humanistic and moralistic terms, blending drama with artistic dedication. As a result, Bradbury has become a vital and respected spokesman for the future; his books (particularly *The Martian Chronicles* and *The Golden Apples of the Sun*) are space-age classics.

At fifty-one, Ray retains the fire and joy and enthusiasm of his youth. A man of immense zest, he refuses to "settle down," refuses to allow his ideas to congeal; he remains vital, flexible, splendidly opinionated, a smiling, happy fellow who treats each day as a fresh adventure. He speaks of moon travel and space stations with the easy familiarity of a man-boy who grew up fired by the inner vision of man's leap into space-an apostle of the rocket at home among the stars.

His *physical* home is in West Los Angeles, a pleasant white upstairs-downstairs house with a garage (for his bicycle; he has never driven a car) and a basement workroom (for his typewriter, books, and files). When I talked to him recently, in the living room of this California home, we tackled the subject of God and space. Ray had much to say.

"I believe that space travel will give us a new image of God," he declared. "Man must stand as God."

"You mean, represent Him in space?"

Ray shook his head. "No, no—not represent Him. *Be* Him. Man is a fusion of the human and the divine. I believe that the flesh of man contains the very soul of God, that we are, finally, irrevocably and responsibly, God Himself incarnate, that we shall carry this seed of God into space."

"What about other forms of alien life?" I wanted to know. "Are you saying that God is with man alone and not with the creatures we'll meet in space?"

In answer, he walked over to a shelf, pulled out one of his books. "I have two stories in this collection relating to priests who must face what they think of as 'godless' aliens on Mars. They come to realize that they are wrong, that all forms of life in God's universe partake of Him." Bradbury's eyes flashed. "How *dare* we consider ourselves God's only true children? In this era of deep-space exploration we have no room for blind ego. A giant spider on Venus may be born of God, as we are, and contain the same sensitivity." Ray laughed. "The missionary of tomorrow is going to have a few surprises in store for him!"

"Ray, do you really believe we'll ever come upon such creatures—or is it just an extension of your science-fictional imagination?"

Bradbury put away his book and settled into the couch; he tented his hands, eyes thoughtful and serious. "We'll meet them out there. Not in our lifetime, perhaps, but in the lifetime of our children. We *are* going out into space. It's our final frontier, and man has always been driven to explore his frontiers. The far horizon is no longer a mountain range; it is now a star cluster. And somewhere out there, amid all the billions of worlds, we'll run into creatures of vast intelligence, alien in shape and attitude but who share the God in man. I surely believe that. This belief is as solid to me as the couch I'm sitting on."

"But how will we be able to communicate with them?"

"The same way we're beginning, even now, to communicate with dolphins. It may take a thousand years, but the gap between man and alien *will* be crossed. We'll find, once we're able to reach other galaxies, that we are far from alone in the universe. And this is not my particular fancy; most of our leading scientists share my views."

I switched from aliens to origins in asking him my next question: "Did you deliberately choose science fiction as a field in which to express your personal philosophy?"

"My functioning in this field is a happy accident," he told me. "As a boy of nine I became an avid fan of Buck Rogers, and I soon devoured all of Burroughs' Martian tales. I was captivated by the world of rockets and space travel. And, instead of growing out of it, I grew *into* it. I matured into manhood reading and writing and relating to science fiction. The first sale I made, in July of 1941, was a science-fiction tale to *Super Science Stories*, a pulp magazine of that period. When I moved into the bigger magazines I took my science-fiction ideas with me."

"But you've written in several fields," I pointed out. "Irish stories, mystery-suspense, terror tales, nostalgic trips into your Illinois boyhood . . . yet you always seem to come back to science fiction. What lures you back?"

"I keep coming back to the field because science fiction is the fiction of *ideas*," he said, "of sociology, psychology, and history, compounded and squared by time. Many people still tend to think of it as comic-strip material, without roots, yet most of our greatest writers have added to the genre—from Plato to Lucian to Sir Thomas More and Francis Rabelais, on down through Jonathan Swift, [Johannes] Kepler, and Edward Bellamy. We all know the work of [H.G.] Wells, [Aldous] Huxley, and [George] Orwell, as well as the 'father' of the field of modern science fiction, Jules Verne—a writer I still read and enjoy immensely. My work follows on a direct line from such men as these, and I'm very proud of my literary ancestors."

Bradbury went on to project some startling ideas of man in relation to a universal image. "A human being is not a shape at all, in the ultimate sense—not a thing of torso, head, arms, not a color, nor does it have to do with a particular place of habitat. Humanity is an *idea*, a concept, a way of doing, a motion toward light and away from darkness. We must never wear a label, not even the label of human being for, in space, we transcend all labels. So we must constantly seek new ways to know and encourage the will toward light in each of us; we must never go back into darkness. We must not, *cannot*, repeat the mistakes of our immediate past in our future. Man must rise up to meet the alien on foreign shores for we are, in reality, taking God out to meet God."

"A lot of science-fiction writers are negative with regard to the future," I reminded him. "They foresee the destruction of man by his own hand. How do you feel about this?"

"I'm an optimist," said Bradbury. "I discard all such dark tomorrows. I have faith in man as God and God as man; I believe we'll be immortal, seed the stars and live forever in the flesh of our children. That's my job as a writer—to show man his basic goodness, to dramatize his struggle up and away from this planet. I reject the doomsayers!"

We got into the area of science fiction as a prophetic form of literature, and Bradbury enthusiastically expanded this view.

"Look," he said, "there's hardly a subject that hasn't appeared in the science-fiction magazines twenty years before it came into public notice in the large-circulation popular publications. In the fields of politics and philosophy, science fiction predates all the mouthings of our present politicos and space philosophers by many years. In fact, it seems to be that every time a government official opens his mouth these days something from a 1928 issue of *Amazing Stories* falls out! Most of today's astronomical theories, printed in learned scientific bulletins, were dramatized in *Wonder Stories* back in 1931!"

Bradbury and I discussed the "death of God" idea current in some segments of our society.

Ray laughed. "If some think we showed God out the front door, they may be startled to find He has quietly infiltrated the basement." Then he got serious again. "If all the universe is God, then are we not extrusions of miraculous matter put in motion to combat darkness, to cherish Being and, with our own extrusions, our metal rockets begot in testpit and factory, to go off in search of yet finer miracles basking under far suns? Man, the ant, will yet build the mountain. We are busy now with the first sand grains that will fill the vast hourglass of our billion-year endeavor."

Then he summed up our conversation.

"Science fiction offers us the quickest route between these two points, a way of shorthand, to educate ourselves to our basic scientific and moral problems without resorting to pomp, preachment, or pushing, and remain entertaining withal. You can't reach people, and deal with fundamental issues of life and morality, without entertaining along the way." Ray walked over to a table in the room on which one of his daughters had placed a small toy rocket. He picked it up, turning it in his fingers. "Today we're still playing at space," he said softly. "Even our moon landings are little more than a halting step at the rim of space. But, with future vision, I look beyond our moon and see man, a Godform, lifted in thunder to seed space and live forever."

The poet, the moralist, the optimist had set me to thinking. I walked away from the quiet, tree-shaded home of Ray Douglas Bradbury and paused for a long moment on the walk outside, shading my eyes to peer into the vault of blue sky.

I heard his words again, echoing inside my head: ". . . not in our lifetime, but in the lifetime of our children . . . we *are* going out into space . . . to the stars."

Far above me, the stars waited, and are waiting . . . for me, for us, for man.

The Bradbury Chronicles
Shel Dorf / 1975

Unknown Worlds of Science-Fiction, 1.1 (January 1975), pp. 34–40, 74, 76, 78.
Copyright © 1975 by Shel Dorf. Reprinted by permission.

Shel Dorf: What was life like for the young Ray Bradbury, in the days that preceded your first writing?
Bradbury: I suppose not much different. I've always lived at the top of my hysteria, as I put it. Enthusiasm. Delirium. I could never wait for things. This is a constant thing with a heck of a lot of children anyway. They just feel steamed up if they don't get a thing on a particular day; or if they don't experience a particular thing, it's the end of the world.

I fell in love with motion pictures, and with comics, and with magic tricks, and with all kinds of illusions, when I was very young. Things like the Oz books. Fortunately, my Aunt Neva had a huge bookcase full of fairy tales and all of the Oz books in my grandmother's house next door. And my Uncle Bion in another house on the same block next door had all the Tarzan and John Carter books. So, between these two libraries, long before I went to the regular library, I picked up on those elements of fantasy which I think influenced me and changed my life.

I was talking with an English professor the other night about what was wrong with our education system in the first and second and third grades—why kids are not reading, and what's wrong with the sort of thing we teach in the first grade. Well, my recollection of the early years was that we were very fortunate in those days to be taught a heck of a lot of Greek and Roman mythology and Norse mythology and some of the Germanic myths. These wonderful stories induced you to want to read. There was something to read, there was something imaginative to grab onto so that you felt the need to learn on your own so that you'd rush ahead into these things.

So all of these things then went into my background and excited me, and I began to read the Oz books when I was seven or eight. And I kept being led around by things which now are considered unimportant.

The Oz books have never been taught in our schools. They're not in a heck of a lot of libraries. They've been looked down on by educators and intellectuals, and I feel at this very moment in history that if we put the Oz books into the first and second grade all over the country, we'd have readers all over the place in no time.

And that also applies to Greek and Roman myths and to things like John Carter of Mars and Tarzan.

Yes, now these are not literature in the usual sense, but they are imaginative, and they do rev up one's imagination, and that's the answer for me, for reading.

SF: Terrific.
B: So this is my background, and I think a lot of it has gone into my work. Of course I'm so glad that I have all the old fairy books that were given to me—the Andersen and Grimm fairy tales—by my aunt when I was three and four years old.

So I would look through those big picture books with their wonderful illustrations, and I fell in love with people like Arthur Rackham when I was a young child. Then the science-fiction books came along with their fantastic covers by Frank R. Paul and works by Mr. [Howard V(achel)] Brown who did the covers for *Astounding* science fiction back in 1930–31–32—and people like [H. W.] Wesso, and Elliot Dold, whose work stands out in my mind. Well, these are all wild and vulgar and beautiful, and fill your mind with images that excite you, make you want to live.

So, thank God, as soon as I saw these things, I fell in love with them, and when Buck Rogers came along, instantly, within the very first strip I just went absolutely crazy. I'd just started with the most *amazing* thing I'd ever seen; I could barely *wait* through each day. That's the way I lived. I lived hysterically, waiting for that hour every afternoon when Buck Rogers came into the house. And then when he went on radio, that was immense, and that was exciting. So I kept moving, then, as a child, from excitement to excitement.

When Blackstone the Magician was coming to town, that was incredible, too. I could hardly wait. I'd just go right out of my head waiting for Blackstone to show up. So all of that energy and passion and madness went right into my writing when I began to do it at the age of twelve.

SF: Was it then the urge to *share* which accounts for your choosing a writing career? Or did you have ambitions to do other things? It seems to me that the physically sedentary nature of writing must have seemed bothersome to one with such energies.

Shel Dorf / 1975

B: I don't think you really think of it at the time. You don't really intellectualize. You don't make obvious decisions. You don't think thoughts, you think *passions*. Writing seemed to come naturally, and I illustrated my own things as I went.

So I did my first comic-strip when I was twelve, which was an adaptation, of course, of Harold Foster. And I was collecting Tarzan all the time then; that was a big thing. Every Saturday night I would go downtown with my dog, and I would buy the Sunday paper (it cost a nickel) and an ice cream cone, and then I'd come home on my roller skates with my dog. And just devour Harold Foster's drawings for Tarzan. Because those were good years, those were terrific years when Tarzan was in Ancient Egypt and when he went back in time through this tunnel and found an ancient Egyptian race. The illustrations of the tombs and the mummies and the sarcophagi were just fantastic, some of his finest work. And so I automatically began to do my own cartoons. I never got very good at it; I'm still a doodler and a Sunday painter, but not good enough to do that incredible work which influenced me.

So, I could have gone many directions. I started doing magic tricks; I went on the stage and had my own little magic show which I put on, and I became an actor on the stage in other things, and I went onto radio, and read the comics to the other kids when I was twelve years old. I hung around the radio station and made a pest out of myself in Tucson, Arizona.

And all of a sudden it's amazing to remember why I love comic-strips so much. Because there I was, broadcasting them every Saturday night with two or three other kids in the local radio station and playing all the parts. "The Captain and the Kids," and "Tailspin Tommy," and "Maggie and Jigs," and things like that.

SF: That's extraordinary. It's not really well-known that you did that. We need more people doing things like that today.
B: I don't know if anyone ever reads the comics to the kiddies on the radio anywhere in the world.

SF: Mayor [Fiorello Henry] LaGuardia got all the publicity. I didn't know that Ray Bradbury did it, too.
B: Yeah, and loved it.

SF: Who were the first people you went to for criticism of your writing?
B: Well, I had to wait until I was in high school, and then I had a wonderful short-story teacher, Jennet Johnson, who taught short story at Los Angeles

High, and she read all my stuff. We were supposed to do ten short stories during the semester and I did twenty. I did double what everyone else did. And I was writing all kinds of junk, including science fiction. She read it all and said, "This is terrible, but you can write." You know, she meant the theme and the material. She didn't understand why I was doing what I was doing, but she understood that I wanted to be a writer, and she encouraged me and loved me. I'm still in touch with her. She's about eighty-four years old, lives out here in Claremont, and we see each other at least once a year. She was the first person and the most important in encouraging me.

Then of course in my last year in L.A. High I went into a bookstore in Hollywood and saw a sign that had been posted by Forrest J. Ackerman announcing meetings of the Science-Fiction League downtown in Clifton's Cafeteria, so I went down and joined and met Henry Kuttner, and Ray Harryhausen, who was my own age and was dreaming of becoming some sort of film-maker.

Ray and I became fast friends. I used to go out to his house. He made a life mask of me and put together a liquid latex horror-mask for me to wear on Halloween back in 1938. And I went to the Paramount Theatre with Ray Harryhausen and Forrest Ackerman, wearing this liquid latex green Martian sort of mask, and had a wonderful time. So you see how crazy we all were.

There's no difference between the generations. Boys are always doing something like this.

But within the Science-Fiction League, then, I met Robert Heinlein and Edmond Hamilton and Leigh Brackett, and each of them at one time or another was a teacher of mine. I used to have meetings every Sunday afternoon for about four years down at Santa Monica on the volleyball courts with Leigh Brackett. She was writing for *Planet Stories* and doing these incredible adventure stories which I envied and admired so much, and still do. And I was trying to do something in science fiction, and I was doing imitations of Leigh Brackett.

They weren't very good. You read some of my early stories in *Planet Stories*. Those were all written at the time I was on the beach with Leigh and she was doing fine work and I was doing lousy imitations just trying to learn how to do it.

Finally I got to a point where I was able to write well enough to take off in my own direction. Later years in *Planet*, if you'll check through my stories, you'll find where I finally began to develop my own ideas and techniques and style and was able to break away from simply being influenced as a student.

But Leigh was one of my *constant* advisors, teachers, and friends. For a brief period there, Heinlein was, too.

SF: What was your first major success—and did it frighten you?
B: It's hard to put your hand on what you mean when you say *success*. I've never thought in those terms. You look at certain areas of your life, and they seem fortunate or loving or good, but you can't point to one thing. These things creep up on you so slowly, anyway.

None of my books has ever sold very well. So there's been no success in large terms that you can point to and say, "Hey, *The Martian Chronicles* was a success!" Well, it's a success over a period of twenty-four years! The first year that book was published it sold only 8000 copies. That isn't really very many copies; it's certainly not a best-seller. It's a very quiet, nice, pleasant sale, because the average book by an unknown writer sells three or four thousand copies, so I sold double that amount. And that is a moderate and quiet and lovely success.

The kind of success that impresses me is collisions between people—meetings between people, heroes that you've always wanted to meet.

I'll tell you a moment in my life that to me meant, I guess, success. I was at a science-fiction convention in Los Angeles in the summer of 1946, as I recall. I was twenty-six years old, and I'd been publishing in *Weird Tales* for about four or five years; almost every month I had stories there and had begun to establish a small reputation for myself. I was being paid around $30 a story, $40, sometimes maybe $45.

And I was attending this convention and I was in the convention hall and I heard a voice at the door behind me, oh, about sixty or seventy feet away, and Robert Bloch had just come through the door and he was looking around and I heard his voice say, "Hey, where is this guy Ray Bradbury? I want to meet him!" Well, you know, that was a wonderful moment for me, and that is what I call success—when someone you have read for years and have never met comes into a meeting of strangers and asks for *you*, then you know you've turned a corner. Those are the moments I remember.

I went back to New York in the spring of 1950 for the publication of *The Martian Chronicles*. On the train was a friend of mine who was on his way to Europe. He couldn't afford to take a sleeping room, so we took the chair car across the United States and we slept in the chairs, of course, because I was too poor to afford anything else.

I arrived in Chicago, and I had been invited to have lunch with a fan there. I was supposed to meet him in the couple of hours between train schedules.

So I went over to the Art Institute to look for my friend at the top of the stairs, and instead there was a crowd of twelve or fourteen people, and I thought, "Well, that can't be my friend; he's not going to be with anyone," and I looked beyond and couldn't find him. And all of a sudden this crowd came down the steps of the museum and I discovered they were all fans and they all had advance copies of *The Martian Chronicles* and they *loved* it, and that's why they were there as a surprise to welcome me to Chicago. That was a moment in my life which was another turning point.

I was suddenly being accepted and loved and read, and here were fourteen strangers showing up to congratulate me on this change in my life. So that to me is a moment of success, and one that I shall remember for the rest of my life.

SF: Beautiful. Ray, were the early years of your writing subsidized by your family? How did you manage to live and pay bills?
B: Well, when I was nineteen I got a job selling newspapers on a streetcorner, and that gave me $10 a week, which was just enough in those days to get by, so I wasn't a burden to my family. I lived at home with my mom and dad, because on $10 I couldn't have afforded an apartment of my own. Still, I was able to pay for my own food and clothing because in those days you could buy a sport coat for eight or nine bucks and a pair of pants for $5. I'd take a girl out maybe once a week; I'd take her to a cheap movie, buy her a malted milk, and that was it.

Then gradually I broke into *Weird Tales* so that in my early twenties I was making $25 or $30 a week writing.

SF: Getting philosophical for a moment: these days the world is filled with a lot of unrest and trouble, and many kids are dropping out and using drugs as a temporary haven for their despair. Have you any advice for counteracting the hopeless feeling some of them have?
B: Well, the counteraction is always action. If you *do* things there isn't time to be despairing. If you move, if you act, if you create something, if you're interested in something, there isn't time to despair. A lot of this despair comes from inactivity, from not knowing what they want to do. Find something. I don't care what it is, to do.

There are so many crazy, lovely things to do in this world. A friend of mine like Roy Squires has more than one activity; he's a lover of antique book collections and he's also a publisher of wonderful small publications that he puts together, reprinting some of the works of Clark Ashton Smith. He's done two things of mine. He gets handmade papers, he sets his own type, he loves typography. You begin to look at people like Roy Squires in this world, and you begin to ask around how many crazy people are there like this in the world, that love paper, that love type, that love putting out their own small publications?

Well, it turns out that there are, at the most, ninety-five or a hundred of these people in the *whole world*. Out of three billion people, there are eighty or ninety lovely people who cannot stay away from paper and typography and setting their own type and making their own small booklets. Which then become collector's items and sell for incredible prices all over the world a year or two later.

That's really what I'm talking about. The younger generation, any of them—if they'd just find that small niche for themselves. It doesn't have to pay much, maybe it won't pay anything, but it will be an activity that's loving and wonderful and that causes them to pump their own adrenaline in their system and feel so good that there's no way of despairing.

Because they are active within their own love, and that means pumping your own drugs into your own systems; you don't need any outside drugs that way. You are so high all the time on the thing that you're doing, whether it's acting or painting or printing your own magazine.

When I was seventeen, eighteen, nineteen, all the extra time I had went into helping Forry Ackerman and the other people at the Science-Fiction League put out various magazines. I helped mimeograph, I wrote articles, I illustrated. When I was nineteen, I had my own magazine, which Forrest Ackerman paid for. An incredible person.

The whole science-fiction activity is a way of making do, of surviving. There are a lot of young publishers there with their own mimeograph magazines, and they have the right answer. They fill their lives with criticizing and reading and illustrating and doing. And that really is the answer to all of this.

SF: I understand that lately you are being consulted by city planners who appreciate your farsightedness. What advice do you give them?
B: Just to take another long look at what they *haven't* been doing. They've been allowing their own communities to disintegrate, because the average

Chamber of Commerce is so fantastically conservative and unable to see the destruction, the boredom within their own planning.

The sort of malls they put up are drab and unimaginative, and all they've done is herd all the little businessmen from their original dwellings into the new ones without thinking how to dramatize them and freshen up what is already there. How to make a mixture of things that's exciting and tantalizing and will attract people. So we're suffering all over the United States, but especially in the large cities, an attrition of people who simply don't come into the downtown area any more except on some sort of business, and who don't stay to shop often enough.

What you try to do with the city fathers, the mayor, the councilmen is to try to take a look at what they're doing in San Francisco in architecture, how they've refurbished some of the streets, how they've put together complexes like the Ghirandelli Square that are wonderful mixtures of things, and learn from these, and put together things for other generations—the old and the young—where we can all go and feel refreshed and excited and want to go more than once a year.

You try to show them ways of revitalizing the center of their towns before the large shopping complexes pull everyone out of the cities, and the city collapses. There's competition between new shopping centers which are a heck of a lot more fun, and that have everything under one roof. Some of these are good and some are not, and even the ones that are not very good work better than the downtown plans of most small cities.

SF: How do you answer those critics of horror stories who look at them as harmful to their children?
B: You just try to get them to take a long look at the horror story, the horror film, the horror comic, and you say, "Look, this has a lot to do with life. This is not a separate thing, and you should consider it as an exercise where a child's mind is trying to test the boundaries of knowledge concerning life and death. This is a natural activity, as most other things are, a way of examining possible futures for each of us, 'cause we all have to go through the process of dying some day. So naturally the child, starting at a very young age, is intrigued by all these things."

That doesn't mean that *all* horror stories or *all* horror films are automatically good. There are some that are fantastically vulgar and poorly done, and I would imagine they might be harmful or destructive to children under a certain age. So, as a responsible parent, you have to save certain of these things as experiences to be gone through at a slightly later age.

I don't think I would recommend to parents that they rush off and take their eight- or ten- or twelve- or thirteen-year-old kids to see *The Exorcist*. I think the film is much too powerful for young children. I would take a long look at a fifteen-year-old, though, and if that fifteen-year-old were exceptionally bright and open and un-hung-up, I'd allow her to see *The Exorcist*, as I have my own fifteen-year-old daughter, because I know she can take it and enjoy it.

But there's a lot of individual decision that has to be made here. And we as parents have to decide which children at what time are ready for what kind of information. We become our own censors, which is the way any really good society works. We shouldn't have to have these things put in from outside. We should be capable of showing judgment on our own.

SF: As a citizen of the world, which single achievement of mankind excites you the most?
B: There are two, actually. They're polarized in my mind.

The most important thing that's happened in the last thirty years is the invention of atomic power and the hydrogen bomb, which has given us a chance to have a heck of a lot more political development in the world. Fewer wars, less war activity, which is giving us a chance to make do with other countries, and that's all to the good. A chance to make peace in the world. We've been forced into it.

That is exciting, because we didn't anticipate that it would happen when we invented these things. But that's the way it has turned out. From our terror of these things, the major powers are being forced into accepting each other, and a long period of peace which will hopefully now ensue will give us time to cure most of the other problems of the world and also make it out into space, which is the second part of my subject.

Space travel, of course, promises incredible benefits for mankind on *thousands* of levels, including the aesthetic and the theological and in so many areas we haven't even begun to explore yet.

And of course the ultimate benefit will be the immortality of mankind that space travel can insure for us. That we can go on from Earth to other planets and on out to the stars and exist for hundreds of thousands and millions of years.

That to me is tremendously exciting.

SF: Do you agree with the *Chariots of the Gods* theory that this planet has been visited by beings from other civilizations in the galaxy?

B: I'm not qualified to have an opinion on that. I think it's an intriguing theory. I don't think anyone knows, including Mr. [Erich] von Daniken, but I think it's a fascinating idea. It makes your hair stand up–some of the photographs, some of the ideas—and I think that if the book causes us to retain some sort of sense of *awe* about the universe, that's fine, that's all to the good.

So we just keep our minds open about these theories and then proceed from there and see what else we can find to tie these things together. If they don't tie up later, we can reject them. Right now we should keep our minds open, for the possibility is a good one.

SF: What is it about the comics that makes you such a fan?

B: Well, I guess the same things I started out with as a child. Today more than ever the sense of humor that goes into them, of course. But that was also true when I was reading "Popeye" when I was eleven, twelve, thirteen years old—and "Mickey Mouse," too.

Today we all read "Wizard of Id" and "B.C." and "Andy Capp" for the same reason—because they criticize the total society and not just a part of it.

But I admire illustration and always did, and I suppose I always will. I get a kick out of well-drawn comic-strips when you're dealing with storytelling, as in the case of "Prince Valiant," or well-drawn comic-strips which deal with humor. And some of the illustration that goes into *Mad* magazine is amazing. Some of the satire, the satirical drawing.

I've been a great collector of people like [William] Hogarth, [Arthur] Rackham, and Gustave Dore, for thirty or forty years. You keep cross-pollinating back and forth between the popular-art comic forms, and the traditional ones we've grown up with and been familiar with.

So it's *looking at pictures* that I've enjoyed, and I'm one of those unusual writers who not only are visually oriented but verbally oriented as well. That doesn't happen too often. Generally if a person can draw or do some sort of picture-writing very well, they're not very good on their feet. They're not good at talking, they're not good at writing.

But I am one of those rare people who seem to be capable of existing in three or four fields at the same time.

The visual thing keeps informing me, and that's why I think my writing is intriguing to a lot of people—because I make pictures on the paper for them, and they're all based on my comic-collecting background and my love of illustration and my love of art. On falling in love with people like [Alessandro] Botticelli when I was in my thirties and with [Jacopo Robusti] Tintoretto, Michelangelo, and [Leonardo] da Vinci and others. These people have continually crammed themselves into my eyeballs and they come running out my fingertips into my stories.

SF: In the early 1960s the Marvel Comics Group revolutionized the approach to comic-magazines by writing at a much higher intellectual level than had been done before. Their characters and superheroes had more humanistic qualities, they had their own hang-ups, and they opened up the field to a much higher audience. Today many college students are avid readers of Marvel Comics. The people who write the comics are also educated, literate people. Do you feel that this type of comic has a special contribution to make?
B: I think we need *every* kind. We need comics to exist at every level for every kind of age group and intellectual group. And *sure,* if you can improve a thing, by all means *improve* it. I think the more the merrier; the more people who come into the field, the better. Over in TV, of course, you've had the huge influence of *Star Trek* on young, bright people all over the country. They've formed groups. Over at Cal Tech, I take it there's a huge following for *Star Trek*. So whenever a thing happens for whatever reason, if people are trying to do things better, that's great.

SF: You've covered this pretty well in an earlier question, but I'll just throw it out anyway. How can we discover that inner fire within each of us that makes life worth the living?
B: I just think you've got to look to your passions and ask your stomach how it feels about something. You see something that excites you, then go with it.

You start maybe with seeing movies. Well, that's a passive thing but it's a beginning, and if you're in love with these things they'll instruct you and fire you and maybe you'll catch onto something else.

You start with movies, you go into comic-strips, you start going to art museums, looking at really good pictures. Then you start looking at book illustration, and you see how *that's* done. Then you begin to look at architecture. That's what *I've* done,

So as a result now people in many fields come to me because they know of my interest and love and excitement in looking at architecture and world's fairs and urban planning. They all begin to latch onto one another. You can't stop, you know. You start in one little field and then you just blaze all over the place.

You start with one passion somewhere, and fuel a kindle in your heart and stomach—it's not inside your head, it's in your heart and stomach—your whole body reacts to this thing, and as soon as that happens, you go with it, whatever it is, and then devour it alive.

If there are books on a particular subject in the library, then you read every damn one of those books, and that kindles the fire more. You find an author who's *your* author, read everything of his. And then in turn from that you'll pick up on other people.

I started with very primitive authors—Edgar Rice Burroughs, and Fu Manchu by Sax Rohmer, and L. Frank Baum. And from these you're led into encounters with Aldous Huxley and [George] Bernard Shaw later in life.

But I wasn't ready for Shaw or Melville when I was a young child—so you go with your primitive passions. That's why these comic-strips and other things that are looked down on are important. You must start with something primitive and not be ashamed of it, and you must express this passion.

SF: I know you're a great movie fan, and I've heard you describe Hollywood as the center of the universe. Would you define what you meant by that?
B: It's the center of the universe in many ways because the films that are made there go out into the world and influence people in many countries to accept our common humanity. I think that's an important thing to do, so that the Russians look at our films and say, "Hey, maybe they're not so bad after all." And we look at the Russian films and say, "Gee, they're human beings!" It's such an important thing to do.

Most of the mass media are located here in Hollywood. It's the center of television, motion-picture-making, and a lot of radio activity and *rock* activity. So like it or not, it's the navel of the world. If this unravels, the world unravels, as far as communication through the visual arts. You may not like it, but there's nothing you can do about it. It's going to stay here for a long time. And all we can hope is that we can keep improving the way we do these things, honestly looking at ourselves, getting these things on film, getting them into better TV production so it isn't all just non-creative.

SF: Which projects occupy your time these days?
B: I'm just finishing work on *Something Wicked This Way Comes* as a screenplay for Chartoff-Winkler [Productions] at Twentieth-Century Fox. It will be directed by one of two directors—either Sam Peckinpah or Jack Clayton, whose film *The Great Gatsby* has just come out. I'm waiting to hear more on this at this time.

And then I'm going right into finishing work on an autobiography that I've been working on for five years with my agent—a book on *writing*, actually—how you get your ideas and how you live with them and create with them.

Then I want to do some more plays, and another book of short stories, another book of poetry, and somewhere along the line in the next five years I'd hope to do a grand opera. I'd like to find the right composer and do something immensely intriguing in the science-fiction field for the musical stage. One of my heroes over the years has been [Giacomo] Puccini, and the influence of his music on my thinking is *immense*. If I can find someone with a commensurate talent, which is not easy to do (the world is not full of Puccinis), I would love to try a grand opera.

Maybe I'll come a-cropper, maybe I can never do this, maybe I'm a fool to even try. But again I'm responding to a desire on my part to try. I have this exciting feeling about it. I've already worked with several composers.

SF: Puccini?
B: Yeah, I've done so much work now with various composers, Jerry Goldsmith, and Billy Goldenberg—a *Dandelion Wine* musical. A cantata with Jerry Goldsmith and Chris Dusipala, which turned out *so* well. And my work with Lalo Schiffren.

I love to be around various artists in various fields, and again here if you're ignorant of it, then you go teach yourself. And you let other people teach you.

I still can't read a note of music, but I can collaborate with musicians, and I've written several songs with Billy Goldenberg which turned out very well. As long as he tends to his music and I tend to my words, then we get together and babble and run around like kids. He sits at the piano up in my living room, and I run around down in the basement typing on the typewriter and run back up to see how he's doing, and then run back down. We spent several evenings that way a year back doing *Dandelion Wine* and came up with three fantastically good songs out of this wonderful, childish activity which all art has to be—this sort of babbling and running and yelling and laughing and having a good time. And if it doesn't happen that way it just isn't any *good*, that's all.

It just has to be very quick and very emotional and *grand fun*, just grand fun.

So I'm intrigued with this area of my life which hasn't filled out completely. I hope I can stick around long enough to experiment in it and see what happens.

SF: What about the television show? You mentioned you were writing the bible for a TV show. . . .
B: Well, I did that, and I don't know what they're going to do. The network has it, and someone else has been assigned to revising some of my ideas, so they finally paid me and said it was brilliant, but who knows if they'll ever use any of it? They're full of praise and not very full of action.

SF: How's your poetry doing?
B: Very well, indeed. Good reviews all over the country, the few that I've seen, and the sales have been remarkably good. We're going into a second printing, which means we may wind up selling seven or eight thousand copies the first year, which for a book of poetry is amazingly good.

SF: Ray, for years, science fiction has been climbing into the mainstream of literature from its humble beginnings in the pulps (Jules Verne notwithstanding). Do you think it will ever reach that status which the literati award Pulitzer Prizes to?
B: By the year 2000 science fiction will dominate the mainstream literature of our time, because it *is* the literature of our time, more important and more exciting and more creative than all the works of [Bernard] Malamud, [Philip] Roth, and [Norman] Mailer put together! We are paying attention to the totality of Mankind, while they are playing around in Brooklyn Heights and Levittown and boring us into the grave.

SF: One last question. In his introduction for *The Vintage Bradbury* (Vintage Books; September 1965), Gilbert Highet states that you are *not* a science-fiction writer, but rather a *visionary*. Do you agree with that statement?

B: I am *not* so much a science-fiction writer as a fantasist, moralist, visionary. I am a *preventor* of futures, not a predictor of them. I wrote *Fahrenheit 451* to prevent book-burnings, not to induce that future into happening, or even to say that it was inevitable. If I thought the latter, I would eat eighteen gallons of ice cream, 189 pickles, and several Clark Bars, and get the hell out of the world tomorrow. I *don't* believe it. I believe we are better than we think we are, and worse than we can imagine, which gives me hope. Yes, hope, hope, *hope!* We will survive our worst attempts to hurt ourselves.

It's Up, On, and Away
Barbara Newcomb / 1980

Christian Science Monitor Eastern Edition, 72:73 (10 March 1980), pp. 20–21, copyright © 1980 by Barbara Newcomb. Reprinted by permission.

Barbara Newcomb: Clifton Fadiman describes you as "a moralist who works most easily in the medium known as fantasy" and a friend of mine once said that you write science fiction which isn't really science fiction.
Ray Bradbury: I'm a magician—when I began to write at twelve, it was only natural that I should put in my stories what I'd seen on the stage and sensed in machinery and read in the scientific magazines. Twenty thousand years ago, sun would fall through a hole in a rock and make a light in a cave appear on the wall, sometimes upside down. This was a natural lens of some sort, and people observed that phenomenon and thought it was magic. But what was once magic becomes science and my stories are really descriptions of that changing state, sometimes moving back and forth between past and present.

BN: You seem to have a somewhat ambivalent attitude toward technology. I think you'd like to warn us about the technological disasters we may be headed towards. On the other hand, you wrote the story "I Sing The Body Electric," about a family that had a robot which brought a sense of love and appreciation to the little girl who missed her grandmother. What are your feelings?
RB: They're mixed, and a fair writer is one who can approach every problem from two directions. An automobile is a destroying mechanism and it's also a happiness machine, depending on how it's used. You should examine both sides, and then write perhaps a third story, which will give us solutions combining both, so that we can get away from the nightmare and move toward the delights in the future, build better cars, better highways, offer more alternatives. . . .

People ask me, "Aren't you afraid of computers, Ray?" I'm not—I'm fascinated. I refuse to be fearful of the object. I examine the object, I revise the object, and in the case of the electric grandmother in ". . . the Body Electric," she's a metaphor for all the good machines that we have in our world, the good reliquaries of time that we are surrounded with everywhere. Disney showed us that delightful humanoid robots can be built to entertain us and to educate us, and I would like to use those robot devices in all kinds of ways in our educational system. They're great teachers. You go into a room with one of them—there's no one there to make you feel self-conscious and stupid—just the machine, and it can teach you over and over and over again until you get it, and it won't call you names, it won't even know you're there. They help dummies like myself and all the other people who must be taught by books alone. But books are little bucks on a piece of paper, aren't they?—robot devices in very simple form come out of a printing machine.

BN: One of the things I find very thought-provoking in your writing is that you'll take an idea, make it happen, and you'll show what the consequences are. It made me wonder if you have one underlying motive for all your writing, or if you have different ideas that you want to get across at different times?
RB: I think I have different ideas at different times, some aggressive, some constructive. You act them out in your stories or your paintings.

BN: Speaking of books, in *Fahrenheit 451*, which you wrote eighteen years ago, you described a society where books were burned and living room walls were television screens. Do you still feel the same kinds of things you felt when you wrote that book? How do you feel individuals can deal with the media in their own lives?
RB: I wrote the book thirty years ago. In the last year, I have written a new version of it, as a play. I took the same plot, the same motives, but I said to the characters, "What have you learned since last I met you?" The firechief, for one, learned why he burned the books. He had thought at one time that books were salvation. He learned that no one thing can be our salvation. Along the way, we lubricate life with knowledge borrowed from others, because if you become too much one thing you tend to become brittle. I tried to broaden myself so that wherever a blow fell I'd have an escape. And that applied to my creativity. I've been an essayist, a poet, a novelist, a short story writer, a playwright. If something doesn't work here, I keep moving.

BN: In your novel *Something Wicked This Way Comes*, you have a time carousel that running forward takes people into the future, and running backwards takes them into the past. In *Dandelion Wine*, which is a very

poetical book, Mrs. Bentley says "You're always in the present," and "Time hypnotizes." How do you feel our concepts of time hinder or help us?
RB: We are the only animal that truly remembers. If we couldn't remember from moment to moment what happened yesterday and the day before, we couldn't invent, we couldn't create the future, so we are the inventors of time, we are the inventors of machines that enable us to live better and to survive natural accidents.

BN: In one of your stories, "Chrysalis," you have a man undergoing a change similar to the one a caterpillar undergoes when becoming a butterfly, and I wondered what your current thoughts are on the next stage for individuals?
RB: That's a huge one, because as we move out into space, I think man will remain a religious creature. Right there is the dichotomy we've been arguing about for a couple of centuries now, the so-called dichotomy between science and religion, which is ridiculous. You can carry the science of physics only to a certain point. With electro-microscopes you can only go so deep into the molecules and atoms, the sub-molecules, and you wind up with mystery because you can't go to the end of where the last particle is. You're back with God again, aren't you? When you go out into the universe with your telescopes, you can only see so far—you end in mystery again. That's where religion takes over; science has only certain perimeters, can explain only certain things, and from that point on it's all theory and you wind up with faith again. So there is no dichotomy, it's all one. So far, certain physical facts seem to be true throughout the universe, but the Prime Mover is still moving, eh? and you have to have something to explain that. That's where the religions of the future will dedicate themselves. They should try not to be too dogmatic, they should try not to lock themselves into brittle theologies. The theology's got to be resilient, and the movement into space is going to force all the believers in the world—Moslem, Buddhist, Christian—to loosen up.

BN: Let me ask you some questions about space. One time you said that you were the only student at Los Angeles High who said, "We're on the edge of space, we're entering a space age," and no one else thought so at the time, but you were convinced. What made you so sure then?
RB: There's a scene in *Moby Dick* where Starbuck says to Ahab, "Sir, what will this chase pay the men of old New Bedford?" and Ahab says, "It does not pay on the barrelhead, it pays here, man, here," and he strikes his chest. We need a

rebirth of idealism. We have to romance ourselves into being tall again, and being proud, and caring about what we do. That's what it's all about. And every child knows this. Why do you think that the lines run around the block at *Star Trek*? That movie has made $50 million in just four weeks! It's the most successful film in the history of the world! *Close Encounters*—$200 million in a few months—is a religious film, because it relates man to the universe. It's got a strong, mighty, huge, overwhelming religious theme. What we're doing with our religions is binding up the mysteries and putting them under a Godhead and trying to make some sense of the miracle, isn't it? And the kids know this. They are ahead of the theologians and educators. We've got to listen. Now that doesn't mean the kids are right about everything. No, no, but they're hungry for that miracle. They're going to science-fiction films because they need answers, and if religion won't give it to them, they'll find their religion in that movie, and it's there.

BN: Let's talk about dimensions. In "Tomorrow's Child" you wrote that dimensions had to do with senses and time and knowledge. Sometimes I wonder "What is reality to Ray Bradbury?"
RB: I think it's a crazy combination. Mammalian creatures are very fragile and vulnerable, and it takes us years to get back to the state where animals are, automatically. A bird learns to fly very quickly, and many insects don't have to be taught at all how to fly. They're alone and no one teaches them and they just take off. A butterfly comes out of the chrysalis, an hour later it's dried its wings, and it's gone. The world is full of fabulous things like that. But for us humans, from the time we're nine until we're twenty-one or twenty-two, we dry our wings and look around, begin to fly a little, fall off, and climb back up. Finally, we're twenty-two and have written five million words, as I did when I was in my teens, and we know the time of waiting is over at last. I was ready to fly, the real self was coming out. The training prepares the real self to be born. We should teach that to kids, say, "Hey, it's going to be a long time before you can be this, that, or the other"—a good basketball player takes about ten years of training.

BN: It's internalized then . . .
RB: Yes, and we need to do all the intuitive things. Take me. I'm a creature who's had sense enough to train himself, and the more free I become, the more I'm able to release these insights that you're talking about.

BN: Let me ask you this question. In one of your stories you have a young man manning a space station, and you have him make a phone call to the him-of-the-future. If you could call the you-of-the-future, what would you say?
RB: A line from a poem of mine, "I remember you, I remember you."

BN: I think of you as a little prophetic. What do you mean when you say "I feel I was put here for a reason"?
RB: Just to reveal truths that are obvious. When people read my stories, they say, "Gee, I've often thought that, but I didn't put it down, or I didn't see it quite that way." There's nothing so remarkable about this ability except that it's a surprise, and I try to surprise myself every day, and see what else is lying around that nobody has noticed and ask, why haven't they? I'll give you a good example. I wrote an article called "The Ardent Blasphemers," comparing Melville and Jules Verne. They're obviously related to each other. One is the dark half of the dark side of the other. The mad captains are identical, one is totally insane, and strikes God, the other plugs into the scientific method and solves the problems of the universe by using the energy of God creatively. One kills the whale, one builds the whale into a nautilus. Well, I sat down and wrote an essay on this, and I sent it off to Clifton Fadiman. Fadiman wrote back and said "Congratulations, you're the first person in the world to notice how they influenced each other." You have to be open to surprise, and never doubt yourself, and if you're wrong, okay, you're wrong, but take a chance and get a thing done. . . .

BN: What if one day we transcend our dependence on machines and are able to communicate and act without them?
RB: We've all thought of this since we were children, haven't we? My fire balloons in *The Martian Chronicles* are pure spirit. They can talk to each other by telepathy and assume any shape that they wish and, since they have no bodies, they are free of sin, you see? Because as soon as you create a body, you have hungers and needs.

BN: You've written stories about modern society like "The Pedestrian," that were disturbing to me, but in your June article in *US News and World Report*, you seemed really excited and enthusiastic about the future. . . .
RB: I'm a terribly practical optimist. I discovered years ago that by doing things, things got done. And your optimism grows out of doing things. The

people who are pessimistic are people who criticize and don't offer solutions. I'm offering solutions, and in some cases I've changed the world. I've written a number of articles in the last ten years about the cities of the future, the towns of the future, how to reinvent them, how to fill them with the things that we need to make us human beings, and I've seen my influence on several small town developments. I would love, if I came to the end of my life, to say that I have contributed to rebuilding of the American small town.

BN: Your feelings about the future—what do you feel are the greatest challenges humanity faces in the next decade?
RB: The great challenge is the usual stupid one—war. The second is energy, and the third challenge is the reconstruction of the small town. The fourth challenge is education, because we're not educating our kids. They don't know how to read and write, and that means they're not going to know how to think. The only way that you can learn to think is by knowing how to write. So everyone's got to be taught how to write essays. I don't care if they're bad or good, just get your thoughts down, keep notes, keep a diary, so that you can see your ideas. You can see what you think that way, and keep a record of your own stupidity year by year. . . .

BN: Or your growth in thinking.
RB: Of course, because ultimately it's no longer stupid.

BN: But It was all part of the process.
RB: Teaching's got to start sooner, because the kids are ready when they're three years old, and a lot of other countries are way ahead of us there. By the time kids get out of the third grade, they should have everything they need as far as reading and writing are concerned. They should really be ready for more serious things. But that's not happening.

BN: I think they have a right to a balanced experience in school.
RB: If we're not careful, we're going to raise a generation that can't think. Then we're going to wonder why we wind up with a lot of bad government.

BN: After I read your article in *US News and World Report*, I thought, "Americans feel like that, they feel as though answers to problems are just around the corner."

RB: Sure. But what we need are creative governments and creative corporations that get in and think about all this too. We've got to create transit systems that really operate for all of us . . . But it's going to take a huge act of imagination by someone to lead the way, and the trouble with most politicians is that's all they are.

BN: What about you?
RB: Going into politics? I can do more, I've already done more, by being outside.

BN: When you write your autobiography, write it like you did *Dandelion Wine*.
RB: That's the way I'm doing it. Actually I've got a first draft, and it's called "The Dogs That Eat Sweet Grass," or "How To Keep and Feed A Muse," and I'm doing it in terms of stories and ideas. What interests me in people is their ideas, and how the experiences they had made ideas. If they can hold onto that, it's up, on, and away.

Ray Bradbury: The Science of Science Fiction
Arthur Unger / 1980

Christian Science Monitor Eastern Edition, 73:1 (25 November 1980), pp. B20–21. Copyright © 1980 by the Christian Science Monitor. Reprinted by permission of the Christian Science Monitor. All rights reserved.

Mr. Bradbury is not only a prolific writer, he is a nonstop talker. A conversation with him is a fascinating, meandering ramble through the intricacies of an ambivalently complex-simplistic mind. His ideas are constantly skewed toward sometimes unique, sometimes amazingly old-fashioned Bradburyesque versions of reality on the planet Earth.

If he had to choose one story that represents the essence of Ray Bradbury, which would it be?

"The one that comes to mind first is 'There Will Come Soft Rains,' which is about a house in the future that goes on living after the city is destroyed around it. All the robots, all the computers, all the poetry-reading machines, all the TV sets, all the toasters and refrigerators go on living after the people are gone. Late at night the house reads poetry to itself and then makes dinners, scrapes the dishes, cleans the rooms. Little mechanical mice come out of the wall.

"Finally, the house burns down and, in hysteria, cries 'Fire! Fire!' and tries to put itself out to save its own life.

"When the fire is finally out and the house is dead, there's one little wall left standing in which the poetry machine repeats a poem—'There Will Come Soft Rains,' by Sara Teasdale: 'Spring herself when she woke at dawn/ Would hardly know that we were gone.'

"It's a lovely science-fictional semifantasy metaphor of the sadness of the world that existed for us in 1950. We'd just been only five years away from the end of the war, the atom bomb. The hydrogen bomb was just being invented. We were more afraid back then than we are now . . . and for good reason. I think things were more nebulous back then. Now we see that there's a power situation existing in the world which may very well exist for quite a few years—if we're lucky—among the three powers. And we may be able to keep ourselves in an uneasy peace. That is my hope. . . ."

Quick, an interruption. Does Mr. Bradbury describe himself as a science-fiction writer?

"No, I call myself an 'idea writer.' The history of ideas is what interests me. The fact is that the first science fiction was written in caves in symbol form. A science-fiction story is just an attempt to solve a problem that exists in the world, sometimes a moral problem, sometimes a physical or social or theological problem. But the people who lived in caves drew pictures of their problems. For instance, if they had a mammoth outside the cave which they wanted to eat—how do you kill and eat a mammoth? So they drew a picture of it all.

"Those were dreams that existed before the fact. And when you solve the problem, the science fiction becomes fact. And then you keep moving on up through science. That whole history of ideas, as ideas alone to start with, and then as they begin to exist in the world and change the world and compete with the world . . . even if you look at, say, the history of castles, the same thing happens. . . ."

Oh, I understand, . . . I think. Is it that science fact has gone beyond science fiction?

"No, not really, because we've only been on the moon for roughly five days out of five billion years of existence for Earth. Our life on the moon is only a few days old; our life on Mars hasn't begun to exist yet. It exists only through our machines. So we're still in a very primitive state. From here on, a lot of science fiction is going to be theological—a combination of theology and science—because a lot of the same problems attract theologians and writers. We're all up to the same thing.

"Everything is an act of faith, isn't it? Friendship is an act of faith. If we agree to be friends, that means we're going to have to behave in a certain way, we hope for a lifetime, and we won't break this invisible pact. But you can't write it down, and there are no guarantees for it. It's faith just as money is faith, . . . and almost everything we do is based on faith."

A change to the more prosaic: Is anybody carrying on the Bradbury tradition in fantasy and science fiction today?

"I am! I'm still at it. But a lot of my friends—some of them my disciples, some pupils, some masters—are at it, too.

"Arthur Clarke is still at it; Robert Heinlein has a new book out—he's a very vital man. He was my teacher when I was eighteen and he around thirty-one. He allowed me to come to his house and he'd read my dreadful stories—a very kind and helpful man.

"Harlan Ellison is writing well—very strange, very neurotic at times. But he loves literature and writing, and when I see that in a person, when I see that kind of enthusiasm for libraries that Harlan has, then I'm on his side, even though I don't understand half of what he does.

"We're totally different people, but we're good friends because I'm a library-oriented person.

"I never went to college, so I raised and educated myself in a library."

Are today's young people confusing horror and fantasy with science fiction? And does it matter?

"I define science fiction as the art of the possible. Fantasy is the art of the impossible. Science fiction, again, is the history of ideas, and they're always ideas that work themselves out and become real and happen in the world. And fantasy comes along and says, 'We're going to break all the laws of physics.'

"So, when you see a film like *Alien*, for instance, it combines the old horror film with science fiction. But it's basically a fantasy about all the monsters that lurk in the back of our minds.

"Most people don't realize it, but the series of films which have made more money than any other series in the history of films is the James Bond series. They're all science fiction, too—romantic, adventurous, frivolous, fantastic science fiction!

"I love *Close Encounters of the Third Kind*, too. And *Star Wars*. I especially love *The Empire Strikes Back*, because it illustrates Zen principles on a very primitive level. . . . There's that great scene . . . where Luke says, 'But I don't believe.' And the Zen master replies, 'That's why you fail. There is no such thing as trying. There is only doing. If you try, you can never do. If you do, you'll never have to try.'"

Is that Ray Bradbury's philosophy?

"Absolutely! Just do it every day, and never think about it."

What books would he recommend to young people—or anybody—who wants his imagination to soar? Which books influenced Bradbury?

"When I was nine, I collected comic strips, which led me into books. I collected Buck Rogers and then later Flash Gordon and Tarzan. I have forty years of Prince Valiant put away. People made fun of me—but all the things that people then told me were foolish have turned out to be very serious subjects later in my life.

"When the Smithsonian put out a paperback edition of its collection of comic books three years ago, I saw that everything they have, I have. How come I was so smart when I was nine?

"It's just a matter of having enough brains to go with your love, anywhere in life. So I read Edgar Rice Burroughs, finally Jules Verne, then moved on to Aldous Huxley."

Would Ray Bradbury recommend reading Ray Bradbury?

"You're darn right I would. I represent so many different fields. My new book represents my interest in eight or nine different subjects. I'm very proud of my curiosity. And that is something, coming from someone who doubted his own intelligence until he was thirty. I bumped into Christopher Isherwood in a bookstore when I was thirty, just after *The Martian Chronicles* had been published. Three nights later he called me and told me I had written an incredible book. And then he brought Gerald Heard and Huxley into my life. So that was the year I discovered I was bright. But it didn't go to my head. I was humbled by it . . . and scared."

Is he brighter now?

He laughs. "Sure. I make better metaphors now. And I just love the delight I get in discovering a new metaphor that works. You just don't know where it is going to come from. I was going through the Vatican Museum a few years ago, and I looked at the bones of the saints in the reliquaries, the crystal jars with the golden tops. And I came home and got to thinking that we are the reliquaries of all time.

"We don't put the bones away in jars; instead we put away all the information of the world, the dust of data, in video cassettes and video discs and into computers. And one day we will be able to take all that information along on a rocket ship to Alpha Centauri and look back and see the total history as the reliquary of all time. And as soon as I had the metaphor, I could sit down and write a poem."

Is there anything left for Mr. Bradbury to do? He has written short stories, novels, screenplays, poems; he has directed plays for West Coast theater groups—what's next?

"I'm working on a new opera called *Leviathan 99*, about Moby Dick in outer space. [He also wrote the script for the John Huston movie based on *Moby Dick*, and claims it is one of the best things he ever did.]

"I've helped create a building which is being built in Florida right now, called 'Spaceship Earth.' It's part of Experimental Prototype Community of Tomorrow which the Disney people are creating down there. It's a permanent world's fair, in effect.

"And I'm working on a new murder mystery. I've loved [(Samuel) Dashiell] Hammett for forty years. I've loved Chandler and Caine. They've all been neglected until the past ten years. Again, I loved them early. So, now I'm writing my own murder mystery—a kind of homage to them."

Mr. Bradbury plans to write the mystery on the train on the way home. Originally from Waukegan, Illinois, he is still thrilled by the breadth of America on each side of his hometown.

"I love to ride on trains. I love to travel on them alone. And I love to write on trains. The greatest moments come on cross-continental trips at midnight, when I watch all the little towns and all the people out on the summer porches and the little kids playing on the swings.

"I wrote a poem coming across country this time because I saw my Grandpa's house going by again and again and again—little towns all the same. It helps you to believe in mankind. It gives you an invigorating rebirth of faith.

"I refuse to believe that these are bad people. On the contrary, I look at those people going by in the night, and I think, 'They're all beautiful. I must write about them. . . .'"

Ray Bradbury: An Interview
Abraham Drassinower and Cheryl Kemkow / 1982

Dial Tone, April 1982, pp. 2–4. Copyright © 1982 by Stanford University. Reprinted by permission.

The crowd filling the seats and aisles of Kresge Auditorium responded to his challenges to intellectualism with enthusiasm. They laughed at his aphorisms—"The only enemy of creativity is thought"—and applauded his calls to celebrate American glory.

Science-fiction writer, novelist, poet and playwright Ray Bradbury lectured at Stanford February 4, 1982. Author of *The Martian Chronicles, The Illustrated Man, Fahrenheit 451,* and the screenplay for *Moby Dick,* Bradbury encouraged optimism and pride in humanity: "The race doesn't have to die, because we don't deserve it. We're too good for that. That's what space travel is all about."

His closing anecdote, concerning his reaction to people who did not approve of the Apollo project the day of the lunar landing ("How long has it taken us to get to the moon? Five billion years! Tonight we reach up and touch the moon and you refuse to celebrate?! To hell with you! To hell with you!") drew a standing ovation.

Later, Mr. Bradbury discovered that the people volunteering to drive him back to his Nob Hill hotel in San Francisco were not among those who stood to applaud him. But Mr. Bradbury happily climbed into our Honda Civic and rode with us for an hour—answering questions, asking them, and volunteering information. He saw us as cynics and potential negative elitists in danger of denying or losing love of life–but young and with a chance of redemption—in short, skeptics. We saw him as a believer—in life, love, sublimation through technology and the American middle class. The conversation was at times antagonistic but without bitterness, and although his attempts to encourage, educate and convince may have been in vain, we parted on good terms.

Dial Tone: What I left your lecture with tonight was that you are advocating a revival of idealism, a rebirth of idealism in the United States. . . .

Bradbury: God knows, yes! We have to believe in ourselves—otherwise, why bother to get out of bed? Why bother to make love to any other individual? If I go to bed with a woman, if I start a love affair doomed to disaster—why? It would be better not to do it.

DT: So your idealism is, in a sense, a device?
B: Right—that's correct. When I was twenty, I never thought anyone would love me. When I was twenty-four, I still didn't. When I was twenty-five, I met my wife and she changed my life forever. All you need is friends, someone who loves you—one male friend who loves you and one woman who loves you—children, and the work to be done to improve the world. That's all you need. There are people who look only at the problems; you can't live like that! It's impossible! I tell myself to go on working, writing my stories, encouraging people like you. I don't give up. All those other people can say, "The world is ending tomorrow—give up!" I just go on doing what I'm doing.

DT: What do you feel the impact of technology is upon the individual—the human surrounded by the created environment?
B: Well, I think technology can teach us humanism. Movies, motion picture cameras, for example, do not "know" but they can teach us humanism. Television broadcasters and television receivers do not understand the information they're getting yet those robot devices teach us how to communicate. You know, books are the same way. Books are indifferent—they have nothing to communicate.

DT: No?
B: No! They are total devices whereby we reproduce, by mechanical means, information. They speak with a technological tongue. When you pick up a book, when you pick up my book, you are learning information. You are learning how to communicate. It's the information that's my concern—not the means.

DT: Sometimes, though, I feel that a technological environment can make things colder, less human. For example, if you go to McDonald's at least there is human contact—you can smile at the person behind the counter and they may smile back—but, if you go to Jack in the Box or an automat, you talk to

a machine and there's no human contact. Could mechanization be, in a way, dangerous?
B: But you don't have to go to Jack in the Box! No one is forcing you. You can go to a little hamburger stand and talk to Sam or Joe or Irv. It's a free country! It's that simple.

DT: Do you have a conception of a utopia—a place where things are "as they should be" and a way that man can be as humanity or even as the United States?
B: Sure, and I'm helping to build it. I work on architecture, city planning, mass transportation. I just attended a conference on mass transit—it's important to me. If you say you've never met an altruist, you've met one tonight! I've been doing this for twenty years and no one's paid me a cent for it. I believe in it. Through social planning and transportation we can get people out of their cars—cars are inhuman devices—we can change the cities and make them better places to live. So, I've become involved; I've given up a lot of things to work on rebuilding our cities.

DT: So you believe in practical reforms to work towards an ideal technologically planned republic? Do you think it's possible to achieve?
B: Walt Disney has created one—it's clean; monorails bring people together. There are more flowers, more places to walk—space and order. Everyone is smiling. There would be more opportunities, more chances for everyone to contribute.

DT: But could that kind of environment be seen as a little artificial? Somehow a city seems more alive and creative. . . .
B: Cities are too dirty, the atmosphere is horrible.

DT: But, in a sense, cities are an expression of how people want to live and that way they are spontaneous and human. Disneyland could be seen as static and sterilized, with no room for individuals.
B: Do you want to live in a ghetto? What we need in the United States is monorails to get us out of our cars. Disney had a lot of ideas and it's not perfectly clean but it's cleaner and they're working on it.

DT: I don't want to sound like a pessimist—I don't think I am—but. . . .
B: Everyone does these days so join the crowd!

DT: What would you do with the darker side of human nature?
B: Try to make it grow by putting it in the light—how do you grow flowers? You offer them sun—most of us want the sun. Give all of us a chance to grow. That's what we should do with the darker side. If I feel I have no control, naturally I'm not going to do anything. We all must work together.

DT: Do you think the United States (as the United States) should take an active role in forming or shaping the future? One of the things that you said tonight that some of the audience reacted to strongly was that at the end of WWII the United States was a benign parental authority who had Germany and Japan "under the heel" but was "nice" and merciful and let them rebuild....
B: They were dangerous! They threatened the rest of the world!

DT: I guess what made me uncomfortable was the "we vs. they" division of the world.
B: They forced it on us—they bombed Pearl Harbor!—what did you want us to do?

DT: Does it always have to be an "us" who changes the world and educates everyone else to follow our way?
B: That's the only way you can grow, my dear! Unfortunately, that's the way we have to do it. If you can think of a better way....

DT: I would think an idealist would be interested in unity—a world community....
B: If you get it done, you get it done. There's nothing wrong with that. If we're going to build it, let's build it. That's the only way we can do it.

DT: So regardless of whether or not it's real, idealism has a primary practical function.
B: Absolutely. There's no way to build a world if it doesn't mean anything. You've got to help civilization.

DT: I'm uneasy turning away from problems and concentrating on self-justification—it just seems you lose touch with reality.
B: It is reality—you are just dwelling on the negative side. If you only see problems and weaknesses you can't move beyond them to a better future. It becomes a modern obsession.

DT: Not necessarily—I'm not sure. What I mean is not sacrificing ideals or the quality of the moment in order to focus on planning or building a future.
B: I'm not sacrificing anything. I enjoy my life. I've realized I can do all of these things and have fun in whatever I do—or I wouldn't do it. I'm not sacrificing. I wouldn't lecture if I didn't enjoy it.

DT: You're allowed to earn a living.
B: I made $10 a week for a long time. No one's "allowed" to do anything—you allow yourself. . . . How fast are we going?

DT: Seventy.
B: That's too fast.

DT: Sorry—I'm worried about my charge warning light—it went on a little while ago.
B: I'm worried about us going out! I'll puke on your dashboard if you don't slow down—maybe you should be worried about that!

DT: You make one feel old.
B: I beg your pardon?

DT: I meant that I don't feel that it's possible for me to be that idealistic anymore—I've lost that.
B: You've got to change that. If you believe, if you love, you stay young forever. You can't let yourself worry, you can't let yourself deny life. When I started, it wasn't easy but, out of love and work, I received everything. I don't know whether it's because I was given abilities or whether I've worked harder. But my life is good, it's full—I write stories, lecture, I enjoy writing plans and working with that. . . .

DT: I saw two of your plays this summer—they premiered in Orange at the Gem Theatre.
B: I have two plays in Los Angeles now. They are being praised by critics, the audience loves them. We put them together for a few thousand dollars and they are comparable to the plays at the major theaters that they spend hundreds of thousands of dollars producing. You talk about love and altruism, you can see it there. I'm very proud of my group—all the people working together—it's wonderful!

DT: You were talking earlier about how a person's broken past would make them a pessimist. If we were to talk about Ray Bradbury, the writer, what was it about his past that produced his attitude toward the world?
B: A combination of things—I had a happy childhood that has grown into the mature adult. I'm well-balanced and I accept—I can look at death, I can look at life too. I was lucky to have a good home. And, as a small boy I discovered Jules Verne, Shakespeare and others and learned to love them. It's through that love that you build a life.

DT: This twentieth-century attitude, this modern pessimism, to what do you attribute it?
B: Guilt, need for approval. They create their own problems. No one looks at the good things we do. . . .

DT: We? The United States?
B: Yes, we solve problems. We're feeding most of the world right now. We have to learn to be proud of ourselves, we have to be confident. We work until we have surpluses and then we can feed the starving. I just can't understand this attitude of just looking for faults—it's anti-American. How can we create? That's not creative. We must learn to accept ourselves—I accept myself. I live in a wonderful place and I'd better appreciate it. I shouldn't feel guilty.

Here in the United States there are problems but they can be challenges. So many of the world's peoples are hampered by their religions—it's sad but true—like the Indians; so many people are destroyed each year by their prehistoric concepts—of animals, of women and such. We can't eradicate things like that, only time can.

In the meantime, all we can do is set examples and eventually they can overcome their constraints and change. Look at Japan—it's now a super-America, and I think it's terrific. They have learned what there is to learn. Why should we have all the fun?

For example, look at the respect that the black man has when he marries, becomes a parent, settles down, keeps a job, raises his children—he becomes a center of influence in his family. Man, he's got his balls back! And you don't have to have poverty, you don't have to have social programs. The black middle class has grown. Millions of blacks have moved into the middle class in the last fifteen years. He's going to support his family, keep his job, raise his children, and make a better society. Why don't people talk about this instead of being negative?

DT: But some people wouldn't accept the ideal of the American middle class as the goal for society.
B: Oh shit! That's what we've heard from Russia for years and they're wrong, they're straight wrong. It is an ideal—I'm middle class and I'm building a better society. That's what they have to learn—that's what the Chinese have had to learn, the French have had to learn. You can't go out and destroy a thing like that. It's where all values come from, where democracy comes from. It's where the ideas come from, the important genius comes from—not from anywhere else. Stop all that talk! We've got to leave that destructive kind of thinking. I'm terrified of it—there's nothing positive in it at all. That leads to totalitarianism.

DT: Could you explain further what you think we should do with the darker side of human nature? I still can't quite grasp it. . . .
B: What you have to do is face it, accept it—by writing, for example. You do what you can do to allow it to come into your writing and learn to understand it.

DT: Do you mean to channel aggressive instinct into creativity?
B: Yes.

DT: Do you think that's possible at a social level?
B: That's what great philosophy is. Every individual has to do this—and start with that—can I ask you a question?

DT: Sure.
B: What do you want to be?

DT: I would like to be a writer.
B: O.K.—write!

DT: I write all the time.
B: All right: and when you are productive you will be a better person, you'll treat your girlfriend better, you'll be less corrupt, less mean. You've got to get

all these things out. You'll be finding out about yourself and that's an exciting adventure. The more you find, the more you look for. At the end of each day—and you've got to write every day. When I don't write for a day I get more corrupt, it's part of a difficult exercise of the spirit . . . what do you write?

DT: I write mostly poetry but I've written some short stories.
B: Say you write a short story—what you have to do is make a list of ten things you love and write about them, then make a list of ten things you hate and destroy them in your fiction. When you understand the dark side you can control it. Murder the things you hate in your stories. I've written a lot of dark stories—that side speaks for itself—and I've killed off a lot of things I hate in my writing—and I celebrate the things I love.

DT: Your love and enthusiasm for literature came through in your lecture tonight.
B: I've written more short stories, essays, poems, novels and plays about other authors than anything else. There's more in one line of something like Emily Dickinson than in entire books. I love Poe, Melville, Hawthorne—libraries are very close to my heart. All the women in my life have been librarians, writers, teachers or booksellers! My wife was a bookseller when I met her and she was also a teacher. I stayed friends with all my teachers, ladies, until they were eighty-five, ninety years old.

DT: I was wondering if you ever worry about reductionism—if anything is lost through the popularization of culture: for example, taking a novel and converting it to a half-hour sitcom. During the modern period it seems that the artist is cut off from society in general—whether this is just elitism or resistance to this tendency for art and communication to be reduced to a common denominator. When you are writing the history of the world for a fifteen-minute ride in Disneyland or for the exhibit of the world's fair, do you ever think about that?
B: You're worrying about unimportant things. All this is not the center of our life; sex is the center! We've got to stop judging. Everything in our life can teach us—even if only on a trivial level. We've got to be prepared to receive education from anywhere we can get it. You've got to stop rejecting things—it's a trap. I learn from TV, I learn from movies. We've got to make sure

nothing fine escapes us. It's a free society—free. So what are you going to do about it?

DT: I guess I would be wary of looking at *The Empire Strikes Back* as the finest cultural artifact our society can produce.
B: Well, you can choose to watch it or you don't have to go see it, look at it or not, read things or not read them.

DT: Should you pursue quality in a society as well as build monorails? Choose [William Butler] Yeats over TV?
B: You can have both! I can read Yeats one minute and then watch *The Empire Strikes Back* and enjoy both equally. What's wrong with that? Do you want me not to do that?

DT: No.
B: All right—then where's the argument? There is no argument.

DT: When you write do you consciously write for a specific purpose or a specific audience?
B: No! I write for myself and to enjoy my own mind—it's brilliant—it's a fantastic mind that I have. I love playing with it. It's a big pinball machine with all these popcorn bits popping around. I delight in entertaining myself. That's what Shaw did, that's what Shakespeare did. One is dark and the other is light. Don't worry about these things. Beat 'em! Join 'em! Go and see *Star Wars* and enjoy it—it's a cartoon. Then the next night go to see Hamlet done by Olivier, then the next night after that go see *Sunset Boulevard* which is a gorgeous film, beautifully made, somewhere in between. Then the next night you go to the ballet—there's room for all of that! You go to a museum—you have the impressionists here on the wall, the renaissance people there; you have to enjoy them all! Why not? I can! I have loves in every age. It could be anything. I take a look and then I develop a taste—a taste for [Claude] Monet and [Pierre-Auguste] Renoir that supersedes that for Toulouse Lautrec—but I still leave room.

DT: But there are some—Europeans looking at America, for example—who would say that great art just isn't produced by a middle class society. . . .
B: Fuck! They're a bunch of jerks! Those intellectuals on that program on Jules Verne in France that I told you about in the lecture said that. But he was

middle class—he changed the world. They're wrong and I'm right! I'm middle class and I've changed the world! I'm creative! Make people fall in love—that's the thing you've got to do. If you don't do that forget whatever you're doing. The power of the world is in love. Stop these qualitative things and just enjoy and live!

DT: Now you're the one who is being a hedonist!

DT: Point scored!
B: No, no, she didn't score a thing! Because I admitted I love sex. I love everything about the sexual side of life and I love food but I don't make a comparison. I used the word because you brought it up in the first place. But I accept me as a hedonist, I accept me as an intellectual, I accept me as middle class, I accept me as cheap and vulgar. I accept me as pragmatic and I accept me as glorious. All these things I accept—except, I refuse to make a distinction between all these selves. I can name them but it all amalgamates itself into creativity—and the poison you accept as a writer.

I collect cartoon strips—you know that? What kind of great art is that? But, I love it. What if I hadn't collected Buck Rogers? What if I had listened to all the people who made fun of me and said, "Don't collect Buck Rogers"? It would have changed my life forever. I never would have become a science-fiction writer if I had listened to all the people who say, "that's middle class"—uh, uh! Can't do that! If you kill my soul, you may as well kill me!

DT: But a lot of times, the family values, the middle-class values, are the ones that restrict and enforce duties—and people can't accept themselves because they have a static value system that judges them and others. That's part of our society too. . . .
B: Every society.

DT: Well, at least ours. . . .
B: That's part of every society—but it's based on real things. I mean, a real baby is a real baby—and that baby has a diaper that needs to be changed and there's a rule and a law there! There are real things in life—like love and death, faithfulness—we try to live up to our friends. Love is a promise; it doesn't exist in the world—where is it? Try to put your hand on friendship—you can't! It's in promises we make to one another.

The Romance of Places:
An Interview with Ray Bradbury
Rob Couteau / 1990

All text copyright © 1991–2002 by Rob Couteau. Reprinted by permission. This interview was conducted in the summer of 1990 in Paris. Excerpts were originally published in the November 1990 edition of the *Paris Voice* (Paris, France) and in the spring 1991 edition of *Quantum: Science-Fiction & Fantasy Review* (Gaithersburg, Maryland: Thrust Publications).

Couteau: My first question concerns the actual process of writing. Do you have any sort of daily ritual which serves as a preparation to writing, or do you just sit down at a certain time and begin?
Bradbury: Well, the ritual is waking up, number one, and then lying in bed and listening to my voices. Then, over a period of years . . . I call it my morning theater; it's inside my head. And my characters talk to one another, and when it reaches a certain pitch of excitement I jump out of bed and run and trap them before they are gone. So I never have to worry about a routine; they're always in there talking.

C: How long do you write for?
B: Oh, a couple of hours. You can do three or four thousand words and that's more than enough for one day.

C: How has the use of the computer affected your writing?
B: Not at all, because I don't use it.

C: You never use a computer?
B: I can write faster on a typewriter than you can on a computer. I do 120 words a minute and you can't do that on a computer. So I don't need anything. . . . That's plenty fast.

C: So you're saying that the technology still hasn't caught up with you.
B: Well, if it won't be any more efficient than my IBM Selectric, why should I buy it? It's for corrections, you know? Then I give it to my daughter and she

has a computer and she puts it in, and she then corrects it in the computer. And we have a record so we have [the best of] both worlds at the same time.

C: How about the imaginative process itself, the building of a story. How do characters and plots first arise? (You've maybe covered this a little just now.) Do they appear spontaneously, or do they first originate in carefully planned, conscious construct?
B: Any carefully planned thing destroys the creativity. You can't think your way through a story, you have to live it. So you don't build a story, you allow it to explode.

C: Do you, for instance, use people and places out of the past, out of your own life?
B: Very rarely. More recently [yes,] in my two murder mysteries, *Death Is a Lonely Business* and the sequel, which just came out, *A Graveyard for Lunatics*. Events in my past life are in there, some people that I knew. But most of my stories are ideas in action. In other words, I get a concept, and I let it run away. I find a character to act out the idea. And then the story takes care of itself.

C: Certain modern writers such as William Burroughs have used characters and settings first observed in dream states as the basis for fictional experiments. Others such as Henry Miller have often spoken of being dictated to by the unconscious. . . .
B: That sounds like my cup of tea. . . .

C: Have you had similar experiences with what might be termed non-ego influences on the creative imagination? I mean there are others: drugs or meditation or whatever. Or dreams.
B: No, dreams don't work. And I don't know anyone who ever wrote anything based on dreams constantly. You may get inspiration once every ten years. But dreams are supposed to function to cure you of some problem that you have, so you leave those alone. That's a different process. But the morning process when you're waking up, and you're half-asleep and half-awake, that's the perfect time. Because then you're relaxed and the brain is floating between your ears. It's not attached. Or getting in the shower first thing in

the morning when your body is totally relaxed and mind is totally relaxed. You're not thinking; you're intuiting. And then the little explosions, the little revelations come. Or taking a nap in the afternoon. It's the same state. But you can't force things. People try to force things. It's disastrous. Just leave your mind alone; your intuition knows what it wants to write, so get out of the way.

C: Where did you fly in from?
B: From New York City. But I'm from Los Angeles.

C: New York's my hometown.
B: Well, it's a good place to get away from. It's a shame. 'Cause I've been going there since I was nineteen and I've watched the whole thing go to hell. I had a lot of friends there. And I love the Metropolitan Museum and the Guggenheim. But I mean, how much love can you have for something? The only livable place is down by Pier 17. South Street Seaport. Have you ever been down there? It's great. And it's very social. It's very safe. A lot of good restaurants. And I go up on this restaurant facing the Brooklyn Bridge, Harbor Lights. A lot of wonderful Irishmen run the place. And I go up and get drunk with them. I lived a year in Ireland. So we get on very well. We talk about The Royal Hibernian Hotel and things like that.

C: You've been the recipient of numerous book awards. You've been received by world leaders such as Mikhail Gorbachev. When the *Apollo* astronauts landed on the moon they paid you homage by naming the Dandelion Crater in honor of your novel *Dandelion Wine*. How has this overall acceptance by people in positions of great responsibility affected your writing and your life?
B: Not at all. You just don't think about it; you shouldn't. The most dangerous thing you can do is to know who you are. See, Norman Mailer's problem is he thinks he's Norman Mailer. And Gore Vidal's problem is he thinks he's Gore Vidal. I don't think I'm Ray Bradbury. So there's a big difference. Just do your work everyday, don't go around thinking, "Gee," you know, "wow!" To hell with that. The work is important; the work is fun. And there's no time, if you get into your work everyday there's no time to think who you are. So . . . these are very nice things, and I was exhilarated by them when they happened. My day with Gorbachev was joyous and I went home immensely happy. But then the next day, you've got things to do. So it hasn't affected me at all.

C: I'm curious about your vision of the future. I'm thinking of a story that first appeared in the early 1950s: "The Pedestrian." In this rather paranoid vision of the future a Mr. Meade is arrested and sent to the psychiatric center for having committed the transgression of walking without a purpose through the streets at night. It is a world in which, you write, magazines and books didn't sell any more and the people sit in rooms mesmerized by television sets. In many ways this tale epitomizes the very dark undercurrent of the 1950s. Yet there are forces at work in the world today that are not that dissimilar. What about your personal vision of the future, especially the political future?

B: Well, it's very optimistic. Look what's happened in the last eight months. Because America stood firm and helped form NATO, and just stayed quietly there, finally the Communists gave up. They *were* an evil empire; you know, Reagan was absolutely right. And they partially still are because they haven't finished disarming.

But who could have foreseen that the end would have come so quickly. And within just a matter of months. We said take down the wall. We implied it many times. Only one president ever said it: Reagan. He's not going to get any credit for it. Everyone hates him for being successful. He'll probably go down in history as the most important president of the century. Because he did in the Communist Empire. Just by holding steady and being very quiet. And when the Communists left the negotiating table three or four years ago everyone said, "Oh, President Reagan, don't do that," you know, "call him back." He said, "They'll be back. They have to come back. Because their economy isn't working, so if we just, if we're not belligerent, don't take advantage of it, don't rock the boat, they'll be back. And eventually the Wall will come down." And that's exactly what happened. So two weeks ago the Russians welcomed Reagan to Moscow, huh? Because he helped them get free of their own system. It's ironic. It's beautiful. And the one president we thought would never be able to do this is the one who did it.

C: How about the opening of the East Bloc? How will it affect science-fiction writing?

B: I don't think it will affect it much. Because we're running ahead of all that. We've always talked about freedom, we've always talked about totalitarian governments. After all, *Fahrenheit 451* is all about Russia, and all about China, isn't it? And all about the totalitarians anywhere, either left or right, doesn't matter where they are, they're book burners, all of them. And so *Fahrenheit* will continue to be a read book, by people all over the world, 'cause there are still totalitarian governments. And book burners. So as long as that's true, or if the threat is true, the book will be read.

C: This past August you celebrated your seventieth birthday. After devoting decades of your life to writing science fiction, have you arrived at any conclusion concerning the function of science fiction either in our individual lives, or in the life of the social collective?
B: Well, it's the most important fiction ever invented, it always has been. People haven't given it credit. Because it has to do with the history of ideas. Of dreaming an idea, birthing an idea, blueprinting an idea, making it into a fact. And then moving on to the next idea.

The history of science fiction started in caves, 20,000 years ago. The ideas on the walls of the caves were problems to be solved. It's problem solving. Primitive scientific knowledge, primitive dreams, primitive blueprinting to solve problems. I never really realized how honorable and how long the history of science fiction is. You look on the walls of the caves, they had pictures of antelopes, and gazelles, and mammoths. And the problem there is: how do you kill them? And that's a science-fiction problem, isn't it? You have to think of it first before you can solve it. Then, you find ways of inventing knives and then spears. A spear is an extension of a man's arm and his imagination. And when you throw it, you're throwing your will, you're throwing your arm, and you're killing the animal. So that's science-fiction dreaming becoming primitive fact. You finally find out how to kill animals. So you can survive. And then how do you build a fire? That's science fiction, isn't it? As soon as you pose the question, that's science fiction. Because you're *imagining* something and trying to figure out, "Gee, if we can bring fire to the cave . . . but it goes out. We find it in the forest after the lightning strikes and we grab it and bring it back, but the next day it's gone. How do you keep it forever?" So you dream that and then you solve it and then you have science-fact. Primitive science, huh? So the whole history of mankind is survival. Science-fiction dreaming science-factual finding. And then moving on to the next problem.

How do you go to the Moon, huh? Science fiction, just forty years ago. Impossible! I had to put up with people saying to me, when I was thirty: "We're never going to do that. Come on, don't be stupid. It's a silly thing to even think about. Why go to the Moon? Why go to Mars?" Well, all of a sudden, just a few years ago, we solved the problem. So the science-fictional dream became the *Apollo* missions. So now we're dreaming of what? We're dreaming of landing men on the Moon. We're dreaming of going out to the other planets, with manned missions eventually, sometime in the next forty or fifty years. Probably land on Mars sometime in the next twenty years. And look at the Hubble Telescope. I take it it's beginning to function now. That's a dream [that] goes a long way back, a long way back. And it was totally impossible. It was science fiction. Now it's out there, looking at the stars. Eventually we'll go to Proxima Centauri. That will be sometime in the next thousand years. Maybe even sooner. If we can make our rockets go half the speed of light, we can get out there in eight or ten years. And that's not bad. Anything longer than that is pretty hard on the human psyche, not to mention the human body.

And then all the other things have occurred. The invention of a Xerox machine, which is a printing press for every human being in the world. That's why they don't exist in Russia. All these technological things are freedoms in the United States right now. Most people couldn't tell you how many airplanes there are, private airplanes. There are 900,000 aviators, private aviators. There are between 200 and 300,000 airplanes, private airplanes, owned by individuals, and 20,000 landing strips. That's a freedom, isn't it? You can go anywhere you want to go. The airplane doesn't exist in Russia. That's one freedom that's denied everyone. 'Cause they're afraid if they had airplanes they'd leave the country. And they have very few telephones. Because they don't believe in communication. That's a freedom. We have a telephone for every person in the country of America. There are no automobiles in Russia. It has yet to be invented. . . .

C: If they can afford them though, right?
B: Huh?

C: You said we have a telephone for everyone in the country. Everyone who can afford a telephone.
B: Everyone has a telephone. Whether they can afford it or not. It's one of those things that people have regardless of their income.

C: Well, how about someone who is. . . . Your answers are piquing my interest in other questions, of course. . . .

B: [Laughs] Okay. . . . No, there are some things that all poor people have, automatically. They have TV. . . .

C: Well, how about a homeless person in New York. . . .
B: Well, no, that's another problem entirely, which has to do with our emptying the lunatic asylums twenty-five years ago. It was a big liberal movement, and a conservative movement, too, because we hated lunatic asylums, we hated the idea of them, and we had medicines which we thought were going to work, right? It was an honorable experiment, but it didn't work. So those people are out there. Now we have to take them off the streets, we cannot leave them out there.

C: I worked in a program in New York that was involved with trying to find housing and jobs for homeless mentally ill people. It was one of the few programs set up to solve that problem. And I did encounter many people who barely got by, who had a home but couldn't afford a telephone or couldn't afford clothing or other things that we all take for granted.
 And what I'm getting at, what I'm leading to is . . . you're talking a lot about the Soviet Union. I'm wondering about your feelings about totalitarian strains within the United States.
B: There are none.

C: You don't feel there are any?
B: No. Of course not. Never have been. We're a free society, we've got television. We have radio. We have newspapers. We have the videocassette, which is coming into play. These are new freedoms.

C: How about right-wing reactionary forces, like the Klan? Wouldn't you say that's a [totalitarian] strain?
B: No, those things exist on both sides. The left wing want to burn certain books too but they don't. We don't allow them to. The Huckleberry Finn liberal groups have been against . . . but we have to oppose that.

C: Well, that's what I'm getting at. Do any of your stories, do they just talk about. . . . Something like "The Pedestrian," which to me when I read it I thought it was such a wonderful thing because I thought it was universal.

It was something that wasn't specifically about China or the Soviet Union, but it was about totalitarian forces that may exist within any individual. . . .
B: Oh, yeah. Every single individual is that same thing. You are, I am. And we have to make sure that we don't misbehave. Well, look what happened with the French Revolution. It started out honorably. And then it passed into the hands of the mob. And so they decided to have revenge and everyone got killed. And then they devoured themselves. Which is neither left nor right. It's just destruction.

C: Your stories do speak, then, to these totalitarian strains that may exist within any individual.
B: Oh, everywhere. Us . . . but our record is clean compared to what's . . . I mean China has burned millions of books in the last twenty years.

C: How about our record not domestically but let's say some of our questionable policies in South America over the last hundred years. Do you think it's that clean?
B: We recognized that. I think most people have discussed it and we're, here and there, trying to do something about it. So that we erase the memory of that. But it's not totalitarian in the sense of what Russia's done when they invade a country and they kill millions of people. We haven't done that.

C: Do we want to erase the record or do we want to face the record?
B: I think we've faced it. We've got plenty of books on it. Our libraries are full of them. And plenty of newspapers to remind us of that.

C: In many ways Mr. Bradbury I see you as—it's perhaps a silly term—but I see you as the granddaddy of science fiction. . . .
B: [Laughs] I've turned into one!

C: And, you know, I mean that even if you were twenty-five or thirty—in essence!
B: [Laughs]

C: If you were to prophesize, what are some of the directions and problems that science-fiction writing will explore in the oncoming decades?

B: Well, we've already done a lot of it. I mean [George] Orwell was certainly a good example, and he'd had terrible personal adventures with Communism. And other people have had encounters with other kinds of totalitarian forces. I think a lot of our thinking and writing in the next twenty years or thirty years—at least mine will be—[will be focused on the need] to get up back in space again, because we've allowed the *Challenger* to destroy our will power. I mean, you know, it really is just a few people [who were killed]. I'm sorry they're dead. It was very hard on them. It's hard on their relatives. It's hard on our psyche. But if we allow it. . . . See, what happened in the twenty-four, forty-eight hours, following the explosion, that film was on the air a hundred times. Well, if you see a thing often enough, you begin to disbelieve in the future. Television is very dangerous. Because it repeats and repeats and repeats our disasters instead of our triumphs.

Look what happened two years ago with the grapes from South America. It was blown all out of proportion. Destroyed an industry. TV did that, not newspapers. What about poison apples, you know? Where the old witch, Meryl Streep, says, "Here's an apple that isn't poisoned." And they destroy the apple industry. What about radon in the cellar? It's a panic a week. So TV. . . . The problem in a free society is how do you control a thing that is supposed to be free? Can you say to them, "One hundred times is enough for the *Challenger*"? That we turn it off for a while? 'Cause we see it still, every once in a while. In one of the news shows, I think it's on CNN, recently, I saw repeated that air accident, at Dresden or Hamburg, where the jet crashed into the crowd and burned up a hundred people right in front of you. They put that on the air every night. So the disaster inclination, the panic inclination of TV is very dangerous. But I don't know what to do about it, except to set an example and say, hey, you know. TV is so vivid, and it rams it down your eyeballs night after night. So . . . I guess all we can ask of the TV networks is a little discretion. So that we won't believe the end of the world was yesterday. And we stopped doing things.

My final point is we haven't been in space. We're finally going back. And it's taken years now. We're afraid to move. We're frozen. So the job of the science-fiction writer. . . . I've been down to Canaveral during the last month. I've had meetings with some NASA people. I want to build a set of bleachers there for 5,000 people with gantries, and Dolby sound and music and my narration, poetry, what have you, and every night at sunset put on a light and sound show like they do here in Paris at various buildings, or in London, to teach us the history of *Apollo*, with all of its incredible intensity and passion and ability to move the soul, so that we can re-teach ourselves how exciting the thing was and still can be. So that from the bottom of the pyramid people pressure the Congress into lopping off some money from the military and putting it over into space travel.

That's always been the problem. The last twenty-five years I've argued about this many times. That we spend so much in the military, and the damned stuff just sits there.

It was important at one time. Now that Russia's beginning to back off I'm hoping that some of that money—and once the Gulf Crisis is over, God help us—will be put into space. Because we need something to lift us, we have a tendency because we all watch the 6:00 local news. See, that's the really destructive news. Because it's all suicides, murders, rapes, funerals, and AIDS. About most of which we can't do anything. AIDS we can do something about. But, the funerals we can't go to. The murders we didn't commit. We didn't have anything to do with the rapes. But that's rammed into your eyeballs every night. I'm trying to get people to watch *McNeil/Lehrer*, who are responsible, informative, and nonpolitical. Very important: nonpolitical. [David] Brinkley on Sunday, with [Sam] Donaldson on the left, [George] Will on the right, Brinkley in between; you know what the labels are. And the more informative programs we can have, with no panic and no disaster every night so that we [have] equilibrium in our society. A lot of people have been looking at the news 365 nights a year; at the end of a year you give up on the human race. I don't want happy endings. I don't want to be Laughing Boy Number One; on the other hand, I don't want to see people going around disbelieving in the future in a country that's one of the best. Done a lot of good things. We've been taking in 500,000 immigrants a year for thirty years now, and some years a million. Now we're going to up again this next year. I mean, where in hell do people go in this world? They come here. They come to America, rather, not here. But they also come to France because it's a place to survive, a good place to survive.

C: A moment ago, you mentioned something about the need to be uplifted and you used the word 'soul'. Is this the long-term function of science fiction or your vision of what we need in the future? Are you talking about a unifying spiritual vision?

B: Yeah, I try to write about it. My stories are warnings, they're not predictions. If they were predictions I wouldn't do them. Because then I'd be part of the doom-ridden psychology. But every time I name the problem, I try to give the solution.

So not only have I talked about the future and the past, but I've been part of creating three malls, in California: the Glendale Galleria; the Horton Plaza, in San Diego; and the Westside Pavilion, at Westwood Boulevard and Pico. In other words, the failure of cities is the failure of chambers of commerce and the failure of the mayors and the city councils who don't understand what cities are. They're in for political power, they're not in to recreate the city, and make it better for everyone. So my dream has been, if they won't do it, some sort of corporate effort has to do it.

And Disney is my hero. I knew him when he was alive. And he created a model, on one level, Disneyland, Disney World, EPCOT; they're social, they're not cities, but they give you examples of ways of living. Of lots of trees, lots of flowers. Lots of fountains and ponds, lots of places to sit, lots of places to eat, so that you can get out of the house again. In a lot of cities people can't get out of the house; they're not safe. So a mall is an environment which is safe, and beautiful—it can be—and creative, and filled with examples of ways of living like you find in the Latin Quarter here, over by Notre-Dame. Those mazes of restaurants, two hundred of them, three hundred, four hundred. So I'm trying to introduce that into American culture, to give people a chance to walk with their families, like down on Pier 17, and be social, and to be happy, instead of being afraid, walking through the streets of New York.

Hollywood Boulevard is a disaster; I'm trying to help them re-build that. Parts of downtown L.A., I have plans for that, if the city mayor would only listen. But he's a big jerk, and he's trying to build an immigrant monument which is stolid and massive and nothing when we need something fluid to connect the areas of the city so the people can leave their cars behind and walk for miles, as you do in Paris here. You don't dream of driving. I mean if you do. . . . I was trying to get here tonight, I was across town playing some tapes, it took me forty-five minutes just to come about a mile to get here. I could've walked it faster, and next time I will.

So again, to give people back their feet, to give back their freedom, should be the job of the cities, except they don't know how to do it and we science-fiction writers know, I know, and I criticized Century City in Los Angeles; twenty years ago they built two new cities, next to each other, and they interviewed me and I said they won't work. And don't build them that way. And I said you don't have enough restaurants. You have to have forty restaurants;

you have to have a thousand tables, a thousand parasols, four thousand chairs, spread all throughout this area, so that people can sit. It's a Mediterranean climate; California, it's beautiful! Three hundred days a year you can sit out. They didn't listen to me. Ten years later, disaster, both cities weren't working. They called me again. And said, "We want an interview." I said, "If you let me tear your skin off, I'll do it." So, they printed everything I said. And I repeated: *Restaurants, restaurants, restaurants,* are the secret of cities. People want to eat. And then after they've eaten, they shop. They don't go out to shop; they go out to eat. They think they're going out to shop, but really, they're going out to eat. And once you do that the whole soul is aerated. Your ambiance changes. And walking around Paris, gee, you turn any corner there's seven restaurants. And little shops. And millions of people on the street every night.

So the social life here is incredible. And Disney was influenced by France. And I try to teach people at home: do what Disney did. He came here, time and again. He sent his best co-workers here to study at the Sorbonne.

C: Is that why you're in Paris so often?
B: Well, I fell in love with it on my own, thirty-seven years ago. I arrived here in 1953 to write the screenplay of *Moby Dick* for John Huston. So this is where I met him, at the Place Athene, and then we moved over to Ireland and I lived there for seven months, finishing the screenplay. But every time, I kept coming back and coming back, and now I spend every summer here, and this is my fourth trip this year. My wife's arriving tomorrow night; she loves it as much as I do.

C: So it's personal love.
B: Yeah, and I'm learning all the time. And the things that I can take back to improve the whole world. The whole world has cities. Most of them don't have as many problems as we Americans do. My hometown, Waukegan, Illinois, is a disaster; the whole downtown section is falling apart. 'Cause the city fathers don't know what a city is. They go in with the wrong reasons. If I became mayor tomorrow of a city, overnight, boy, I'd be in there planning, and changing, and building, and improving, and my motive would be to make the city. And that would give me a personal feeling of triumph, which is more than enough, instead of just pure power, which the average mayor wants: he wants to be mayor.

C: When did you first become intrigued with cities?
B: When I was eight years old and saw the covers of science-fiction magazines. They're all architectural. We love science fiction because it's architectural. All of the big science-fiction films of the last twenty years are architectural. *2001*, when you see the rocket ship flying through the air, it's a city; it's a big city up there. And in *Close Encounters of the Third Kind*, when the mother ship descends, it's not a ship, it's a city. It's so beautiful. And when the aliens come out of the ship, you want to go back in with them; and go away forever. And when one of the characters does, your heart goes with him.

So, we love architecture; we love the romances of places. And Paris: identifiable objects—London, Rome—if you took the Eiffel Tower out of Paris and the Arc-de-Triomphe, half the city would be gone, because [of] the objects, the romance of objects. And I've written articles which have influenced the building of these malls at home. I wrote an article called "The Aesthetics of Lostness." We travel for romance, we travel for architecture, and we travel to be lost. There is nothing better than to walk around Paris and not know where in hell you are: "Gee, where is this. . . . No, I'm lost"—and you say, "Hey, that's good." And you're safe. Lost and safe. And you can't do that in New York City. Once upon a time you could. There's hardly a place where you can do that. Someday, someday, if I have my say. If I have my influence. But while we're waiting for that, the mall is the temporary answer. It is a city away from the city, because the city doesn't know what it's doing. Corporations know what to do. Because they have to know; they have to make a profit. Profit is a great motive. But cities don't have to make a profit. Governments don't have to make a profit, do they? The experiment doesn't work, they say, "Oh, what the hell; let's tax people." But corporations, you've got to make sure you know what you're doing, because otherwise you're out of business.

C: So what would you see as the ideal formula in the creation of a city if we were to take these various elements: the corporation, the citizenry that is affected, and the local government? How would the formation of a city come about?
B: First of all, you tell the cities: "hands off." That's what Disney did.

C: The local government, you mean.
B: Yeah, 'cause they don't know what they're doing. They have no knowledge; they don't have the individual knowledge that a corporation should have. You

pick the people from your environment who know a city block, who know the local parish, who know the local aesthetics, whatever it is.

C: So who would pick them? Would the citizenry. . . .
B: Disney; myself. If you were to give me a project tomorrow, let's say in. . . .

C: How about the people affected? Would they have a choice in the selection?
B: Yeah, they would have a choice of being excellent instead of having the city dead. If I could do something to help my downtown in Waukegan, which is. . . . All the shops are closed, so [to] the people who own the closed shops, you say, "How'd you like to open them again? Well, come on and sit in with us, have some input here. It's like, you didn't know what to do in the first place, and the city is dead, we have to start from scratch."

C: So you would leave it in the hands of nonelected officials?
B: Yeah, elected officials don't know anything about cities and how to build them.

C: But how are we to select who is going to make these decisions that will affect us. . . .
B: Let the corporations get together. That's how they build most of these malls. And they turn out very well. And they're getting better all the time. Because more and more restaurants, more and more really fine shops of all kinds. And there's excellence. . . .

C: Let me give you a possible conflict here. What if the local citizenry is at odds with the planning of the local corporations?
B: Well, they've got to be part of it, of course, sure. But if they don't want it, then you don't build it. It's that simple.

C: So you do see a partnership of some kind between the two.
B: Oh, yeah. But the main thing is to have the people who know how to [do these things]. I know several people who know how to build these things.

C: In researching for this interview, I've noticed that commentators have often made note of your ambiguous, or at least changing, relationship with technology. The obligatory remark is that you chose to downplay its role in favor of literary stylistic innovations while everyone else was exploring it.

And then when other writers were catching up with your own stylistic concerns you gained a certain faith in technology and even, for the first time, flew in an airplane after many years of avoiding them. Is this an oversimplification and do you care to comment on your current feelings regarding high-tech?
B: Well, you know, when you're twenty it's easy to be negative. And we just came out of, we were going through World War II and coming out of it. And so it was a negative time. And then the atom bomb came along and I got married in those periods: 1946, '47, I was courting my wife. And there was that day which you didn't experience because you weren't born. But there was the time, in the middle of the summer of '46 or '47, when they were going to explode the first super-nuclear warhead, out in the islands. But the scientists weren't quite sure whether the earth wouldn't catch on fire. What if the earth caught on fire and the whole thing went up? Well, the night before, you know, I think everyone in the world thought about it, everyone that could hear about it on the radio, because there was no TV in those days and [it was] primitive, a few thousand sets in the United States. So you become a philosopher that night, don't you? What if this is the last night of the world? So, it didn't happen, thank God. But nevertheless, it was a negative time, and out of that I wrote a lot of things that went into *The Martian Chronicles*. Including "There Will Come Soft Rains," the house that lives on after the people and talks to itself. So it's all part of a time, and my being very young, in my twenties.

And then, as time progressed, and I learned more about those positive inventions that give us freedoms—the Xerox machine is the freedom to have your own printing press. I couldn't afford one, there weren't any such animals, they had mimeograph machines, but they were too expensive when I was nineteen. So a friend of mine gave me money to publish my own magazine, *Futuria Fantasia*, and it cost eighty dollars to put out each issue. But I was only making eight dollars a week, selling newspapers on a street corner. So you see, it was impossible. And most people don't own mimeograph machines; they borrow them. Or they'd do the things at work. But everything's changed now.

We have the Xerox machine, everywhere; el cheapo, you can put out your own magazine. And now we have the Fax machine, which is another printing press. Not only can you send things, but you can print things in your own house. So the ability to acquire knowledge and dispense it is a thousandfold.

C: Was your faith in government shaken as well, at that time? After all, those were elected officials. . . .

B: I think that politically the world is mad; always has been, probably always will be. It's a bunch of chickens everywhere. They're all chickens. Look at what's been going on with our budget problems in America the last few weeks. I know a few senators. Al Simpson of Wyoming (R) I love; wonderful man. Terrific sense of humor. And very opinionated. But so many of them have no opinions.

C: You do have mixed feelings about government then.
B: Oh, God, yes; oh, sure! There should be no tax raises; more money should go back to the people. Again, no one wants to talk about it, but during the last eight years we've got employment for nineteen million people, new jobs; no one wants to talk about it. I said, "Wait a minute, that's good!" You want them to go back on relief? Then your deficit goes up. No one has done any research on how much of the deficit's already been retired through interest. We're paying interest on this deficit, every year. How many hundreds of billions of dollars of interest have been paid and don't they equal the principal? We could retire the whole thing tomorrow and forget it. There would be no profit, that is, the interest, but in effect, it's semantics here. The principal has long since been retired. So we should get on to the next problem. And because of giving the money back to the people, which we did, with lower taxes, we've got all these jobs, we've got a new tax base, we're taking in more revenue now than ever before in the history of the country. No one talks about that. Every year now we've got forty billion extra dollars beyond what the revenue used to be. Now who's spending that? Where's it going? Has anyone researched that? They don't talk about it on TV. It's there. And it's every year. Who's spending our money and what is it being spent on? These people are irresponsible.

Frank Lloyd Wright, Jr. was a friend of mine, years ago, and he was part of an endeavor I had to build rapid transit in L.A., which had been destroyed. It was all there, thirty years ago, we destroyed all of it, now we've got to rebuild it; well, it's impossible. And anyway, he gave me the rule which applies to politicians. Put one million dollars out on the table to build a building, and it will disappear. Now put two million dollars out for the same building; it'll be spent. If you're foolish enough to put two million out there and the architect will be: "Well, what the hell—Gimme!" So these people can't be trusted with money; they're drunk. And they think they can throw money at a problem. That isn't it.

The problem of education is: where do you apply the money? It's in the first grade. And it's in the kindergarten. And if we don't teach reading and writing we lose the generation and we lose our civilization. It has nothing to do with money. It has to do with the will to teach. The will to care. And you can't buy that. And we should test all the teachers and fire half of them next year. Because if you let boys grow up to the age of ten and twelve and they can't read, they're bored silly, then they begin with dope, and they begin with the gangs. And if we could solve the problem of gangs and drugs tomorrow with education, it's got to start in kindergarten. And they've got to know how to read by the time they're out of first grade. The administrators don't care; I have listened to people lecture on this, and I'm one of the few that says, "Fire the teachers." Test them and fire them. And then all the first and second grade students must be tested immediately. And if they can't read, then you intensify the effort with your money there. Because there's no use in having enriched programs up in the eighth grade if they can't read them! I mean, it's madness!

C: Do your future plans involve a political role of some type?
B: No, no. There's no power there, and you become one of those dummies. And they won't let you . . . if you're inside the political scheme you can't do anything. You're not allowed to speak up.

C: I agree with you.
B: Yeah. The good things in our country are coming from the outside, corporate effort. EPCOT is a permanent world's fair, which I always wanted to have when I was twelve. 'Cause I saw the Chicago World's Fair, in 1933, and discovered they were going to tear it down in two years. Why tear down something so beautiful that is a centrifuge for the young, to whirl people into life, so that when they come out of a museum, or a world's fair, they want to live forever? That happened to me, with the fiction that I read, and the world's fairs that I saw. And then, finally, I was invited to create the interior of the United States Pavilion at the New York World's Fair in 1964. Can you imagine how excited I was? 'Cause I'm changing lives, and that's the thing. If you can build a good museum, if you can make a good film, if you can build a good world's fair, if you can build a good mall, you're changing the future. You're influencing people, so that they'll get up in the morning and say, "Hey, it's worthwhile going to work." That's my function, and it should be the function of every science-fiction writer around. To offer hope. To name the problem, and then offer the solution. And I do, all the time.

Interview with Ray Bradbury
Donn Albright / 1991

Gauntlet, 1991, pp. 139–43. Copyright © 1991 by Donn Albright. Reprinted by permission.

Gauntlet: Based on what you said in the Afterword to *Fahrenheit 451*—does it bother you when magazines (i.e., *Scholastic Magazine*) reprint your stories in an abridged form?
Bradbury: I try to prevent that. In fact, if they're doing it, I was not aware of it. In many cases when they approach me I say "You can't cut anything, you've got to print the whole thing." But I haven't gone back to check. Maybe they've done this and I don't know it.

G: Your first stories predated McCarthyism. What prompted you to explore censorship?
B: Well, book burnings in Russia and China over a period of time; and Hitler's book burning in Germany; and the history of the burning of libraries at Alexandria—two by accident, I believe, and one on purpose. Thousands of volumes lost. And since I'm a library person and I've grown up in libraries and been educated by them and never made it to college, the library, to me, is central to my life.

G: Had you experienced censorship yourself at this time and have you experienced censorship of your work since then?
B: I haven't had any trouble. The last time was thirty-five, forty years ago. Nothing in recent years at all. I have good relationships with my editors everywhere in the world, so the problem just doesn't occur.

G: Were you upset when, for instance, with "The Screaming Woman" the *Philadelphia Inquirer* wanted to change the ending?
B: Well, slightly. But on the other hand I was very poor, so I wasn't in a position to argue. I needed the money. I had a growing family. There are times in your life, not pleasant, where your moral stance is undermined by the fact that you have no money in the bank. But that was such a minor thing. And actually, I love to see both versions of the story.

G: Are there any other stories that were changed during that time period?
B: I think *Collier's* changed the ending of "Sound of Thunder" slightly, but I can't remember what they did to it. I called them on the phone and reversed the charges and talked for a long time, saying "If you're gonna make a change, call me first, let me make it. You shouldn't do it—it should be in my own style."

G: With more special interest groups today—feminists, gays, blacks, to just name a few—is the danger of censorship greater than when *Fahrenheit 451* was written?
B: A little bit, but not much. If we listened to all these groups then we wouldn't have anything to read or anything to look at. It's okay for them to speak up, but you don't listen to them 'cause if we censor all the things the gays want changed and all the women's lib things changed and all the Jewish groups want changed and all the Catholic groups, after a while you have empty shells. You cannot listen to any of them. They have the right to speak, but you have the right not to listen.

All of which reminds me of all this problem with the government funding of arts and talk of censorship. It's just not true. That's not censorship. Censorship is when the total society is prevented from doing what it wants to do. They're not saying that. They're just saying that they're funding you just as a gallery does; a gallery has the right to choose what it wants to hang on its walls. That's not censorship—that's selectivity. So if you don't like a particular gallery, go to another one, and if that doesn't work, form your own gallery. I've done this myself. People didn't want my plays thirty-five years ago, so I formed my own theater group and we all worked free. I worked with people like F. Murray Abraham who got $50 a week working in my plays at the Coronet Theater. And I got nothing for my efforts. I put my money in and lost it all.

So the answer to all this so-called talk about censorship . . . first of all, it doesn't exist. Government funding has the right to say what it wants to fund. There's not enough room to hang every artist.

When I put on my plays at the Coronet twenty-five years ago I wanted government funding. I didn't get it. Who got it? Black groups with dreadful plays. They lost $500,000 and I didn't get a penny. So I have a right to feel left out, right? So that's what's wrong with government funding. It can't please everyone, so you shouldn't do it. If you want to act, if you want to put on plays, form your own group! You don't need much money. Just put it on in little tiny theaters, put it on in store fronts, do it in the parlor. There are eighty small theaters in Los Angeles—you can get your plays put on there. There are all kinds of galleries *everywhere* in the United States that hang photographs and paintings. And lacking that, you can get twenty artists together, they each put in twenty bucks, you rent your own gallery and you don't have to worry about the government. And then there's no one to censor you at all, if you want to use that word.

G: Do you see the day when the basic premise of *Fahrenheit 451* becomes a reality?
B: No, but I see the other danger that I pointed out—how the totalitarian concept came about. If people can't read, if your educational system fails and people can't read or write, then they're at the beck and call of everyone with a flimsy idea. And also, if the magazines and newspapers follow up on that sort of inability to read, then your total culture becomes ignorant and idiotic. All of our magazines today are beginning to look like—*USA Today* or *People*; moronic at the lowest level. So when I'm lecturing to the magazine editors of America I'm gonna take along copies of *Forbes, Fortune, Time, Good Housekeeping, Gourmet* and hold them up as examples of lousy magazines. They've all become lousy. Why? Because you can't find the articles. And *Gourmet* is the only magazine I've seen recently where you have four or five articles clumped in the middle where you can find them—surrounded by a lot of ads, but nevertheless, when you get to a certain page then you have a lot of articles following page after page. *Forbes* has become unreadable. All the women's magazines are a mess; they're an insult to the intelligence.

The major magazines have all gone to hell. *Omni* is beginning to look that way. We see in *Time* magazine little obituary and news bites and that's the way *USA Today* looks. You've got all kinds of little news bites on the front page and all the way through—there's no information. They just say that the Saudi Arabian countries did such and so; Saddam Hussein did this and that, but no explanation. Everything is supposed to be easy. Looking at *Time* it's becoming more fragmented. And the more you do that the dumber the people get; you don't lift them up, you don't use big words.

People try to change my short stories, take out the big words and put in small ones. I won't allow it. And if I catch them doing it, then I cancel the contract. So, the danger is not censorship. The danger is what's *not* going on in our school system. We're not teaching reading and writing in kindergarten, first and second grade. Then that's followed through by your culture later; the magazines fall in with that and say, "This being true, let's simplify the language," and the next thing you know you have no readers and you have nothing worth reading. So that's censorship from a different angle. It's not imposed from above; it happens from below through the ignorance of teachers who don't want to teach.

G: What's your feeling about the 2 Live Crew controversy; explicit lyrics in music and explicit sex in moves?
B: All this talk about arresting people for selling pornographic records bothers me. What we should worry about is movies broadcast at the wrong hours. Wait until the kids go to bed, then you have the right to put anything on the air you want. As for record stores I think that under a certain age . . . kids learn about sex early enough, and to learn the wrong sex, dirty sex, that's not what sex should be. It should be beautiful. You should have wonderful love affairs, and long before we're married. But my goodness, can't they be decent instead of indecent? So all I'm saying . . . instead of arresting people, they should say, "Look don't let anyone in this particular store under a certain age. They can't buy the record."

G: Just like they did with pornographic magazines. . . .
B: Sure. Sure. We have laws on alcohol and a lot of other things.

G: Who are more dangerous—censors of the right (Donald Wildmon, Jesse Helms, for example) or so-called "Yuppie liberals," those in political in-groups like gays, blacks and feminists?
B: Well, all of them. It's the left and right, liberal and conservative. The liberals . . . in fact, the history of the world, in recent times, is liberals burning books all over the world. Chinese Communist liberals, left-red radical liberals burn millions of books and millions of librarians and teachers. So, that's the worst thing in modern history. Russia's done it over a period of time, maybe not as much as Red China, but the record, if anything, is worse among the liberal nations than what it is in what you'd call more conservative nations.

G: At what point does irresponsible journalism in tabloids like the *National Enquirer* infringe on First Amendment rights of others, if at all?

B: Well, they're such a joke, it's hard for me to believe anyone takes them seriously. And you have the right to sue, so I suppose . . . most of us are never going to appear in these magazines so we haven't anything to worry about. I don't think they infringe on anyone. A lot of these people like to be infringed on; they're public figures and they want people to know about their dreadful affairs.

G: Are you a First Amendment purist or do you see limits to free expression? Just where do you draw the line at what should be censored, like kiddie porn for example?
B: Well, of course—that's reprehensible. If you get those guys in jail they'd be killed by the other prisoners and one sympathizes with that. You can't mess around! I mean, just because you want to fiddle with some nine-year-old boy or girl, should you be allowed to do it and can you take pictures of this and sell them? No, I don't think so.

G: Do you perceive the [Salman] Rushdie affair as having long-term ramifications on the publishing of controversial work?
B: Well see, what's happened, and is going to continue to happen and which is really dangerous because it sways our opinion, is that we're doing all of our thinking by television nowadays. The *merest* incident is blown out of proportion. This case last October of a woman reporter being in a locker-room . . . well she'd shouldn't be in there in the first place. She can interview them right outside the door. It's blown out of proportion by the TV people who want a story. And she wants it and all the other people want it. Our lives are being controlled by television interviews and news breaking.

 The situation two years ago of the so-called poisoned grapes from South America. Two poisoned grapes and they weren't even sure if they hadn't been injected with a needle up here, to make a story. Okay, a whole industry is destroyed. Not completely and forever, but for a couple of months *millions* of dollars are lost because of something that may have been a lie. We need the "Panic of the Week" club. So this kind of panicked thinking in America. . . .

G: It makes news.
B: Yeah and then you've got the poison on the apples, the skin of apples. Meryl Streep's out there screaming and yelling. It's all nonsense. Destroy the apple industry. Then you've got radon in your cellar, huh? Everyone's got

radon in their cellar. So what! There's something in every house. I've got black widows in my spider den downstairs here.

The great danger is that we're allowing television to dominate our lives. So that every week, we're rushing back and forth between things. We're looking to TV to tell us what we're thinking. And that . . . to hell with that! That really is terrible.

G: In your writing do you have any taboos—some line you personally won't cross?
B: No, I never think about that sort of thing. They may be there, but I don't know what they are. I don't really know. I don't want to know anything about my writing at all. I just do it. Let other people decide what my taboos are.

A Few Words with Ray Bradbury: The "Fahrenheit" Chronicles—It Did Happen Here

Judith Green / 1993

San Jose Mercury News, 30 October 1993, Final Morning Edition, Living Section, p. 3C. Copyright © 1993 by *San Jose Mercury News*. Reprinted by permission.

Question: You've been working on this project [a new music-theater adaptation of *Fahrenheit 451*] for some time.
Answer: I've been creeping up on theater for forty years now. But yes, this piece has been around for eight or nine years.

Q: Whose idea was it?
A: It was their idea. (Bradbury wrote the book. The songs are by Georgia Bogardus Holof and David Mettee.) I asked them to send me a tape, because if I meet people I like them and then it's hard to turn down a project. I like songs without faces. But eventually, they caught up with me. I heard "Cross the Border" (which now ends Act 1 of the musical) and that hooked me immediately.

Q: But this isn't the only version of *Fahrenheit 451*, right?
A: There's a rock opera in Prague. There's another in England by John Butcher—he's a member of Parliament. And there was a chamber opera in Sydney, Australia. It's by Benton Broadstock, which sounds like something out of Dickens, doesn't it? It was lousy, but I haven't had the heart to tell him.

Q: Do you call *Fahrenheit 451* science fiction?
A: I call it political fiction. I call it "the art of the possible." We're talking about political correctness here. It's about Hitler and Stalin and China, where they burned God knows how many books, killed God knows how many teachers.

Q: You said you wrote it when you were very angry.
A: I wrote it in 1953. I was angry at (Senator Joseph) McCarthy and the people before him—Parnell Thomas and the House Un-American Activities Committee and Bobby Kennedy, who was part of that whole bunch. I was angry about the blacklisting and the Hollywood 10. I was a $100-a-week screenwriter, but I wasn't scared—I was angry.

Q: So it comes out of the same events as *The Crucible* (Arthur Miller's play about the Salem witch-hunts).
A: Yes, but I was writing about book-burning three or four years before *Fahrenheit 451*. It's a theme in my stories as far back as "Pillar of Fire" and "The Exiles."

Q: Did you like Truffaut's film?
A: There were two things that always bothered me. He left out the mechanical hound (an implacable robot who assists the firemen in sniffing out books and readers). And he left out the girl next door.

Q: I thought that was Julie Christie.
A: Yes, but he also had her play Montag's wife, in a different wig, and you couldn't tell the difference between them. I'll tell you one thing he did, though. He allowed the girl to live.

Q: In the story, she dies—or disappears.
A: I did that. And a lot of people have told me I was wrong, and I decided they were right. I wouldn't rewrite the novel at this point, but the musical allows me to change the ending.

Bradbury Talk Likely to Feature the Unexpected

Anne Gasior / 1994

Dayton Daily News, 1 October 1994, City Edition, Lifestyle/Weekendlife Section, p. 1C. Copyright © 1994 by *Dayton Daily News*. Reprinted by permission.

Question: How many times have people attempted to ban your work?
Ray Bradbury: Very rarely, occasionally by little frogs in little puddles. It's never anything serious.

This comes up in any society where people have different opinions. You're a Catholic and I'm a Baptist and we may have problems. If you're a homosexual and I'm heterosexual, we may have problems. You're black and I'm white. You've got all these differences and people get sensitive and they want to change all the books. And you have to tell them to go sit down somewhere.

Q: In Beavercreek, a mother tried to have your story "The Veldt" taken off reading lists because she said it could influence children to kill their parents. Do you believe that?
RB: Not for a minute. People provoke themselves. It's a rare book that makes people behave.

Q: Have you ever read anything you felt should not be on the shelves?
RB: I wouldn't want to ban them, but there are some modern books that describe depraved sexual things and bodily functions and you read them and slam them down and say, "Well, I hope no one buys this." In open society, they have the choice.

Q: What is your definition of censorship?
RB: Censorship is when the government controls things, and you cannot publish or sell or find in a library the books that you want. It comes from the top, it comes from the government.

Q: How can censorship be combated?
RB: Speak up and say whoever's doing it is wrong, very quietly. If you're a librarian and someone insists you take a book off the shelf, and maybe they come in and take it off the shelf. When they leave, you put it back. And when they come back a week later and they take it off again, you put it back. And you keep putting it back and finally they get tired and they leave. It's that simple.

Q: Is censorship in this country a growing trend?
RB: No. We've never had that danger in this country. I didn't write *Fahrenheit 451* about us. I wrote it about Stalin and Mussolini and Hitler.

Q: What do you plan to talk about when you come to the University of Dayton?
RB: I may not even talk about book banning if I don't feel like it. I don't prepare anything ahead. I have a dozen subjects to talk about because I write plays and poetry and essays, short stories and novels and screenplays and teleplays and operas. I'll get lost, and the audience will have a wonderful time. And I'll get a standing ovation, and they'll go home.

Q: What are you working on now?
RB: I'm working on a screenplay of *Fahrenheit 451* that will star Mel Gibson. It will be better than the original because they left a lot of things out of the first film.

Q: How does the story of *Fahrenheit 451* stand up in 1994?
RB: It works even better because we have political correctness now. Political correctness is the real enemy these days. The black groups want to control our thinking and you can't say certain things. The homosexual groups don't want you to criticize them. It's thought control and freedom of speech control.

Q: Did you have to update the story at all?
RB: No, my society caught up with me. My society updated itself. I predicted all this forty-two years ago in the book. Go back and look at the fire chief's speech about what's going to happen to society, that the newspapers are all going to be moronic like *USA Today*. *Fahrenheit 451* was supposed to be a warning, not a prediction. But my society has caught up with it.

Q: What would you put on your suggested reading list?
RB: All the plays of George Bernard Shaw. I go back to Shakespeare constantly. I go back to the great poets. And there are a lot of women in my life. Edith Wharton has been part of my life for at least forty-five years, and she's been discovered in the last few years because of *The Age of Innocence*. Willa Cather, Eudora Welty, these are all very important women writers. And then you pick up the short stories of Steinbeck and Hemingway. F. Scott Fitzgerald is certainly our greatest American writer in the last sixty years.

Q: You don't mention anyone contemporary.
RB: There isn't anyone writing right now that's any good, except me. They're all dead. But it's all right because the libraries are full of books. If you haven't read *Hamlet*, then it's a new play. I'm so tired of novels about middle-aged men in their menstrual crisis where they can't decide whether to go back to their wife or girlfriend or boyfriend. That's real junk.

Q: How would you classify what you write?
RB: I'm a magician who writes about ideas. I'm not a science-fiction writer. People who call me that are wrong. Most of what I write is fantasy or magic realism or plays about my Mexican American background. There is so much that I've done.

Question: Will the ideas dry up?
RB: Never. I've got five hundred short stories that haven't been finished. I'm working on two novels and a screenplay and twenty-two new short stories right now. I've gotten it all done every day of my life since I was twelve, and I'll keep doing it as long as God doesn't hit me with a baseball bat.

Playboy Interview: Ray Bradbury
Ken Kelley / 1996

Playboy, 43.5 (May 1996), 47+. Copyright © 1996 by *Playboy*. Reprinted by permission.

Playboy: Many people don't take science fiction seriously, and yet you maintain that it is the essential literature of our age. Why is it so important?
Bradbury: In science fiction, we dream. In order to colonize in space, to rebuild our cities, which are so far out of whack, to tackle any number of problems, we must imagine the future, including the new technologies that are required.

Playboy: Yet most people don't consider science fiction to be part of mainstream literature.
Bradbury: It isn't part of the mainstream—science fiction is the mainstream. It has been since Sputnik. And it will be for the next ten thousand years.

Playboy: So how did Sputnik change things?
Bradbury: People, especially kids, went crazy over science fiction after Sputnik lit the sky. Overnight, instead of an apple on the teacher's desk, there was a book by Asimov. For the first time in history, education came from the bottom up as kids taught their teachers.

Playboy: Why do kids respond to science fiction more than adults?
Bradbury: Obviously, children's imaginations are piqued by the implications of science fiction. Also, as a child, did you want to have someone tying your shoes? Like hell you did. You tied your own as soon as you could. Science fiction acknowledges that we don't want to be lectured at, just shown enough so we can look it up ourselves.

    The way to teach in this world is to pretend you're not teaching. Science fiction offers the chance to pretend to look the other way while teaching. Science fiction is also a great way to pretend you are writing about the future when in reality you are attacking the recent past and the present. You can criticize communists, racists, fascists or any other clear and present danger, and they can't imagine you are writing about them. Unfortunately, so much old science fiction is too technical and dry.

Playboy: Beyond kids, science fiction is the purview of men, for the most part. Why aren't women as interested?
Bradbury: There are two races of people—men and women—no matter what women's libbers would have you pretend. The male is motivated by toys and science because men are born with no purpose in the universe except to procreate. There is lots of time to kill beyond that. They've got to find work. Men have no inherent center to themselves beyond procreating. Women, however, are born with a center. They can create the universe, mother it, teach it, nurture it. Men read science fiction to build the future. Women don't need to read it. They are the future.

Playboy: Some women don't like it when you make those distinctions. In fact, in *People,* you said that CD-ROMs are more for men than for women—and you were denounced as sexist on the letters-to-the-editors page shortly thereafter.
Bradbury: Oh well. Unscrew them.

Playboy: What does "unscrew them" mean?
Bradbury: That they'll never get any sex again. [*Laughs*] Listen, men are nuts. Young men are crazy. We all love toys. I'm toy oriented. I write about toys. I've got a lot of toys. Hundreds of things. But computers are toys, and men like to mess around with smart dumb things. They feel creative.

Playboy: But computers aren't just toys. They're tools for the future.
Bradbury: People are talking about the Internet as a creative tool for writers. I say, "B.S. Stay away from that. Stop talking to people around the world and get your work done." We are being flimflammed by Bill Gates and his partners. Look at Windows '95. That's a lot of flimflam, you know.

Playboy: Why is it flimflam?
Bradbury: Because it doesn't give most people anything more than what they already have. On top of that, when they buy it they have to buy other things to go with it. So you're talking about hundreds of dollars from people who can't afford it. The Windows thing isn't bought by women. I bet if you look at

the sales figures, it's 80 percent men. Crazy young men or crazy older men who love toys.

Playboy: For a man who has built a career looking into the future, you seem skeptical of technology—CD-ROMs, the Internet, multimedia—
Bradbury: It's all meaningless unless you teach reading and writing. It's not going to do a bit of good if you don't know how to read and write.

Playboy: But reading is involved—on computers, people can interact with works of fiction, choosing to move the plot any way they want to.
Bradbury: Don't tell me how to write my novel. Don't tell me you've got a better ending for it. I have no time for that.

Playboy: When you talk about the future, you tend to talk about space travel. Do you really think it's in our future?
Bradbury: It must be. First of all, it's a religious endeavor to be immortal. If the earth dies, we must be able to continue. Space travel will give us other planets to live on so we can continue to have children. It's that simple, that great and that exciting.

Playboy: Will we really be forced to escape earth? Will we be able to in time?
Bradbury: We are already on our way. We should be back on the moon right now. And we should be going off to Mars immediately.

Playboy: Yet there doesn't seem to be a rush into space anymore. NASA's budget is being whittled away as we speak.
Bradbury: How come we're looking at our shoes instead of at the great nebula in Orion? Where did we mislay the moon and back off from Mars? The problem is, of course, our politicians, men who have no romance in their hearts or dreams in their heads. JFK, for a brief moment in his last year, challenged us to go to the moon. But even he wasn't motivated by astronomical love. He cried, "Watch my dust!" to the Russians, and we were off. But once we reached the moon, the romance started to fade. Without that, dreams don't last. That's no surprise—material rewards do last, so the history of exploration on earth is about harvesting rich lodes. If NASA's budgeters could be convinced that there are riches on Mars, we would explode over-

night to stand on the rim of the Martian abyss. We need space for reasons we have not as yet discovered, and I don't mean Tupperware.

Playboy: Tupperware?
Bradbury: NASA feels it has to justify everything it does in practical terms. And Tupperware was one of the many practical products that came out of space travel. NASA feels it has got to flimflam you to get you to spend the money on space. That's B.S. We don't need that. Space travel is life-enhancing, and anything that's life-enhancing is worth doing. It makes you want to live forever.

Playboy: How much is NASA to blame for the apathy about the space program?
Bradbury: The NASA bigwigs have been their own worst enemy. I've pleaded with them for twenty years to let me do a film for them. Most of the early films NASA made about the Mercury and Apollo projects were inept. I want to fuse poetry and fact in a way that, as my various presentations at world fairs did, leaves the audience in tears. But NASA never does transcendent, poetic or explosive things to sell itself—nobody cares about NASA in Congress except, notably enough, Bob Packwood.

Playboy: Do you still see Packwood as a visionary even though he was forced to resign in disgrace?
Bradbury: He's still a visionary. I wish he were still in Congress. I sent him a telegram a year ago and told him to stand firm because those women are jerks. They wait twenty years. They are offended twenty years later. Don't hand me that. There are very few other senators like him, and it's a shame he's gone.

Playboy: What's the biggest mistake NASA has made?
Bradbury: It should have done the space shuttle before the Apollo missions. The shuttle is a big mailbox, an expensive experimental lab. It's not nearly as exciting as it should be. It should have been launched first to circle the earth, which is all it's doing. After that, it should have been sent to the moon, and the program could have ended there. Then we could have built a colony on

the moon and moved on to Mars. We need something larger than ourselves—that's a real religious activity. That's what space travel can be—relating ourselves to the universe.

Playboy: When the space program started, did you expect all that to occur?
Bradbury: Yes. But it didn't. NASA is to blame—the entire government is to blame—and the end of the Cold War really pulled the plug, draining any passion that remained. The odd thing to me is the extraordinary number of young people the world over who care about these things, who go to see science-fiction films—*2001, Close Encounters* and *Star Wars*—who spend billions of dollars to watch the most popular films ever made. Yet the government pays absolutely no attention to this phenomenon. It's always the last to know.

Playboy: Do you think we will at least return to the moon?
Bradbury: I hope we do it while I'm still alive, which means within the next ten to fifteen years. But I think it is a forlorn hope. I hope we'll have a manned expedition to Mars, though the politicians put it way down on their list. But it would be so uplifting for the human spirit. It's hard to get the government to act the way it should.

Playboy: How did you feel when Viking landed on Mars?
Bradbury: There was this festive feeling, like a surprise party, at the Cal Tech Planetarium the night the Viking ship landed. Carl Sagan and I and a lot of others stayed up all night. Suddenly, the first photographs of Mars started coming back on the giant screen. We were all exhilarated—dancing, laughing and singing. Around nine in the morning, Roy Neal from NBC News came by and held this microphone in front of my face. He said, "Mr. Bradbury, you've been writing about Mars and its civilizations and cities for all these years. Now that we're there and we see that there's no life, how does it feel?" I took a deep breath—I'm so proud I said this out loud to him—and replied: "You idiot! You fool! There is life on Mars—look at us! Look at us! We are the Martians!"

Playboy: You must have felt much the same way when Galileo reached Jupiter last year.
Bradbury: These scientists are incredible. Every time I go to a place like the Jet Propulsion Lab and someone shows me a telescope, he says, "Isn't it won-

derful?" I say, "No, it's not." He says, "What do you mean?" I say, "You are wonderful. You invented this. You are the genius."

Playboy: What is your motivation for writing?
Bradbury: I had decided to be a magician well before I decided to be a writer. I was the little boy who would get up on-stage and do magic wearing a fake mustache, which would fall off during the performance. I'm still trying to perform those tricks. Now I do it with writing. Also, writers write because of a need to be loved. I suppose that's greedy, isn't it?

Writing has helped me in other ways. When I started writing seriously, I made the major discovery of my life—that I am right and everybody else is wrong if they disagree with me. What a great thing to learn: Don't listen to anyone else, and always go your own way.

Playboy: Do you admit that that's an unrepentant, egotistical view?
Bradbury: Unfortunately, I don't think I keep my ego in check very well. I try to remember that my voice is loud, which is an ego problem. But at least I don't suffer from a self-deluding identity problem like, say, Carl Sagan does.

Playboy: What is the problem with Sagan?
Bradbury: With each passing year he grows stiffer because he goes around thinking he's Carl Sagan. Just as Norman Mailer thinks he's Norman Mailer and Gore Vidal thinks he's Gore Vidal. I don't think I'm Ray Bradbury. That's a big distinction. It doesn't matter who you are. You mustn't go around saying who you are, or else you get captured by the mask of false identity. It's the work that identifies you.

Playboy: Some critics say that you rely too much on fantasy and not enough on science to be a respected science-fiction writer.
Bradbury: I don't care what the science-fiction trade technicians say, either. They are furious that I get away with murder. I use a scientific idea as a platform to leap into the air and never come back. This keeps them angry at me. They still begrudge my putting an atmosphere on Mars in *The Martian Chronicles* more than forty years ago.

Playboy: A review by Christopher Isherwood launched *The Martian Chro-*

nicles. Did you know him?

Bradbury: The entire scenario set in motion was a fluke. Summertime, 1950, I recognized Isherwood browsing in a Santa Monica bookstore. My book had just come out, so I grabbed a copy off the shelf, signed it and gave it to him. His face fell and my heart sank, but two days later he called and said, "Do you know what you've done?" I asked, "What?" And he simply told me to read his review in the *Times*. His rave turned my life around; the book immediately made the best-seller lists and has been in print ever since.

He was very kind in introducing me to various people he thought I should know, like Aldous Huxley, who had been my literary hero since *Brave New World* came out.

Playboy: What was Huxley like?
Bradbury: He was very polite. Most Englishmen, most intellectual Englishmen, are very polite, and they treat you as if you're the genius, which is a sweet thing to do. Years after we met, I was a panelist along with Huxley discussing the future of American literature. However, I was disappointed when he refused to admit that science fiction is the only way for fiction to go.

Playboy: He was already extolling the virtues of psychedelics by then. We presume he offered you some,
Bradbury: I gave him the right answer: No, thanks. I don't want anyone lifting the trapdoor on my head—it may not go down again.

Playboy: Who are the best new science-fiction writers?
Bradbury: I'm so busy with a full agenda, I just don't have the time to hunt around for any. Do you realize that hundreds of novels come out every year now?

Playboy: Are you ducking the question?
Bradbury: OK—I admit I don't want to read in my own field.

Playboy: Why not?
Bradbury: Because it's incestuous, and you can't do that. You should read in your own field only when you're young. When I was eight, ten, twelve, six-

teen, twenty-five, I read science fiction. But then I went on to Alexander Pope and John Donne and [(Jean-Baptiste Poquelin)] Molière to mix it up.

Playboy: What about some of the more famous science-fiction names, such as Kurt Vonnegut?
Bradbury: I know him and we get on fine. We had a wonderful day together in New York a few years ago, and he had a nice sense of humor. But I haven't read anything since *Player Piano*, and that was forty years ago. So I can't give you any comment.

Playboy: How about Robert Heinlein?
Bradbury: I met him at Clifton's cafeteria in downtown Los Angeles. I had just graduated from high school, and Heinlein was thirty-one years old. He was well known, and he wrote humanistic science fiction, which influenced me to dare to be human instead of mechanical.

Playboy: What about those writers who popularize science in nonfiction books, such as Stephen Hawking and his *Brief History of Time*?
Bradbury: We have his book, but I'm not going to kid you and say I read it. My wife claims she has, but I don't believe her. I don't believe anyone has read it. I'm positive the guy is a genius and it's wonderful he has done what he's done.

Playboy: You have also written nonfiction, such as *Green Shadows, White Whale*, about your attempt to adapt *Moby Dick* with director John Huston. Were you attempting to get even for a disastrous experience?
Bradbury: Writing that book was gloriously cathartic. What got me started was that Katharine Hepburn's bad book about the making of *The African Queen* excluded so much and was quite scant about Huston's character. Her skimpy failure made me furious and propelled me to begin my own book.

Playboy: Was it that she was too easy on Huston?
Bradbury: Yes, and that upset me.

Playboy: How did you get the job to adapt *Moby Dick* in the first place?

Bradbury: Huston invited me to his Beverly Hills Hotel suite, put a drink in my hand and flattered me with enough Irish charm that, before I knew it, I'd agreed to spend six months in Ireland writing the script. Acting ability runs in Huston's bloodline.

Playboy: So he was on good behavior.

Bradbury: And I was fooled. I should have just admitted that he embodied the monster I realized he was and then quit. What kept me going despite the merciless cruelty he showed toward me and everyone else near him were three things: the love I felt for Herman Melville and his whale; my awe of John Huston's genius, as proved in *The Maltese Falcon*—he had directed the perfect movie; and my deep appreciation of how very few people in the world are lucky enough to get that kind of opportunity. Now I'm left with the bittersweet knowledge that, thanks to him, I learned so much that I otherwise wouldn't know. Nobody else in Hollywood would have given an unproven newcomer the chance to write a major script.

Playboy: Did that experience influence your decision not to write the screenplay for the movie adaptation of your next hit novel, *Fahrenheit 451*?

Bradbury: No. In 1955, Charles Laughton got me thoroughly drunk before he told me how bad the stage play I'd adapted for him was and convinced me I should give it up. So years later I told François Truffaut, "You do it." I'd had it.

Playboy: Were you happy with Truffaut's effort?

Bradbury: It was very good, but he was a coward about doing certain things. He didn't put in the Mechanical Hound, which should be included, because it's a metaphoric adventure thing. The tactical stuff is really miserable. The flying men should be cut out. They're not flying anywhere except down. And the casting was a mistake. Not all of it. Oskar Werner I like very much.

Playboy: Who didn't you like?

Bradbury: Julie Christie playing the girl next door. She couldn't play it. She was supposed to be sixteen. So Truffaut did the trick. He had Julie Christie play the wife and the girl next door, which was confusing. Sometimes you weren't quite sure who was talking.

Playboy: How do you feel about having a second opportunity to turn the novel into a movie now that Mel Gibson is interested?

Bradbury: I've wanted to redo *Fahrenheit 451* ever since it came out in 1966, because Truffaut left out so much from the novel. I sat bolt upright when I was told that Warner Brothers wanted to make the new version with Mel Gibson.

Playboy: Along with Orwell's *1984* and Huxley's *Brave New World*, your book presents a bleak view of the future. Were you trying to write a cautionary story?
Bradbury: That's fatal. You must never do that. A lot of lousy novels come from people who want to do good. The do-gooder novel. The ecological novel. And if you tell me you're doing a novel or a film about how a woodsman spares a tree, I'm not going to go see it for a minute.

Playboy: It's hard to imagine that the man who wrote *Fahrenheit 451* was not trying to predict the future.
Bradbury: It's "prevent the future," that's the way I put it. Not predict it, prevent it. And with anger and attacking, yes. You have the fun of attacking the thing you think is stupid. But your motives are hidden from you at the time. It's like, "I'll be damned. I didn't know I was doing that."

For instance, when a bright Sony inventor read about my seashell radios in that novel, he invented the Walkman. That was one good thing to emerge from that book—the banishment of most picnic-ruining ghetto blasters. But I had no idea I was doing it.

Playboy: *Fahrenheit 451* seems to have predicted the unpredictable for years.
Bradbury: Yes. When O. J. Simpson prowled the freeway pursued by cop cars and helicopters, Russell Baker wrote in his *New York Times* column words to the effect: This is the last act of *Fahrenheit 451*! I watched the reruns and thought, My God, he's right. In the final pages of my novel, Montag is running ahead of the book burners and sees himself on TV screens in every home, through each window, as he flees. When he eludes the Mechanical Hound, the society he left behind gets frustrated and kills a proxy Montag on television to satisfy the panicked need.

Even more depressing is that I foresaw political correctness forty-three years ago.

Playboy: In *Fahrenheit 451*, too?
Bradbury: Yes. [At one point, another character,] the fire chief, describes

how the minorities, one by one, shut the mouths and minds of the public, suggesting a precedent: The Jews hated Fagin and Shylock—burn them both, or at least never mention them. The blacks didn't like Nigger Jim floating on Huck's raft with him—burn, or at least hide, him. Women's libbers hated Jane Austen as an awfully inconvenient woman in a dreadfully old-fashioned time—off with her head! Family-values groups detested Oscar Wilde—back in the closet, Oscar! Communists hated the bourgeoisie—shoot them! And on and on it goes. So whereas back then I wrote about the tyranny of the majority, today I'd combine that with the tyranny of the minorities. These days, you have to be careful of both. They both want to control you. The first group, by making you do the same thing over and over again. The second group is indicated by the letters I get from the Vassar girls who want me to put more women's lib in *The Martian Chronicles*, or from blacks who want more black people in *Dandelion Wine*.

Playboy: Do you respond to them?
Bradbury: I say to both bunches, "Whether you're majority or minority, bug off!" To hell with anybody who wants to tell me what to write. Their society breaks down into subsections of minorities who then, in effect, burn books by banning them. All this political correctness that's rampant on campuses is b.s. You can't fool around with the dangerous notion of telling a university what to teach and what not to. If you don't like the curriculum, go to another school. Faculty members who toe the same line are sanctimonious nincompoops! It's time to stop the trend. Whenever it appears, you should yell, "Idiot!" and back them down. In the same vein, we should immediately bar all quotas, which politicize the process through lowered admission standards that accept less-qualified students. The terrible result is the priceless chance lost by all.

Playboy: So you disapprove of affirmative action?
Bradbury: The whole concept of higher education is negated unless the sole criterion used to determine if students qualify is the grades they score on standardized tests. Education is purely an issue of learning—we can no longer afford to have it polluted by damn politics. Leave pollution up to the politicians [*laughs*].

Playboy: How did you feel being so prescient?
Bradbury: Thoroughly disgruntled.

Playboy: Is the public well informed about these issues?
Bradbury: The news is all rapes and murders we didn't commit, funerals we don't attend, AIDS we don't want to catch. All crammed into a quarter of a minute! But at least we still have a hand with which to switch channels or turn off altogether. I tell my lecture audiences to never, ever watch local TV news.

Playboy: What about magazines? You have been an avid magazine reader since you were a kid. How would you rate the current crop?
Bradbury: Magazines today are almost all stupid and moronic to start with. And it makes me furious that I can't find any articles to read anymore. I used to enjoy *Forbes* and *Fortune*, but now the pages are completely cluttered by ads. That's what caused me to explode three years ago when I spoke to a gathering of the country's leading editors and publishers.

Playboy: Why did you explode?
Bradbury: Let's say the slow burn grew hotter the more I thought about what a chance I had. So I took along my props—copies of *Forbes*, *Fortune*, *Good Housekeeping*, *McCall's*, *Vogue* and *People*. I went up on stage and said, "Let's talk about the real problems with your magazines." I held up *Good Housekeeping*, flipped through the pages and said, "Find the articles—you can't." I held up *McCall's* and *Vogue* and said, "Look, the same thing." I held up *Forbes* and *Fortune*—"Look at this," I said. "You've got a half-page article here, you've got the start of an article on the left, then you look to the right and it's a full-page ad." I threw them off the podium. Then I held up an issue of *People* and said, "Do you really want to read a magazine like this? To hell with Time Inc.!" and threw it down. I paused and lowered the boom, saying, "The magazines of this country have to take over education—even more than the corporations—because you want readers in the future, don't you? Can you keep downgrading people's intelligence and insult them with the shit you're publishing? You should make sure the schools teach reading, or you're out on your ass in a couple of years. You won't have any readers—doesn't that scare you? It scares me. Change your product and invite me back to talk to you again." I stopped and waited, figuring that maybe they would do something if I managed to scare them enough.

Playboy: Did they?
Bradbury: I got a standing ovation. Afterward, Christie Hefner came over

and congratulated me—I didn't even know *Playboy* would be there. *Playboy* is in fact one of the best magazines in history, simply because it has done more than any other magazine. It has published the works of most of the important short story writers of our time, as well as some of the most important novelists and essayists—and just about every important American artist. The interviews have included just about everyone in the world with something important to say. Nowhere else can you find such a complete spectrum, from the semivulgar to the highfalutin [*laughs*]. I have defended *Playboy* since the beginning. Its editors were brave enough to say, "The hell with what McCarthy thinks" when they ran excerpts from *Fahrenheit 451*. I couldn't sell that to any other magazine because they were all running scared. And I must add another important point—one I'm sure that many other guys growing up in the sorry years before *Playboy* existed will agree with—which is that there would have been a lot fewer problems if *Playboy* had been around back then. I wish I'd had *Playboy* when I was fourteen.

Playboy: To sharpen your writing skills?
Bradbury: Come on! Those pictures are great. There was nothing when my generation was growing up. Like it or not, I rest my case, except to add that Hugh Hefner is one of the great sexual revolutionaries.

Playboy: Why do you shy away from eroticism in your own writing?
Bradbury: There is no reason to write pornography when your own sex life is good. Why waste time writing about it?

Playboy: It has always struck us as strange that most science fiction is relatively sexless.
Bradbury: There are certain kinds of people who write science fiction. I think a lot of us married late. A lot of us are mama's boys. I lived at home until I was twenty-seven. But most of the writers I know in almost any field, especially science fiction, grew up late. They're so interested in doing what they do and in their science, they don't think about other things.

Playboy: What is the most challenging literary form you have worked in?
Bradbury: I'm trying to write operas. I'm still learning. I'm writing a musical based on *Dandelion Wine*, which I've been working on for thirty years with various composers. I'm doing a new thing now with Jimmy Webb. We've been mess-

ing around with these things for eight years. Juggling the pieces, trying to figure out where you shut your mouth and let the song take over.

Playboy: What brought you to Hollywood in the first place?
Bradbury: The Depression brought me here from Waukegan, Illinois. The majority of people in the country were unemployed. My dad had been jobless in Waukegan for at least two years when in 1934 he announced to my mom, my brother and me that it was time to head West. I had just turned fourteen when we got to California with only forty dollars, which paid for our rent and bought our food until he finally found a job making wire at a cable company for fourteen dollars a week. That meant I could stay in Los Angeles, which was great. I was thrilled.

Playboy: With what aspect of it?
Bradbury: I was madly in love with Hollywood. We lived about four blocks from the Uptown Theater, which was the flagship theater for MGM and Fox. I learned how to sneak in. There were previews almost every week. I'd rollerskate over there—I skated all over town, hell-bent on getting autographs from glamorous stars. It was glorious. I saw big MGM stars such as Norma Shearer, Laurel and Hardy, Ronald Coleman. Or I'd spend all day in front of Paramount or Columbia, then zoom over to the Brown Derby to watch the stars coming or going. I'd see Cary Grant, Marlene Dietrich, Fred Allen, Burns and Allen—whoever was on the Coast. Mae West made her appearance—bodyguard in tow—every Friday night.

Playboy: The story is that you pestered George Burns to give you your first show-business job. Is that true?
Bradbury: Yes. George was kind. He would read the scripts I'd write every week. They were dreadful, and I was so blindly and madly in love with the film and radio business in Hollywood that I didn't realize what a pest I was. George no doubt thought he could get me off his back by using my words for one of the eight-line vignettes he had Gracie close their broadcasts with. I wanted to live that special life forever. When that summer was over, I stopped my inner time clock at the age of fourteen. Another reason I became a writer was to escape the hopelessness and despair of the real world and enter the world of hope I could create with my imagination.

Playboy: Did your parents approve?
Bradbury: They were very permissive, thank God. And strangely enough, my parents never protested. They just figured I was crazy and that God would protect me. Of course back then you could go around town at night and never risk getting mugged or beaten up.

Playboy: What do you think of modern Los Angeles—earthquakes, riots, O. J., fires and all?
Bradbury: The big earthquake actually renewed optimism throughout L.A.—it fused us, just as all the other calamities did. You pick up the first brick, then the second and so on. I've never seen so many people helping so many other people. A small boy came to my door to tell me my chimney was about to collapse—I didn't know. The next day a stranger from up the street dropped in to give us the names of some really good builders and repairmen. They turned out to be superb—jolly, bright and inventive library people, readers! They lived with us for more than a month. They became family—we missed them when they left. I've heard similar things from everyone around us and in the San Fernando Valley, where things were twenty times worse.

Playboy: Were you surprised when, after the earthquake, the freeways were rebuilt within a few months?
Bradbury: And almost before anything else? No. Here a human without a car is a samurai without his sword. I would replace cars wherever possible with buses, monorails, rapid trains—whatever it takes to make pedestrians the center of our society again, and cities worthwhile enough for pedestrians to live in. I don't care what people do with their cars, as long as they give them up three quarters of the time—roughly the amount of time people spend every week superfluously driving places they don't want to go to visit people who don't want to see them.

Playboy: That's easy for you to say; you have never driven a car.
Bradbury: Not a day in my life.

Playboy: Why not?
Bradbury: When I was sixteen, I saw six people die horribly in an accident. I walked home holding on to walls and trees. It took me months to begin to function again. So I don't drive. But whether I drive or not is irrelevant. The automobile is the most dangerous weapon in our society—cars kill more

than wars do. More than fifty thousand people will die this year because of them and nobody seems to notice.

Playboy: Until recently, you were the futurist afraid to fly in airplanes, never mind spaceships. What was it that cured your phobia?
Bradbury: A car breaking down in so many small Southern towns and the chauffeur taking three miserable days just to get through Florida. After the second tire blew, I got the word. In a loud and clear voice from the heavens above I heard the message: Fly, dummy, fly! [*Laughs*] I was afraid for forty years that I'd run around the plane yelling, "Stop! Let me off!" But I fly all the time now. I just sit back relaxed, occasionally peep out the window and peruse the magazines.

Playboy: Was your faith in law enforcement shaken because of Stacey Koon and Mark Fuhrman?
Bradbury: We've become what I call a Kleenex society—I saw the public's reaction as the symbolic chance to blow its collective nose on the whole police force of the United States, holding all cops responsible for incidents in Los Angeles. Of course I knew there was a problem in the LAPD. On the other hand, three of my daughters have been raped and robbed by black men, so I have a prejudice, too, don't I? And if I ever were to find the bastards, I'd kill them. I've seen violence used by police, and I've seen it used against white people, too.

Playboy: Did the Rodney King riots shock you?
Bradbury: I was more than shocked—I was terribly upset, and terribly angry at Mayor Bradley. The friend I've known for ten years was the man who went on television half an hour after the trial was over and used terrible language to say he was outraged. Boom!—next thing you know, the mobs burned the streets. Thus far I haven't had the guts to tell Tom Bradley, face-to-face, "you did it!"

Playboy: Did you have any idea there was so much rage in Los Angeles' black community?
Bradbury: I don't think anybody knew.

Playboy: Did you feel any empathy for the rioters?
Bradbury: None. Why should I? I don't approve of any mob anywhere at any

time. Had we not controlled it in L.A., all the big cities in this country would have gone up in flames.

Playboy: If Los Angeles is an indicator for the nation, what is the future of other big cities?
Bradbury: Along with man's return to the moon, my biggest hope is that L.A. will show the way for all of our cities to rebuild, because they've gone to hell and the crime rate has soared. When we can repopulate them, the crime rate will plunge.

Playboy: What will help?
Bradbury: We need enlightened corporations to do it; they're the only ones who can. All the great malls have been built by corporate enterprises. We have to rebuild cities with the same conceptual flair that the great malls have. We can turn any bad section of town into a vibrant new community.

Playboy: How do you convince corporate leaders and bureaucrats that you have the right approach?
Bradbury: They listen because they know my track record. The center of downtown San Diego was nonexistent until a concept of mine, the Horton Plaza, was built right in the middle of bleakest skid row. Civilization returned to San Diego upon its completion. It became the center of a thriving community. And the Glendale Galleria, based on my concept, changed downtown Glendale when it was built nearly twenty-five years ago. So if I live another ten years—please, God!—I'll be around to witness a lot of this in Los Angeles and inspire the same thing in big cities throughout the country.

Playboy: You have said that you want to influence children. Is that your most important audience?
Bradbury: I feel like I own all the kids in the world because, since I've never grown up myself, all my books are automatically for children.

Playboy: How does it feel to have an impact on children?
Bradbury: It's mutual delight and love made manifest. For one thing, kids love me because I write stories that tell them about their capacity for evil. I'm one of the few writers who lets you cleanse yourself that way.

Playboy: Would you say you're nostalgic for childhood?

Bradbury: Yeah. Once you let yourself begin to be grown-up, you face a world full of problems you can't solve. The politicians and specialists—adults, all—have a hard enough time trying to figure out where to look. It doesn't have to be that way. The greatest solutions in society are reached by corporate thinking, ruled by a motive to either make a profit or go out of business. There's great incentive to strive for excellence. On the other hand, bloated bureaucracies like city governments don't have to make a profit—they just raise people's taxes when they need more money. If you want to get anything done, it should be through a corporation. Disney is a prime example.

Playboy: Didn't the Eighties—the decade of Wall Street junk-bond scandals and bankrupt banks—establish that corporate chiefs can be little more than thieves?

Bradbury: I'm talking about top-flight people like those at IBM, Apple, AT&T. If corporations don't take over the educational system soon, we'll end up with all black-and-brown cities surrounded by white-flight small towns, which are under construction even as we speak. You can't blame whites for getting the hell out. City governments have neglected the biggest factor in our criminal environment—education. Kindergarten. First grade. If we don't change those immediately, we'll raise another generation of empty-headed dummies. If you let boys grow up as that, when they reach the age of ten they're bored, drop out, take dope, rob stores, rape—all that good stuff. Our jails overflow with illiterates who have been ignored by our city leaders. Jails should be run as schools, where kids are taught the basics, instead of spending a billion dollars a day just to keep them locked up. The government should stop sending schools money until they prove they are teaching reading and writing. We should fire half the teachers right now. This is an emergency—we're raising a criminal culture in all races and every walk of life by not teaching kids how to read and write. That scares me more than anything, yet I don't hear anyone else talking about the primary grades—where our future lies. The corporations I mention are getting involved more and more in magnet school relationships with local schools. The reasoning is hardly utopian—it's actually a selfish endeavor since they must educate the kids who grow up to be a part of their companies.

Playboy: A future when our children are taught to be useful employees of big companies? It sounds like a robotic race in some science-fiction story.

Bradbury: You mean the way Japan-bashers portray that society? Listen, you can't turn really bright people into robots. You can turn dumb people into robots, but that's true in every society and system. I don't know what to do with dumb people, but we must try to educate them along with the sharp kids. You teach a kid to read and write by the second grade and the rest will take care of itself. To solve the drug problem, we have to start at the root—first grade. If a boy has all the toys in his head that reading can give him, and you hook him into science fiction, then you've got the future secured.

Playboy: How does it feel to get older?
Bradbury: On my seventieth birthday, when I reflected that so many of my friends were dead or dying, it hit me that it was high time I got more work done. Ever since that time, I have done the active, smart thing by increasing my productivity. I'm not on the rocks or shoals yet, but the last few years have been a devastation of illnesses and deaths of many good friends. [*Star Trek* creator] Gene Roddenberry was a loss that deeply grieved me.

Playboy: How well did you know him?
Bradbury: Gene was an intimate friend. We'd been friends for many years when he asked me to write for *Star Trek* more than twenty-five years ago. But I've never had the ability to adapt other people's ideas into any sensible form.

Playboy: What did you think of Roddenberry's final flourish, when NASA honored his will's request and released his ashes into space on one of its missions? Sound tempting?
Bradbury: That was interesting. At one time, I had planned to have my ashes put into a Campbell's tomato soup can and then have it planted on Mars. [*Laughs*] But in recent years, I have come to realize that I have a lot of fans and lovers out there. So I plan to design a big, long, flat gravestone that will be inscribed with the names of my books and lots of dandelions, as a tribute to *Dandelion Wine*, because so many people love it. At the bottom of the slab there will be a sign saying PLACE DANDELIONS HERE—I hope people will, so a living yellow meadow can bloom in the spring and summertime.

Playboy: Do you believe in God?
Bradbury: I believe in Darwin and God together. It's all one. It's all mysterious. Look at the universe. It's been here forever. It's totally impossible. But,

then, the size of the universe is impossible. It goes on forever, there's no end. That's impossible. We're impossible. And the fact that the sun gave birth to the planets, and the planets cooled, and the rain fell and we came out of the oceans as animals. How come dead matter decided to come alive? It just did. There is no explanation. There's no theory.

Playboy: You almost sound like a fundamentalist preacher. You say you believe in Darwinism, but you sometimes sound like a creationist.
Bradbury: Or a combination of both. Because nobody knows. Science and religion have to go hand in hand with the mystery, because there's a certain point beyond which you say, "There are no answers." Why does the sun burn? We don't know. It just does—that's the answer. Why were the planets created? We don't know. It happened. How come there's life on the earth? We don't know. It just happened. You accept that as a scientist and as a religious preacher. The scientist can teach us to survive by learning more about how the body works, what disease is, how to cure ourselves and how to work on longevity. The preacher then says, "Don't forget to pay attention to the fact that you're alive." Just the mere fact, the glory of getting up every morning and looking at the sunrise or a good rainfall or whatever, and saying, "That's wonderful." That's just wonderful. The Darwin theory can't be proved; it's a theory. We think it is true.

Playboy: Do you think it's true?
Bradbury: Nobody knows. I can't give you an opinion about it. It's only a theory, you see.

Playboy: Do you go to church?
Bradbury: No. I don't believe in the anthropomorphic God.

Playboy: Do you think our souls live on or do we cease to exist when we die?
Bradbury: Well, I have four daughters and eight grandchildren. My soul lives on in them. That's immortality. That's the only immortality I care about.

Science-Fiction Supernova
Sandy Hill / 1997

Charlotte Observer, 12 October 1997, Art Section, p. 1 F. Copyright © 1997 by *Charlotte Observer*. Reprinted with permission from the *Charlotte Observer*.

Question: You don't consider yourself a science-fiction writer, even though others call you that. How do you see yourself?
Answer: I am a collector of metaphors. Any idea that strikes me I run with. I've published in the last seven years two murder mysteries, *Death Is a Lonely Business* and *A Graveyard for Lunatics*. Then during the last six years I've published a book on Ireland and (written) *Moby Dick* for the screen. I have published two books of essays, *Zen and the Art of Writing*, which I like to think is one of the better books on writing, then *Yestermorrow*, on how to cure current problems and make our society work.

I wrote *The October Country*, which is weird fantasy. There is no science fiction there. And "Halloween Tree," which is a history of Halloween. And *Dandelion Wine*, which is my childhood in Illinois. *Something Wicked This Way Comes*, which is also my childhood plus fantasy. So when you look at the spread of things, there is only one novel that is science fiction. And that's *Fahrenheit 451*.

In other words, science fiction is the art of the possible, not the art of the impossible. As soon as you deal with things that can't happen you are writing fantasy.

Q: I know you never have trouble coming up with ideas. Walk me through your daily inspiration and writing process.
A: I just wake up with ideas every morning from my subconscious percolating. At seven in the morning I lie in bed and I watch all the fragments of ideas swarming around in my head and these voices talk to me. And when they get to a certain point, I jump out of bed and run to the typewriter. So I'm not in control.

Two hours later I have a new short story or an essay or part of a play.

Q: You use a typewriter, not a computer?
A: Oh, I hate computers. Who needs one? Why would I need a computer when I already have a typewriter? I have an IBM Selectric, which corrects automatically when you want it to correct. And it makes duplicates. So all this nonsense is a way of making money for Bill Gates and all his partners.

We're talking about a billion-dollar industry here. They are flimflamming everyone into thinking you've got to have what you don't need.

All you need is a pad and pencil. Sit yourself in a room, get out your pad and pencil and write a short story. You don't need any of this junk.

I was at a meeting at the library last January. I signed the guest book, and on the page next to me I saw that Bill Gates had been there and signed in. And I wrote underneath his name, "I don't do Windows." It's nonsense.

If you need them for certain kinds of research, swell. But I'm not a researcher. I don't research things. It is all in my head to start with.

Q: What is your position on the Internet?
A: That it's old-fashioned. You've gotta type things. That's ridiculous. I was in Buenos Aires a couple of weeks ago and they did this interview (on the Internet). They type a question to you. You type an answer back. That's thirty years ago. Why not do it on the telephone, which is immediate? Why not do it on TV, which is immediate? Why are they so excited with something that is so backward?

Q: When you've finished typing your short stories, do you revise?
A: No. Never. A few words, but that's not revision. That's just cleaning up.

Q: What are you passionate about?
A: Everything. If you're in love, you're in love.

Q: There is a scene in *Dandelion Wine*, where a young boy is lying on the ground and is suddenly just intoxicated with the wonder of the world. And he thinks, "I'm really alive!" Was that a strong sense you had from an early age?
A: Absolutely. That particular event occurred when I was thirteen years old and I suddenly looked at the shiny hairs on the back of my wrist and I said, "My God, why didn't someone tell me about that."

Q: The opposite of that aliveness is a sense that someday you are going to die. Did you have that sense?

A: That provokes you into creativity. That is the ricochet board that you work against. The sense of death has been with me always. It's a wall there and you bounce life off of it. And you create because there is the threat of extinction, so every new book is a triumph over darkness.

Q: You said once that "the great thing about my life is that everything I've done is a result of what I was when I was twelve or thirteen." What does that mean to you?
A: Or even younger, when I was three, when I was five, when I was nine. All the things that I loved have been part of my writing. *The Hunchback of Notre Dame* when I was three years old; *The Phantom of the Opera* with Lon Chaney when I was five in 1925. . . . When I was nine, I collected all the Buck Rogers comic strips. Edgar Rice Burroughs, the *Tarzan* books, *Warlord of Mars*. I memorized those books. The *Oz* books when I was nine, ten, eleven. . . .

King Kong in 1933 when I was thirteen, H. G. Wells, Jules Verne. All those things. My childhood was packed with metaphors. Plus the Bible. Plus the hundreds of other films during that time.

(In 1934, the family moved to Los Angeles.) I was a real freak. I hung around the studios when I was fourteen so I could see famous people. I intruded on the life of George Burns when he and Gracie Allen were doing their radio show. I wrote scripts for the show every week and gave them to George. They used one routine.

I did radio acting. I read the comic strips to the kiddies when I was twelve years old.

Out of all those images and metaphors, I became a good screenwriter, because a good screenwriter is making storyboards like comic strips. So I am a natural outgrowth of the impact of all these wonderful art forms.

Q: How do you want to be remembered?
A: As someone who never had to take a vacation, as someone who played through life and had a great time.

Q: What would your critics or enemies say about you?
A: They would be envious of my joy. You know, there are people in this world who hate it if you express joy in the sunset because they don't see it the same way. They think maybe you're pulling rank on them, maybe you are being

one up, maybe you see things they don't see. And of course that would make you the enemy.

Q: You said that when you were a young man you learned a lot about style from female writers. What is different about female writers?
A: They are more sensitive. They see life differently than men do. They accept life much more openly. They are not angry all the time. Men tend to react to life a little too violently. All the murders are committed by men. Most of the bad accidents on highways are caused by men.

We're two different races. So you have to learn about the other half of the human race, the other race, from people like Katherine Anne Porter, Willa Cather, Jessamyn West, Edith Wharton. I've been reading her since high school, long before she was discovered by this generation. That is a pretty good list right there.

Q: I understand you are writing a third detective story?
A: Yes. I'm writing a sequel to the other two. It's called *The Rattigan* [*Let's All Kill Constance*]. It is the name of one of the women in the other two novels. She keeps coming back to life on me.

Q: How is it going with the film adaptation of your short story "The Wonderful Ice Cream Suit"?
A: The filming has gone beautifully. I'm very happy about it. For the first time in my life they are filming exactly every word and every scene that I wrote. Unbelievable.

Q: That must be especially nice after the disappointing TV version of *The Martian Chronicles*. Now Steven Spielberg's company plans a new film of *Martian Chronicles*, and Mel Gibson is doing *Fahrenheit 451*. Are you heavily involved in these projects?
A: Yes. I'm doing all the screenplays.

Q: What else are you doing?
A: I'm working on another play, another book of essays. And I have two other books coming out in the next month. One is about dogs, called *Dogs Think Every Day Is Christmas*. The cat book is called *With Cat for Comforter*. They are two books of poetry, illustrated.

Q: What kind of advice would you give beginning writers?
A: Fall in love and stay in love. Explode. Don't intellectualize. Get passionate about ideas. Cram your head full of images. Stay in the library. Stay off the Internet and all that crap. Read all the great books. Read all the great poetry. See all the great films. Fill your life with metaphors. And then explode. And you're bound to do something good.

Q: What things do you do that aren't related to writing?
A: I have my four daughters and eight grandchildren. There is plenty to do. And tending to your wife. Going to movies, going to plays. We spent the summer in Paris. That was wonderful. It's a terrific place to be. It's very creative. I get up at three in the morning and write there.

Q: Do you think this is just a gift that you've got?
A: Yeah. Unfortunately for a lot of people, they're not born with the same genes and chromosomes. And no matter how hard they write or how often, they can't get the same results. So that's God-given, isn't it? I'm very fortunate.

Q: All writing is self-revelatory to some extent. What does your work say about you?
A: Everything we've already said. I've been at the circus all my life and I never came out.

An Interview with Master Storyteller Ray Bradbury

Jason J. Marchi / 1998

Hollywood Scriptwriter (January 1999). Copyright © 1999 by Jason J. Marchi and © 1998–2002 by New Century Cinema Group LLC. Reprinted by permission.

In October 1998, New Century Writer Executive Director, Jason J. Marchi, conducted an exclusive interview with Ray Bradbury for the cover story of the January 1999 issue of the *Hollywood Scriptwriter*.

Jason J. Marchi: You're busier than ever these days.
Ray Bradbury: Thank God.

JJM: How is the writing for Gibson going?
RB: It's been a crazy week. Problems with everybody. With Gibson, and Universal on *The Martian Chronicles*, and Disney on another project. So, it's good to talk to you.

JJM: You're in the midst of several movie projects now.
RB: Three movie projects and four novels.

JJM: Tell us about the film projects.
RB: Well, *Fahrenheit 451* is one. I've turned in a screenplay on that. And there have been six more screenplays since then, by other writers. And for Universal, I've turned in three screenplay versions of *The Martian Chronicles*. But they've assigned an idiot to revise it. That's the problem I'm having right now. And for Disney I'm promoting *The Wonderful Ice Cream Suit*, which is a beautiful film, so that's good news. I'm going to all these film festivals all over the United States, and people love it. So that's good.

JJM: You've both adapted your own work for the screen or had your work adapted by others. Have you had any luck maintaining control over these adaptations?

RB: Well, mainly on television with *The Ray Bradbury Theater*. I had total control, so it was a wonderful series of programs. I did sixty-five scripts.

JJM: Since we're talking about adapting work for the screen, was it easier when you first started writing for Hollywood than it is to adapt your work today?
RB: It's always been bad because the producers think they know what they are doing and they don't.

JJM: It was that way when you were writing the film version of *Moby Dick* for John Huston?
RB: That was different. But that was difficult too, because John Huston didn't know the novel any better than I did. So it was a process of reading and rereading and trying to understand. But John didn't comprehend the book any more than I did. And back then there weren't any producers around, thank God.

JJM: Mel Gibson will definitely be directing the new film version of *451*?
RB: Yes, he will. [*Editor's note: According to Amy Archered of* Variety, *in early February 2000 Mel Gibson announced that after thirteen rewrites he has decided to shelve the filming of Fahrenheit 451 because, "The opportunity for that one has passed me by."*]

JJM: Who will be playing the main characters in the film?
RB: He hasn't cast it yet. They haven't told me. You'll find out at the same time I do.

JJM: You spent some twenty years trying to get your book *Something Wicked This Way Comes* made into a movie.
RB: That's right.

JJM: Did you push to have *451* remade, or did Mel Gibson first approach you?
RB: Mel Gibson came to me.

JJM: Tell me about your version of the script for Gibson that's different from the 1966 François Truffaut version?

RB: I went back to the novel and I adapted the novel. He didn't do that. He used parts of it, but he left out a lot. So I put back all the missing pieces.

JJM: What process did you use when referring back to the novel to write the film adaptation?
RB: Well, you know, when there's good dialogue there you use it. I'm a screenwriter automatically.

JJM: *451* has had many lives—short story, play, novel, musical, and Truffaut's 1966 movie. Why another movie version of *451*?
RB: You'll have to ask Mel Gibson. But, first of all, it should reflect the novel. The original version by Truffaut was very good. It had a lot of good stuff. I watched part of it on TV the other night again. I hadn't seen it in years. And it has a very good cast except for Julie Christie who played Clarrise as "the girl next door," which was totally wrong. Clarrise has to be sixteen years old and naive. And Julie Christie was not sixteen and not naive.

JJM: So you're hopeful that Gibson's version of *451* will be a more true rendition of the novel.
RB: Well, I hope so. You never know.

JJM: You've been writing for about sixty-eight years now.
RB: Just about, yes.

JJM: Do you think that *451* is your most definitive work?
RB: All of them are. They're all my children.

JJM: Is *451* your favorite?
RB: No. They're all my favorites. I have four daughters, I don't play favorites with them. I have eight grandchildren, I don't play favorites with them. And I've got six hundred short stories, and I don't play favorites with them.

JJM: My former English professor, Gary Goshgarian, who teaches literature at Northeastern University, has the following question from his students. It comes up every time he teaches the *451* novel in class, which he's been doing for twenty-five years now. What happened to Clarisse in the novel? It's not clear how she died. She just vanishes near the end.

RB: Well, everyone's talked about this, so in my stage version I brought her back alive, and in my musical I brought her back alive. And in Truffaut's film she comes back alive. So that will happen also in Mel Gibson's movie. She was too good a character to lose.

JJM: Then why did you leave her out of the end of the novel?
RB: If I were revising the novel today I would do what I did in the stage play—let her come back on-scene for a moment.

JJM: I've read that one of your methods of writing is to listen to your characters when they speak to you of their own volition. Do your characters, like Clarisse, still talk to you after all these years? Still ask for changes to their stories?
RB: Oh yeah. I'm working on a murder mystery now with a character called Constance Radigan. She's been in my first two murder mysteries, and I killed her off in the first one. As I was revising that first murder mystery, she came back and knocked on the door and said "I refuse to stay dead. Put me back in!" So I put her back in and now she's in three books.

JJM: What do you do differently today when adapting your work from when you first started?
RB: Nothing. I still adapt right from the original work. I go right to my short stories, right to my novels, and they come right off the page. I had lunch with Sam Peckinpah twenty years ago, and he wanted to do *Something Wicked This Way Comes*, as a screenplay, and I said "Sam, how you gonna do it?" And he said, "Rip the pages out of the book and stuff them in the camera." And he was right. All of my work is photogenic. I'm a child of cinema. I grew up seeing thousands of films. That goes into your blood stream, and when you begin to write you write for the screen automatically.

JJM: Your family moved to Los Angeles when you were fourteen. Had you not moved to Hollywood, and gotten so much direct exposure to the Hollywood community, do you think you would have become a different writer?
RB: Hollywood was a good influence because I was madly in love with films, and the films had a direct influence on me. I don't know, really. If I'd stayed in Waukegan, Illinois, what would have happened to me as a writer? That's a

hard thing to guess. But Hollywood was perfect. I was exposed to movies when I was one year old.

My mother was a fiend for movies. I went to the movies twice a week when I was one and two, and when I was three I saw *The Hunchback of Notre Dame*, with Lon Chaney. When I was five I saw *The Lost World*. And then *The Phantom of the Opera*. I saw thousands of films. All silent films and sound films. So, now I think, if I hadn't been anywhere near Hollywood, films would have influenced me.

JJM: So you fell in love with films very early.
RB: Oh God, yes! One year old.

JJM: You've adapted quite a bit of your own work. Other than Herman Melville's *Moby Dick*, have you adapted the works of other writers?
RB: Very few. Very few. I don't want to do other people's work.

JJM: So it's not a good idea to adapt other people's work?
RB: You can't do that. It's not yours. You can't write other people's ideas.

JJM: I think lots of school children across the country would like to hear that. I remember some of my teachers forcing the students to write about the subjects the teachers were interested in.
RB: If the teachers do that they're stupid. Let the kids come up with lists of their own ideas. Their own fears, their own hopes, their own desires, their own loves. And they can write about those.

JJM: I love talking about short stories, but many of our readers are interested in writing directly for Hollywood. What's your advice for dealing with the difficulties of breaking into film writing?
RB: Don't do it! There are thousands of scripts out there already. The competition is terrible, and most of it is crap. It looks easy, but you should be writing short stories and novels instead. You've got young writers with visions of $100,000 and $200,000 screenplay fees and that's what's luring them on. It shouldn't be that. You should love literature. You should live in the library. Forget about films. That came late in life to me. I was in my thirties.

JJM: You've inspired so many young people to become writers, filmmakers, actors—Leonard Nimoy, Steven Spielberg, George Lucas to name a few, but who first inspired the writer in you?
RB: L. Frank Baum; the Oz books. Edgar Rice Boroughs; Tarzan. And John Carter; Warlord of Mars. Jules Verne. And Buck Rogers—the daily strips that appeared in the newspapers everyday in 1929 when I was nine years old.

JJM: Can we still learn from these writers today?
RB: Some of them. It depends on your age. You can't read Edgar Rice Burroughs when you're in your late teens because you're too old. But when you're ten, my God, Tarzan is just wonderful. But you can read Jules Verne because he still reads well at any age that you pick him up. And the Oz books aren't bad, but I wouldn't advise reading them past the age of eighteen.

JJM: Who else might we read and learn from today?
RB: Robert Heinlein was a friend of mine when I was nineteen and he was thirty-one and just starting his career. He has published a hell of a lot of fascinating material. All of his early short stories were great influences on me because his stories were very human. And they taught me to write about human problems, instead of technological or robot problems.

JJM: What makes your work so memorable? Is it the strong metaphors which have become a signature of your style, your voice?
RB: Yes, metaphor is really it. I was influenced by all the Greek myths, the Roman myths and all those metaphors. The Old Testament, the New Testament—both are full of metaphors. Egyptian mythology; metaphors. The great poetry of the world, it's all metaphors. The great motion pictures, all metaphors. (JJM note—Here Ray gives one of his "Huh" punctuations.) So I've grown up on a diet of metaphors. If young writers would find those writers who can give them metaphors by the bushel and the peck, then they'll become better writers, to learn how to capsule-lize things, and present them in metaphorical form.

JJM: Is it wise for writers who want to write screenplays to watch modern films and try to emulate what they see?
RB: Well, you've got to be careful. There's a lot of crap out there. Most of the science-fiction films alone are abominations, you know. They're mindless.

So you can't learn from those kinds of films. You've got to find something like *Close Encounters of the Third Kind*, which at least has a philosophical, religious metaphor at its center. But there are very few films like that.

JJM: It sounds like writers should be going back to the classics to get the education they need to learn to write.
RB: Yes. Go back and reread ALL the great short story writers of the last one hundred years: Edgar Allan Poe, Nathaniel Hawthorne, Herman Melville, Washington Irving. They all wrote with metaphors. And then in our time we have a lot of science-fiction writers who've done some very good work. Heinlein is one. Theodore Sturgeon. The short stories of Henry Kuttner. Then, you've got to read over in other fields. Read Rudyard Kipling. Read [William] Somerset Maugham's short stories. Read *The Friendly Persuasion* by Jessamyn West, she's a wonderful writer. Willa Cather. Edith Wharton. There are a lot of wonderful women writers who would be good influences on writers. You've got to spread yourself out, and educate yourself with all kinds of stories.

JJM: You've given us some wonderful metaphors to describe the writing/editing process over the years: "Throw up in the morning, clean up at noon. Step on a land mine upon waking and spend the rest of the day putting yourself back together." And my favorite: "You are the spectrum gathering all the white light of experience and in turn throwing your spectrum onto the page." Do you have any new ones to share with us today?
RB: I can't think of any. [Laughs]

JJM: Okay. You've said to avoid Hollywood. But let's say a young writer really wants to break into Hollywood, how can it be done?
RB: Well, first you mustn't. You can't learn to write that way—by writing directly for the screen. Wait until you're thirty. But in the meantime write two hundred short stories. You've got to learn how to write! Screenplays are not writing. They're a fake form of writing. It's a lot of dialogue and very little atmosphere. Very little description. Very little character work. It's very dangerous. You'll never learn to write. You've got to learn how to write well and then you can survive. You must write all kinds of things. Essays, poetry, short stories, novels, stage plays, and screenplays. That's what I do. All those things.

JJM: But starting with short fiction.
RB: Yes. A story a week for five years and then you'll know something about writing.

JJM: Should a writer get an agent to help sell his work?
RB: When he's learned how to write, yes. [Laughs] You've got to wait until you have a decent short story to show an agent.

JJM: Is it hard to sell short stories today?
RB: There are plenty of markets. Science-fiction markets. Detective markets. The science-fiction market is wide open. We're publishing at least two hundred science-fiction books a year from Ballantine, Dell, Avon, and Bantam. Two-hundred books by new writers. Some are books of short stories, and a lot of them are short novels. So, there's a field where you can break in. It's wide open, if you have any talent. *Hitchcock Magazine* is still being published. So is *Ellery Queen*. And *Amazing Stories*.

JJM: Do you think playwrights get better treatment than screenwriters?
RB: Oh, it depends. A really good film gets a lot of attention. Take the film *As Good As It Gets*. Mr. [James L.] Brooks is getting a lot of attention not just because he directed the film but because he wrote a good screenplay. Take the film *Moonstruck*. The young American/Irish writer got a lot of attention when that film came out. So it depends on the film.

JJM: With your busy schedule, are you still receiving three hundred letters per week?
RB: Sometimes it's three hundred, sometimes just one hundred or two hundred.

JJM: And you answer most of them?
RB: I try to pay attention to all those letters that are really sincere.

JJM: It's very nice of you to take the time to answer all those letters.
RB: Well if someone sends you a love letter, you've got to answer back, don't you?

JJM: You said you have new books in the works.
RB: Yes, four new novels. One is a mystery, one is a fantasy, one is a sequel to *Dandelion Wine*, and one is a romance. A little bit of everything.

JJM: Speaking of sequels. I've found a rumor circulating on the Web that you might be writing a sequel to the *451* novel.
RB: Never! Never. Never never never. It answers its own questions.

JJM: Any last thoughts you'd like to ad?
RB: Just one. I wish we could get more productions of my opera *Fahrenheit 451*. It's a beautiful opera, and I'm very proud of it.

JJM: Thank you Ray, for today and for all your years of inspiration to all your fans.
RB: Thank you, Jason! And God bless you.

Ray Bradbury
Joshua Klein / 1999

The Onion a.v. club. Copyright © 2001 by Onion, Inc. Reprinted by permission. [Interview conducted in 1999.]

The Onion: I'm one of many to have grown up reading your work. How does it feel to be canonized?
Ray Bradbury: I don't think about it. Just get your work done and never think about that sort of thing.

O: Still, it must be exciting to know that students are required to read your books in school.
RB: Yeah, occasionally. I was at a ceremony yesterday to give an honorary degree to Ray Harryhausen, my old friend, the animator of dinosaurs. So, things like that, the two of us get one heck of a lot of love and affection from people. That's good, yeah.

O: Really, though, there are so few authors who are actually on reading lists. Isn't that a validation?
RB: It's amazing. I never thought it would happen. I wrote stories to please myself, and it's very gratifying to see that *Fahrenheit*, or *The Martian Chronicles*, or *Something Wicked* are in schools all over the country.

O: It's also relatively unusual for a science-fiction writer.
RB: I'm not a science-fiction writer. I've only written one book that's science fiction, and that's *Fahrenheit 451*. All the others are fantasy.

O: What's the distinction for you?
RB: Fantasies are things that can't happen, and science fiction is about things that can happen.

O: Well, you had originally set *The Martian Chronicles* in 1999, which then was a long way off. For all you knew, what you wrote about was not completely out of the realm of plausibility.

RB: My Mars is fantastic, you see. It's not real, so it's a fantasy. I've just had to change all the dates for the new edition. [Laughs.] I've set our colonization of Mars ahead to 2050.

O: Why did you originally estimate 1999?
RB: Well, it seemed like a long way off. It was fifty years ago! The space age was nowhere in sight, and I thought that that gave it enough time. [Laughs.] At least we got to the moon.

O: It must be weird to see the present catch up to your future.
RB: Oh, no. They haven't caught up. We've only been on the moon for a few hours. I'm way ahead of them.

O: I was thinking strictly chronologically. The whole world is now the date you chose, regardless of whether any of the changes you predicted actually occurred.
RB: Oh, yeah. Of course.

O: Does the fact that it's already 1999—"the future"—and you're still writing put your career into perspective?
RB: Oh, no. I just get my work done. That's the important thing.

O: *Fahrenheit 451* is one of the definitive anti-censorship books. What do you think of the renewed efforts to restrict or regulate the content of books, movies, music, and the like?
RB: That's not censorship. You have to have taste. You know, there's a hell of a lot in movies that doesn't have to be there. I'll give you a good example: Mel Gibson is doing a new version of *Fahrenheit 451* next year some time. There are nine screenplays—nine screenplays! Now, if you know the book, you can just shoot the book off of the page. It's an automatic screenplay. Well, I gave them one screenplay, and there are eight more by various screenwriters. And to give you an example of what should not go into a film—and it's not censorship, it's taste—there's one of the scenes by this other screenwriter. The fire chief comes to visit Montag, and Montag's wife, Mildred, says to him, "Would you like some coffee?" And the fire chief then says, "Do bears shit in the woods?" Do you want that in a film?

O: It's certainly not necessary.
RB: No, it's not. It's not in the book. It's not me. So, that's not censorship. It's just their bad taste.

O: Is it hard to watch people changing what you wrote?
RB: Oh, sure, because I don't have control. Once you sell those things to the studio, they can do anything with it that they want. You have the privilege, of course, of not selling it to them. But Mel Gibson is a fine director and a fine actor, and I trust him to do a good job. But at the right moment, when they start production, I'll make a list of things that don't go into the film. And if he doesn't [listen], I'll call a press conference.

O: Compared to most of the films out there, the example of bad taste you brought up is pretty mild.
RB: [Laughs.] There are a lot of "fuck" words in there, too!

O: I guess it's just a business, and that stuff sells.
RB: They think they need it, but I have a new film out now, *The Wonderful Ice Cream Suit*, and. . . . Have you seen it?

O: No, it played only briefly.
RB: No, it didn't. That was only the premiere. You can rent it for a dollar. They didn't put it in a theater. They were experimenting with videocassette sales, which I don't approve of. It belongs in theaters. It's the best film I've ever made, and there's not one curse in the whole film. And it's about people who could very easily curse, you see? But you don't need those swear words.

O: Do you think screenwriters are just too lazy to write without profanity?
RB: Oh, they're just trying to show off. It's just male macho crap.

O: But that sells tickets.
RB: No, it doesn't. At least, I don't think it does. They imagine it does. It all started with *Saturday Night Fever* about twenty years ago. In the very first scene, the guys drive up and call him a "fuckhead." That's the point where I got up and left the theater with my wife. I said, "I don't need that." That's where it all started, about twenty years ago.

O: It's one thing if it's a matter of personal taste, but isn't it bad if someone else imposes their own tastes? Isn't that a dangerous direction to go, or can the task be handled responsibly?
RB: I'll handle it for them. If they want, I'll kick 'em!

O: Well, you complained that you don't have control over the rights to your book. . . .
RB: But I can take a press conference, though. I'm a danger to them if they're not careful.

O: I suppose the new *Star Wars* film went out of its way to avoid bad language and blood.
RB: And it's doing very well. In fact, it's doing better than it deserves, I gather. I haven't seen it, so I can't judge. It looks like a lot of special effects. People go to see that.

O: You've always written about people first and foremost, and I think that accounts for the longevity of your stories.
RB: Also, I deal in metaphors. All my stories are like the Greek and Roman myths, and the Egyptian myths, and the Old and New Testament. If you speak in tongues, if you write in metaphors, then people can remember them. The stories are very easy to recall, and you can tell them. So it's my ability as a teller of tales and a writer of metaphors. I think that's why I'm in the schools.

O: But there's a whole new generation of fantasy and science-fiction writers that don't write in metaphors. They write visually, as if they're writing a screenplay.
RB: I don't read them, so I can't judge.

O: Though you have expressed disdain for a lot of the cyberpunk novels.
RB: They look boring to me. But I haven't read them. Again, it's a male macho fad. Women don't care for this sort of crud.

O: Why do writers gravitate toward the macho stuff?
RB: I don't know. I have no knowledge. I just hear these things. I don't have time to read these books.

O: Are you always working, then?
RB: [Laughs.] Are you kidding? I've got six new books coming out in the next two years. I've been writing every day of my life for sixty-five years.

O: That's an admirable habit.
RB: Oh, it's not mine. It's God-given. It's not discipline; it's passion. Passion is the discipline.

O: Do you think contemporary writers have a similar passion?
RB: Of course they do. You just have to look around for it, though. There are people writing in every field: essays, poetry, plays. But you have to search them out.

O: Do you think the average person these days has enough passion for reading to search these things out?
RB: Sure, my fans.

O: But besides your fans. Are people reading enough?
RB: Well, there are twenty thousand new books published every year.

O: But do people really purchase them?
RB: They wouldn't be published otherwise.

O: It seems as if everybody winds up reading the same things.
RB: Well, there's a lot of junk around. Barbara Taylor Bradford, Judith Krantz, and what have you. And they sell in the millions. It's always been true. There have always been soap operas and summer-reading books. That goes back a hundred years. Look at *Gone with the Wind*. That was a big bestseller sixty years ago. But, you know, it's very shallow. It's a woman's book, and they read for the adventure of a woman trying to make do with these beasts called men.

O: Do you find it inspirational that people are still attracted to your writing through all the changes in fads and tastes?
RB: Nope. I write just for myself. My tastes are the same. I've always loved Tarzan, I've always loved John Carter of Mars, and I still collect Buck Rogers comic strips. I still love Prince Valiant. It doesn't change.

O: Still, it must be difficult to weather cultural changes, because we're all inundated with external stimuli.
RB: But you can cut it all off. You don't have to turn on the TV set. You don't have to work on the Internet. It's up to you.

O: Many people act like they're compelled to consume these distractions.
RB: But they're not. Not for a moment. Everything is generated through your own will power. You don't have to do anything you don't want to do. This is a democracy. You go where you want to go and do what you want to do.

Joshua Klein / 1999   189

O: A lot of young people may not have the maturity to make such decisions.
RB: Well, better they decide on me. That's all I ask.

O: On the subject of computers, I found a quote from you that says, "I don't understand this whole thing about computers and the superhighway. Who wants to be in touch with all those people?" That's from 1995.
RB: That's right. And I haven't changed my mind. Bill Gates was at the library ahead of me two years ago. He signed in the guest book, and I wrote underneath his name, "I don't do Windows."

O: Have computers been a benefit?
RB: Yes and no. It depends on how you use it. Some things you use it for, searching for certain kinds of facts, are good. But if you're not careful, it turns into just one more toy.

O: It is a good way for people to share certain passions.
RB: That's a lot of nonsense. Go out and meet people! Don't get on a machine and do it.

O: You have written a good deal about the future—or what was then the future—so surely it must be interesting that some of your predictions have come true.
RB: *Fahrenheit* is full of 'em. A lot of things are unpleasant, like local television news. I'm sorry I predicted that. But here it is. It's all crap. At least we don't have a totalitarian government like what they had in the book. But through lack of education, we're not teaching kids to read and write. So there is the danger that you raise up a generation of morons.

O: But the fact that a book like *Fahrenheit 451* is taught in schools—and that students are required to read it—may help prevent the rise of a totalitarian government.
RB: Oh, no, because the responsibility is at the kindergarten and first-grade level. And if you don't do the work there to teach people to read, they're not going to read *Fahrenheit*.

O: What can be done to make students more interested in reading?
RB: That's not it. It's the teachers who have to do the job in kindergarten and first grade. Once you teach them to read and write, then the students will be

curious. But the education system has failed, and all the money that Washington sends out in the next two years has got to go to local schools, first grade, and kindergarten. Then we can cure the problem.

O: What do you think went wrong?
RB: The teachers stopped teaching. They're lazy, and they don't want to be graded. And yet we're all graded constantly.

O: As a writer, do you feel like a teacher yourself?
RB: You must be. You can't be self-conscious about it, but Dr. [Albert] Schweitzer said years ago, "Do something good and someone might imitate it." So if you like my writing, you may very well imitate my passion.

Future Tense Sci-Fi Legend Bradbury Going Strong
Jim Cherry / 2000

Arizona Republic, 31 August 2000, p. 24. Copyright © 2000 by Jim Cherry. Reprinted by permission.

Rep: You lived in Arizona as a boy?
Bradbury: I lived there when I was six in 1926, and for a year when I was twelve. I was a curious kid. When I was six and lived in Tucson, I was on the university grounds all the time, especially the natural science building, which was full of snakes and tarantulas and Gila monsters. They used to throw me off campus, and I'd creep back and hide. Tucson's a very special place to me.

R: Do you think your peripatetic childhood had an impact on your becoming a writer?
B: I think that I was born to be a writer—it was genetic. You can't teach that; what you can teach is good habits. When you read my books you can't imagine anyone else writing them.

R: There seems to be a spiritual quality that runs through your work. Do you subscribe to the Eastern idea of an impersonal God or the Western idea of a personal one?
B: I have a delicatessen religious outlook—"I'll take some a' deez, some a' doze and some a' deez." I believe in American Indian ideas, ideas of the Far East; they're all fascinating and nothing is proved.

R: Do you "write drunk and revise sober" or compose everything carefully in your mind before setting it down?
B: It's got to be an explosion. I get an idea and then, bang! I'm at the typewriter, and two hours later it's done. All of my short stories have taken two or three hours.

R: You don't consider yourself a science-fiction writer. Instead, you're a fantasy writer, is that correct?
B: Correct.

R: There's a timelessness to your work.
B: It's mythological—I write Greek myths, Roman myths, Egyptian myths. It's metaphorical, but there's no science in them. The only book I've written that's science fiction is *Fahrenheit 451*. That's political and psychological science fiction.

R: In that way, your book is like *A Clockwork Orange*.
B: Oh, don't say that! That's a sick book! I hate *A Clockwork Orange*. It's so vulgar. The characters don't lift you up in any way.

R: Do you have any idea how many copies of *Martian Chronicles* you've sold?
B: Oh, I don't know, it's never been a bestseller. It only sold five thousand copies its first year. But, it's been a cumulative bestseller. You sell fifty thousand to one hundred thousand paperbacks a year for fifty years and you have quite a few million. None of my books sell worth a damn when they first come out.

R: How many movies have been made from your books?
B: Oh, four or five. *Illustrated Man*, which is no good; *Something Wicked This Way Comes*, which was very good. *Fahrenheit 451*, which had things missing but was still a good job. *Martian Chronicles* on TV was a bore, but we're going to do it over next year as a theatrical movie.

R: Do you hand the book over to the movie studio and let them do their thing?
B: No, I have to be in there, or I won't let them do it.

R: Did you see computers and the Internet coming?
B: I could see them coming, but nobody could predict some of the problems that would be connected to that.

R: Such as?
B: Well, all this business with Napster, and stealing all that music—thieving millions of dollars of music away from people without paying for it. That's ridiculous. They should be destroyed. They're behaving like the Russians and Chinese, who've been stealing my books for forty years.

R: What do you think of alien visitors and UFOs?
B: No such, no way. It's ridiculous; there's absolutely no proof anywhere, at any time.

R: You've never driven a car?
B: I never learned. I was too poor. Writers can't afford things like that. My wife and I didn't have enough money to buy a car till we were thirty-seven and thirty-eight—then she learned to drive. Becoming a writer is a very slow process and there's not much money in it for a long time.

R: Your musical *Dandelion Wine* is set to play in L.A.
B: I did it first at Lincoln Center thirty years ago; now we're bringing it back, at the Colony Theater in Burbank.

R: What are you working on now?
B: I have a new book of essays called *A Chapbook for Burnt-Out Priests, Rabbis and Ministers*, a book of philosophic essays, a new book called *One More for the Road*, a novel *From the Dust Returned*, and a book of poetry. That's more than enough, don't you think?

Conversation with Ray Bradbury
Steven L. Aggelis / 2002

Interview conducted 9 October 2002. Copyright © 2003 by Steven L. Aggelis. Reprinted by permission.

Aggelis: You've been interviewed numerous times. I've got a bibliography of 335 interviews. If you could interview anyone, living or passed on, who would you interview, and why?
Bradbury: George Bernard Shaw. He was the greatest playwright of our century. There was no one anywhere near him when it came to play writing. And his book of prefaces, which I have two copies of, is around three or four thousand pages of the essays he wrote introducing his plays, on any subject you want to name. So, if I were to interview anyone, it would be George Bernard Shaw.

A: What's the latest on your work in film?
B: There's nothing going on except one project, "A Sound of Thunder," which started filming in Prague, in October. And on all the other films or events, I have no news.

A: What were some of the problems you were having with "A Sound of Thunder"?
B: Well, the director who had been on the project for a year, all of a sudden, said: "Why don't we get rid of the butterfly?" When I tell that story people say: "The butterfly? Good Grief! That's the center of the story. If you get rid of the butterfly, there's no story." So, we fired him. We have another director now.

A: I would like to discuss your latest short-story collection, *One More for the Road*.
B: OK.

A: The story "One More for the Road" addresses plagiarism and censorship, and also mentions the city of Tallahassee. I contacted you from Tallahassee in

February 2002 about the *Conversations with Ray Bradbury* project and, over the ensuing few months, we discussed the issue of plagiarism. When did you write this story and what was your motivation?
B: Ho ho! I can't remember. Once the writing process is back, I really can't remember.

A: You said Tallahassee stuck out in your mind. One time you had car trouble there.
B: I was down . . . twenty years ago, I was going for the opening of EPCOT, the Disney project in Florida, and I lectured in New Orleans one day, and the next day I was supposed to leave on the train for Miami, and they canceled all the trains. So, I had to hire a limousine driver in order to go south for the opening of EPCOT. Well, I wound up with this limousine with a driver, a colored driver who was about twenty years older than myself (I think he was seventy-five years old, at least, and I was in my early sixties.), and we started out on the road to head south into Florida. And at Tallahassee we blew a tire in the middle of the freeway. So, you can imagine what fun it was to change a tire right out in the middle of the freeway, with the cars whizzing by. And we finally got the spare put on, but it was not a good spare. It only lasted a few miles. So, we pulled into Tallahassee, and we tried to find a place that carried a different sized tire. Limousine tires aren't the same size as ordinary tires. So, it took us two hours of prowling around until finally we got decent tires for the limousine. And we got on the road, and a couple of hours later the engine of the limousine broke, and we drifted into a motel, and the car died right there in the motel parking lot. And I moved into the motel for the night with two six-packs of beer for the last night of the World's Series. And the next morning, the damn limousine was dead forever, and there was no way of getting further south for the opening of EPCOT. So, I called the local taxi cab company—I still had about 150 miles to go to get down to EPCOT. Well, the taxi driver showed up, and he turned out to be the town sheriff as well as being the cab driver. So, the town sheriff took me the rest of the way down to EPCOT. And I got a full lecture on the splendors and the glories of Florida on the way, and it cost me an additional $200 to get to EPCOT. So, Tallahassee is burned into my mind from that splendid day when the car blew a tire there. These things happen, and I write a story within minutes of it happening. I never brood over anything.

A: In "First Day," four elderly gentlemen are stationed around their alma mater's flag pole, because of a pact they made to meet on the first day of school, fifty years after their graduation. They do not speak, but wave to each other and leave. Charles Douglas, the protagonist, concludes that they were to meet on the *last* day of school, not the first, but, when he returns home, he tells his wife, Alice, "We talked our heads off!" What exactly is the moral of this particular story?

B: The moral, of course, is you mustn't plan things like that. It's a romantic idea. It actually happened to me on the last day of school, back in 1938. All my buddies, all my best pals, we all promised each other that fifty years later we'd all get together and have a reunion. Well, I'm the only one who remembered, I think, and that's why I wrote the story—because I'm a born romantic, hopelessly sentimental. And of all the people who took that oath, I was the only one who remembered. I didn't go there on that day, but I thought about it. So, naturally, I wrote the story, because I was sad remembering our friendship and the fact that we would never get together again.

A: The story "Beasts" seems to address the effect of pornography on personal relationships and society. The story depicts men wading through the sewers for flesh, like lemmings swimming to their destruction. Is this an accurate take on the story? Please elaborate.

B: What happened is that many years ago I belonged to a gymnasium, and you get to talking to all kinds of people. And there was a gymnast there—I used to swim, and then lie out in the sun and take some sunlight, and you get to talking to people when you belong to the gymnasium—and he told me about a phone number I could call. And it was a combination of numbers that fused, you could hear voices from around the city and around the country, of people calling in with terrible needs. Phone sex. All sorts of strangers who took that way of connecting with people—not meeting them, but having this sort of terrible meeting on the telephone. I never called the number. I never had enough courage. I didn't want to know that truth about people. I thought it was horrible such a number existed, and that people would be using it—tens of thousands of them, or hundreds of them, or dozens of them. So, the story was born out of knowing that such a number really existed, and that kind of phone pornography occurred in the world. It's a metaphor that connects with the phone. That's all.

A: "Fore!" and "Well, What Do You Have to Say for Yourself" both deal with marital infidelity, but are handled quite differently. In "Fore!" Glen Foray, the golf driving range manager, acts on behalf of Mr. Gingrich by punching Gingrich's adulterous wife in the mouth. In "Well, What Do You Have to Say for Yourself," the couple resolves their differences between themselves. Do certain circumstances justify specific reactions, or should Glen Foray go to jail for assault?
B: Ha! It's only a story!!

A: It's a purging; it's a way to get the hairball out.
B: That's right. But, you mustn't read too much into a story like that. You read it because it's the sort of thing you would like to have happen in the world, if there was any justice.

A: "The Cricket on the Hearth" seems to lead the reader to accept government surveillance in personal households. Was this your intention?
B: No, no, not for a moment. It's a thing that actually happened about fifty years ago during the McCarthy era. I had a writer friend, a lady friend, whose husband, James Wong Howe, was the most important cinematographer in movies. I knew Jimmy very well. They had been in love for many years, but they were not allowed to marry because there was a law in California up until 1949 or 1950 that Chinese were not allowed to marry Americans. That law was changed, and they were able to marry at last. During the same period, they were under surveillance because she was, on occasion, I believe, a member of the Communist Party, so they thought that their home was bugged. And she told me about it, and I said, "Are you sure?" And she said, "Yes." There were these mysterious sounds on the telephone, and that was a bad period, around 1952 or 1953, when almost anything was possible. And I knew a lot of people who were temporarily involved with Communism and were not what you would call "diehard." They were people with good hearts who thought Communism promised them a good future. All of us at one time or another, when we were young, fall into that category—not necessarily Communism. I belonged, when I was nineteen, to Technocracy Incorporated. They had a good heart, and had a wonderful plan, but it was completely impractical. I belonged to it for about a year, and then I realized I was boring the hell out of everybody, by lecturing them. Anyway, when Sanora told me about this possible bug, a cricket on the hearth, I was so upset I wrote the

story. So, the story is very old. I never sold it. And I finally took it out of my file forty-eight years later. So, censorship is nothing I approved of, ever.

A: It almost seemed, when I read the story, that the couple's behavior changed after the "cricket" was gone, that the wife, particularly, missed it.
B: She's being semi-facetious, or sometimes a certain kind of threat or almost danger becomes part of our lives, and when it's gone, we get bored. While it was there, it was more stimulating, and when it was gone, they missed it, because it was stimulating.

A: "My Son, Max" addresses homosexuality. Was the husband justified in shocking his wife because she had defended her son's position, versus her husband's stance, over the last year, since Max came out of the closet?
B: The father there is a man who's had the future taken away from him, when he realized there could be no future if his son turned out the way his son said. It means there would be no grandchildren. So, the shock of realizing the family was destroyed caused him to behave that way. It's very natural. I was very fortunate in raising four daughters, and I have four granddaughters and four grandsons. But, if someone had said to me at a certain point, fifty-two years ago, "You're not going to have any grandchildren," that would have been a terrible shock. And God knows how I would have reacted to it. So, what the father does is perfectly natural, to put himself on some sort of even keel with the world, now that the future has been destroyed.

A: Stepping out of *One More for the Road*, and looking at your collection *Long after Midnight*, there were a couple of stories that dealt with homosexuality (Bradbury laughs "Ha!"), and both are compassionate representations of a particular culture—"Long after Midnight," the story of the apparent suicide of a transvestite, and "The Better Part of Wisdom," the story of a grandfather who happens upon his grandson in a homosexual relationship.
B: That one story where the grandfather comes to visit his grandson, the memory he has of his childhood—there was a thing that happened to me when I was twelve. I had a friendship with a boy who moved in next door, and we were great pals. We wandered everywhere, like gypsies, totally innocent, you know. When you're twelve years old, you don't know anything about the world. You don't know about sex, you haven't discovered your body. So, your feelings are pure—absolutely pure. And two boys wandering around with

their arms over each other's shoulders. The world is glorious; it's simply glorious. And the grandfather remembers this, and that makes him a little bit more tolerant of his grandson, and realizing that the same thing could have happened to him, but never did. He had that one summer where he wandered around with his best pal. The best pal went away forever, and that was it. But it was absolutely pure and complete. So, I thought it would be wonderful to build a story around a real memory I had of childhood, and place it forward in relation to a grandson.

A: The transvestite in "Long after Midnight," it seemed to me that it was a suicide, but I had someone read it and say, "How do you know that someone didn't pick this person up and find out who it was and then lynched this person?"
B: That story's based on a real story that was in the *L.A. Times*, and it so saddened me to think that someone would commit suicide by hanging himself. And then the next day they discover it wasn't a girl after all. It was a man dressed like a woman, who must have had, God knows, an unhappy life and killed himself by hanging. So, the terrible irony of the story is in the fact that you have the police sympathetic in one moment because they think they're taking down the body of a girl, and then later discover it's not a girl at all. So, you have a shift in feelings implied, and you, the reader, then suffer the difference.

A: According to some literary critics such as Michel Foucault, a work should be thought of as author-less—that what really matters is the relationship between the reader and the text. And the skillful writer uses this principle to intentionally create gaps so that the reader must fill them in, thus acting as a co-creator, actively participating in the creation of the story. What would you say about this? Can Ray Bradbury stories be read without being aware of Ray Bradbury?
B: Oh, dear me! That's too complicated. I don't believe in theories like that. If you thought of that sort of thing, you would write self-conscious stories that wouldn't be any good. You can't think about what you're doing. Just get the story down.

A: Just put it on paper.
B: Yes, that's all. And whatever people think about, let them think. Because you, yourself, don't know when you're writing it why, exactly, you're doing it, but you write the story.

A: One of the last stories I want to discuss from *One More for the Road* is "Where All Is Emptiness, There Is Room to Move," which sounds Eastern in its orientation. What was your inspiration and moral for that story?

B: When I was in Mexico fifty-seven years ago, traveling around, I was supposed to go down the coast to Vera Cruz. And there was a harbor there that had been silted in with sand. And the sand had collected in such a way to build a barrier, so that ships couldn't get in or out. Well, the people couldn't afford to clear the sand barrier, and the port died. And the ships that were in the port stayed there, and the ships that were outside could never come in. So, you had a ghost town. The town eventually was evacuated by the people, who went elsewhere. It's a perfect town for someone to use as a bombing target for a motion picture. So, there's an irony there of Hollywood taking advantage of an actual disaster that occurred to the town, and moving in to further destroy it. So, that's basically what the story is.

A: Was Jackie Robinson's entry into professional baseball the inspiration for "The Big Black and White Game"?

B: No. That's a true story that happened to me when I was twelve years old. I saw that game, and I saw the cakewalk at the end of the day, that evening in the big tavern there at the lakefront in Wisconsin. All the colored people got together. The women in those most beautiful gowns, and all the colored men in tuxedos. And there must have been—oh, forty or fifty couples, a hundred colored people, dancing the cakewalk there, in the tavern, that night, after the big black and white game. So, the memory of it stayed with me for all those years, and I finally had to write about it. Everything in that story is the truth. So, it wasn't inspired by anything else—only that time when I was twelve.

A: Were both "The Golden Kite, The Silver Wind" and "The Meadow" pro United Nations pieces?

B: No. Starting when I was thirteen, I hung around Paramount Studios, Columbia, United Artists, MGM, and I saw them building and destroying the sets. So, I remembered that when I was twenty-six years old—and I wrote a short story then, based on the destruction of those sets. And they were metaphorically representative of the world. But, that's mainly it. It wasn't about politics at all.

Steven L. Aggelis / 2002

A: What would you say to one's assertion that, in *Dandelion Wine*, Leo Auffman and his "Happiness Machine" are fashioned around the story of Philo T. Farnsworth and his electronic transmission of images, his television?
B: No, I didn't know anything about him till later in life. I still don't know all that much. But, when I was young, of course, I had no way of knowing what he was up to because very few articles appeared anywhere—I believe there were one or two articles in *Popular Mechanics*, that sort of place. So, no, I knew nothing of him.

A: Henry Adams compared the dynamo to a cathedral. How much Henry Adams is in "Powerhouse"?
B: I didn't read him till later. I lived in Venice, California, with my parents, from 1942 on the powerhouse property. We had a little bungalow and right next door across the wire fence was this powerhouse. I would go over on occasion and look at the various electrical devices humming there. It was a small place, where the power came to be reduced to a smaller voltage before it was sent back out. I was amazed at my feelings there at night, that the interior of the powerhouse felt like a church. It reminded me of the interior of a cathedral, a small metaphor for something very large. So, I wrote about it because I lived next door to it.

A: I'd like to ask you a couple of questions about films. I know you're very much a film person.
B: I've seen every film made. I'm a super expert.

A: Which films over the last few years do you consider fabulous works of art and why?
B: A film came out about five years ago called *As Good As It Gets*, with Helen Hunt and Jack Nicholson, and directed by Brooks who wrote the fabulous screenplay. It had incredible performances. And it achieved an impossible goal, because you start with a man who is completely unpleasant, played by Nicholson, and you begin by not liking him at all, maybe even hating him. And over a period of two hours you get to love him and understand him and his relationship with the waitress that he falls in love with. So, if you haven't seen it, I think it had twelve Academy nominations and won eight Oscars. Everyone in the film, and the film itself, and the screenplay won Academy awards. And that's fabulous. Have you seen it?

A: I enjoyed the film. I have yet to see *A Beautiful Mind*. My professor has really encouraged me to see that film.
B: No. I turned it off. We have a copy here, but it was too self-conscious. I hate films that are "good" for you. I don't like people who set out to do me a favor: "Look at this film and it will do good for you." See, *Fahrenheit* does good for you without trying. And the important thing about *Fahrenheit* is that I wrote a James Bond adventure, but the core of it has a lot to do with my love of reading and libraries, and about book burning. But, I don't hit you over the head with it, at least I don't think I have. I don't recommend my book or my film of *Fahrenheit* because it will do you good. That would be terrible. I don't want to do good for anyone. I want the good to come incidentally.

A: On the flipside, which films over the last few years do you consider worthless works of art and why?
B: Well, most of them. I mean, films that have won Academy awards the last few years—like *American Beauty* is filled with terrible people. They all deserve to die. The one person who does something decent, the husband, at the end, when he refuses to go to bed with his stupid daughter's girlfriend, he's rewarded with a bullet through the brain. Well, come on! So, I hated that film. And it got all kinds of Academy awards. Same way with *The English Patient*. It's a story of a dreadful man who destroys everyone. He destroys his best friend, who commits suicide, by trying to kill him. He kills his mistress, indirectly. She dies in a plane crash. He's carrying her dead body back across enemy lines. He's shot and burned, and finally commits suicide. So, it's a real happy story, isn't it? And it got all kinds of Academy awards.

A: Well, Mr. Bradbury, is there anything, a question, I haven't asked you (Bradbury laughs "Ha!") that you would like to respond to?
B: If I start doing that, we'll be here all night. Bye bye.

Index

Abbott and Costello, 37
Abraham, F. Murray, 140
Ackerman, Bettye, 70
Ackerman, Forrest J., 88, 91
Adams, Henry, 201
African Queen, The, 57, 63, 157
Albee, Edward, 29. See also *Who's Afraid of Virginia Woolf?*
Alcoa Premiere, 68, 69
Alien, 109
Allen, Fred, 163
Allen, Gracie, 38, 163, 172
Alley Oop (comic), 37
Amazing Stories, 20, 21, 33, 83, 182
American Beauty, 202
American Scholar, 35
Andersen's fairy tales, 86
Anouilh, Jean, 23
Apollo missions, 127, 131, 153
Arnold, Jack, 60
As Good As It Gets, 182, 201
Asimov, Isaac, 150
Astounding, 33, 86
Austen, Jane, 160

Baker, Russell, 159
Baldwin, James, 29; *Giovanni's Room*, 40
Barton, James, 70
Baum, L. Frank, 96, 180. See also *Oz* books
Beast from 20,000 Fathoms, The, 54–55
Beautiful Mind, A, 202
Bellamy, Edward, 82
Belmondo, Jean-Paul, 74
Best American Short Stories, The, 4
Bible, 12, 172, 180
Bion (uncle), 21, 85

Blackstone the Magician, 20, 86
Bloch, Robert, 89
Bogart, Humphrey, 63
Botticelli, Alessandro, 95
Brackett, Leigh, 21, 88–89
Bradbury, Ray: on automobiles, 31–33, 34, 43, 164–65; on censorship, 13, 19–20, 139, 140, 141–43, 147–48; on city planning, 32, 43–44, 91–92, 105, 114, 132–35; on comics, 37, 87, 94–95, 109, 172; on creative people, 9–10, 55–56; on death, 11–12, 36–37, 51, 172; on education, 42–43, 44, 45–47, 85–86, 137–38, 141–42, 160, 167–68, 189–90; on God, 51–52, 81, 83, 102, 168–69, 191; on government, 136–37; on Halloween, 20, 36; on homosexuality, 20, 39–40; on horror films, 11–12, 36–37, 92–93; on idealism, 112–13, 115–16; on intellectuals, 38, 48, 50; on magazines, 141, 160–62; on the middle class, 34, 118, 120–21; on motion pictures/movies, 96, 179, 180–81, 201–2; on newspapers, 10–11, 14, 141; on political correctness, 148, 159–60; on science fiction, 17–19, 22, 30, 48, 79, 82, 83, 98, 108–9, 126–27, 129–30, 150–51, 156, 162, 170, 182; on sex, 19–20, 119, 162; on space travel, 81, 84, 93–94, 112, 126–27, 130–31, 152–54; on technology, 100–1, 113, 135–36, 152, 189; on television, 14, 49–50, 130, 144; on writing, 3–7, 17, 23–27, 29–30, 46–47, 87, 118–19, 122–24, 155, 170–71, 174, 178, 182, 187–88, 191; on writing for film, 54–55, 176–77, 178, 179, 181

Works
- "Aesthetics of Lostness, The," 134
- "And So Died Riabouchinska," 69
- "And the Rock Cried Out," 78
- "Anthem Sprinters, The," 66
- "Ardent Blasphemers, The," 104
- "Beasts," 196
- "Better Part of Wisdom, The," 198–99
- "Big Black and White Game, The," 200
- "Bullet Trick, The," 67
- *Chapbook for Burnt-Out Priests, Rabbis, and Ministers, A*, 193
- "Chrysalis," 102
- "Cricket on the Hearth, The," 196–97
- *Dandelion Wine*, 22, 23, 76, 101–2, 106, 124, 160, 162, 168, 170, 171, 201; musical, 78, 97, 98, 193
- *Dark Carnival*, 57
- *Death Is a Lonely Business*, 123, 170
- *Dogs Think Every Day Is Christmas*, 173
- "Exiles, The," 146
- *Fahrenheit 451*, 19, 57, 73–75, 80, 99, 101, 125, 140, 141, 145–46, 148, 158–60, 162, 170, 173, 175, 176, 177–78, 184, 185, 189, 192, 202; opera, 183
- "First Day," 196
- "Fore!," 197
- *From the Dust Returned*, 193
- *Futuria Fantasia*, 136
- *Golden Apples of the Sun, The*, 27, 80
- "Golden Kite, The Silver Wind, The," 200
- *Graveyard for Lunatics, A*, 123, 170
- *Green Shadows, White Whale*, 157
- *Halloween Tree, The*, 78, 170
- *Harper*, 72
- "I See You Never," 4
- "I Sing the Body Electric," 70–71, 100–1
- *Illustrated Man, The*, 55, 57, 68, 71–72, 73, 74, 75, 76, 80, 192
- *It Came From Outer Space*, 59–60
- "Jail, The," 68–69, 70
- "Jar, The," 70
- "Lake, The," 25
- *Let's All Kill Constance*, 173
- *Leviathan 99*, 110
- "Life Work of Juan Diaz, The," 70
- *Long After Midnight*, 198
- "Long after Midnight," 198, 199
- "Looking for Death," 69–70
- "Lost City of Mars, The," 77
- "Marionettes, Inc.," 69
- *Martian Chronicles, The*, 27–28, 56, 57, 67, 77, 80, 89–90, 104, 110, 136, 155–56, 160, 173, 175, 184–85, 192
- "Meadow, The," 200
- *Moby Dick* screenplay, 28, 60–67, 78, 157–58, 170, 176
- "My Son, Max," 198
- *October Country, The*, 25, 170
- *One More for the Road*, 193, 194–98, 200
- "One More for the Road," 194–95
- "Pedestrian, The," 17, 104, 125, 128–29
- "Picasso Summer, The," 75–76
- "Pillar of Fire," 146
- "Powerhouse," 201
- *Ray Bradbury Theater*, 176
- *Screaming Woman, The*, 76, 77, 139
- *Something Wicked This Way Comes*, 52, 77, 78, 97, 101, 170, 176, 178, 184, 192
- "Sound of Thunder, A," 140, 195
- "Sun and Shadow," 27
- "There Will Come Soft Rains," 107, 136
- "Tomorrow's Child," 103
- "Veldt, The," 73, 147
- *Vintage Bradbury, The*, 98
- "Way in the Middle of the Air," 8–9, 19
- "Well, What Do You Have to Say for Yourself," 197
- "Where All Is Emptiness, There Is Room to Move," 200
- *With Cat for Comforter*, 173
- *Wonderful Ice Cream Suit, The*, 175, 186
- "Wonderful Ice Cream Suit, The," 173
- *Yestermorrow*, 170
- *Zen and the Art of Writing*, 170

Bradford, Barbara Taylor, 188
Bridges, James, 70
Brinkley, David, 131
Broadstock, Brenton, 145
Brooks, James L., 182, 201
Brown, Howard Vachel, 86
Buck Rogers, 20, 37, 48, 82, 86, 109, 121, 172, 180, 188
Burns, George, 38, 163, 172
Burroughs, Edgar Rice, 52, 82, 96, 110, 123; *John Carter of Mars*, 20–21, 85, 86, 180,

Index

188; *Tarzan*, 20–21, 172, 180; *The Warlord of Mars*, 20–21, 37, 172, 180
Butcher, John, 145
Buttram, Pat, 70

Caine, James M., 110
Cather, Willa, 72, 149, 173, 181
Challenger, 130
Chandler, Raymond, 110
"Chandu the Magician," 37–38
Chaney, Lon, 172, 179
Charm, 4
Chartoff-Winkler Productions, 97
Chester, Hal, 54
Chicago World's Fair, 20, 22, 138
Chile, 39
China, 34, 125, 129, 142
Christie, Julie, 146, 158, 177
Clarke, Arthur, 108
Clayton, Jack, 97
Clockwork Orange, A, 192
Close Encounters of the Third Kind, 103, 109, 134, 154, 181
Coleman, Ronald, 163
Collier's, 140
Corwin, Norman, 52, 56

Daniken, Erich von, *Chariots of the Gods*, 94
Darwin, Charles, 168–69
Da Vinci, Leonardo, 95
Día de los Muertos, 36
Dickens, Charles, 13
Dickinson, Emily, 119
Dietrich, Marlene, 163
Disney, Walt, 21, 43–44, 101, 114, 132, 133, 134, 135, 167
Disney studios, 175
Dold, Elliot, 86
Donaldson, Sam, 131
Donne, John, 157
Dore, Gustave, 94
Douglas, Kirk, 73
Dracula, 11, 12, 36, 37, 51
Dusipala, Chris, 97

Eiffel Tower, 45, 134
Ellery Queen, 182
Ellison, Harlan, 109

Emerson, Ralph Waldo, 52
Empire Strikes Back, The, 109, 120
English Patient, The, 202
EPCOT, 132, 138, 195
Exorcist, The, 93

Fadiman, Clifton, 100, 104
Fantasia, 21
Farnsworth, Philo T., 201
Finney, Albert, 76
Fire Island, 15, 40
Fitzgerald, F. Scott, 149. *See also* Great Gatsby, The
Flash Gordon, 37, 109
Fleming, Ian, 38
Forbes, 141, 161
Fortune, 141, 161
Foster, Harold, 87
Foucault, Michel, 199
France, 131, 133
Frankenstein, 17, 37
Frost, Robert, 38
Fuhrman, Mark, 165

Gates, Bill, 151, 171, 189
Gavin, John, 70
Gerard, Merwin, 77
Germany, 115
Gibson, Mel, 148, 159, 173, 175, 176, 177, 178, 185, 186
Goldenberg, Billy, 97–98
Goldsmith, Jerry, 68, 97
Gone with the Wind, 188
Good Housekeeping, 20, 141, 161
Gorbachev, Mikhail, 124
Goshgarian, Gary, 177
Gourmet, 141
Goya, Francisco, 13
Grant, Cary, 163
Great Gatsby, The, 97
Grimm's Fairy Tales, 11, 86
Grove Press, 41

Hamilton, Edmond, 21, 88
Hamlet, 149
Hammett, Samuel Dashiell, 110
Harper's Bazaar, 4, 15, 27

Harrison, Joan, 68
Harryhausen, Ray, 54, 55, 56, 57, 88, 184
Harvard University, 46
Hasse, Henry, 21
Havilland, Olivia de, 77
Hawking, Stephen, *Brief History of Time*, 157
Hawthorne, Nathaniel, 119, 181
Heard, Gerald, 110
Hefner, Christie, 161
Hefner, Hugh, 162
Heinlein, Robert, 21, 88, 89, 108, 157, 180, 181
Helms, Jesse, 142
Hemingway, Ernest, 149
Henry V, 61
Hepburn, Katharine, 157
Highet, Gilbert, 98
Hillyer, Robert, 27
Hitchcock, Alfred, 60, 68, 69, 70; *Rebecca*, 73
Hitchcock Magazine, 182
Hitler, Adolf, 48
Hogarth, William, 94
Hollywood, 7, 96, 163, 178–79
Holof, Georgia Bogardus, 145
Hopkins, Gerard Manley, 47
House of Un-American Activities Committee, 146
Howe, James Wong, 197
Hunchback of Notre Dame, The, 172, 179
Hunt, Helen, 201
Hussein, Saddam, 141
Huston, John, 28, 40, 56, 57, 59, 60–61, 62–63, 64–67, 79, 133, 157–58, 176
Huxley, Aldous, 27, 38, 48, 67, 82, 96, 110; *Brave New World*, 156, 159

Ionesco, Eugene, 29
Ireland, 15, 28, 30, 40, 59, 64, 158
Irving, Washington, 181
Isherwood, Christopher, 110, 155–56

Japan, 115, 117
James Bond stories, 38, 47, 48, 109
Jane Wyman Theatre, 67
Johnson, Jennet, 21, 87–88
Johnson, Lyndon B., 33
Jones, Chuck, 78
Jones, Leroi, 40

Kafka, Franz, 29
Kennedy, Bobby, 146
Kennedy, John F., 152
Kepler, Johannes, 82
King, Rodney, 165
King Kong, 172
Kipling, Rudyard, 53, 181
Kirsch, Bob, 47
Knight, Arthur, 68
Koon, Stacey, 165
Krantz, Judith, 188
Krishnamurti, Jiddu, 52
Kuttner, Henry, 21, 88, 181

LaGuardia, Fiorello, 87
Lancaster, Burt, 73
L.A. Times, 47, 156, 199
Laughton, Charles, 158
Laurel and Hardy, 163
Lean, David, 37, 56
Le Corbusier, 43
Little Orphan Annie Secret Society, 38
Lloyd, Norman, 68, 69
London, 45, 134
Los Angeles, 15, 31–32, 43–44, 45, 132, 163, 164, 165–66, 172
Lost World, The, 179
Lucas, George, 180
Lucian, 82

Mad, 27, 94
Mademoiselle, 4
Mailer, Norman, 98, 124, 155
Malamud, Bernard, 98
Maltese Falcon, The, 57, 66, 158
Mann, Thomas, 41; *Death in Venice*, 39–40
Marvel Comics Group, 95
Maugham, William Somerset, 48, 181
McCall's, 20, 161
McCarthy, Joseph, 146, 162
McCarthy era, 19, 139, 146, 197
McNeil/Lehrer News Hour, 131
Melville, Herman, 58, 61, 63, 64, 96, 104, 119, 158, 180; *Moby Dick*, 28, 179
Mettee, David, 145
MGM studios, 77
Michelangelo, 95

Index

Miller, Arthur, *The Crucible*, 146
Miller, Henry, 123
Mirisch brothers, 62
Moby Dick, 28, 40, 45, 50, 57–59, 60, 61, 102, 110, 157
Molière, Jean-Baptiste Poquelin, 157
Monet, Claude, 120
Moonstruck, 182
More, Thomas, 82
Morley, Christopher, 48
Mulligan, Bob, 28
Murphy, Audie, 63
Mussolini, Benito, 148

NASA, 152–54, 168
Nation, 35
National Enquirer, 142
Neal, Roy, 154
Neva (aunt), 20, 21, 85
New Republic, 35
New York City, 43, 124
New Yorker, 4
New York Review of Books, 47
New York Times, 159
New York World's Fair, 22, 138
Nicholson, Jack, 201
Nimoy, Leonard, 180
1984, 158
Nolan, Bill, 77

Olivier, Lawrence, 21, 60–61
Omni, 141
One Step Beyond, 77
Orwell, George, 82, 130; *1984*, 158
Oz books, 85–86, 172, 180

Packwood, Bob, 153
Pakula, Alan, 28
Pakula-Mulligan Productions, 77
Palance, Jack, 73
Palomar College, 46
Paris, 132, 133, 134
Paul, Frank R., 86
Peace Corps, 35
Peacock, Thomas Love, 48
Peck, Gregory, 60, 62–63
Peckinpah, Sam, 77–78, 97, 178
People, 141, 151, 161

Phantom of the Opera, The, 172, 179
Philadelphia Inquirer, 139
Piranesi's Imaginary Prisons, 45
Planet Stories, 88
Plato, 82
Playboy, 15, 51, 162
Podhoretz, Norman, 47
Poe, Edgar Allen, 20, 37, 119, 181
Pope, Alexander, 157
Popular Mechanics, 201
Porter, Katherine Anne, 173
Prince Valiant (comic), 94, 109, 188
Puccini, Giacomo, 97

Rabelais, Francis, 82
Rackham, Arthur, 86, 94
Rains, Claude, 69
Rand, Ayn, 48
Reagan, Ronald, 125
Rebecca, 73
Rechy, John, *City of Night*, 41
Red Badge of Courage, The, 62–63
Renoir, Pierre-Auguste, 120
Richard III, 61
Robinson, Jackie, 200
Rocklynne, Ross, 21
Roddenberry, Gene, 168
Rohmer, Sax, 47; Fu Manchu stories, 96
Roth, Philip, 98
Rushdie, Salman, 143
Russia, 19, 34, 118, 125, 127, 129, 142

Sagan, Carl, 154, 155
San Diego, Calif., 166
San Francisco, Calif., 92
Saturday Evening Post, 20, 54
Saturday Night Fever, 186
Saturday Night Post, 14
Schiffren, Lalo, 97
Scholastic Magazine, 139
Schweitzer, Albert, 190
Science Fiction League, 88, 91
Serling, Rod, 70, 71. See also *Twilight Zone, The*
Shakespeare, William, 58–59, 78, 117, 120, 149; *Hamlet*, 149. See also *Henry V* and *Richard III*
Shaw, George Bernard, 23, 48, 96, 120, 149, 195

Shearer, Norma, 163
Simpson, Al, 137
Simpson, O. J., 159, 164
Smight, Jack, 71, 72, 73, 74, 76, 77, 79
Smith, Clark Ashton, 91
Sontag, Susan, 47
Spielberg, Steven, 173, 180
Squires, Roy, 91
Stalin, Joseph, 148
Star Trek, 95, 103, 168
Star Wars, 109, 120, 154, 187
Steiger, Rod, 73
Steinbeck, John, 38, 149
Stevens, Robert, 69
Stevenson, Robert Louis, 21; *The Strange Case of Dr. Jekyll and Mr. Hyde*, 52; *Treasure Island*, 52
Straw Dogs, 78
Streep, Meryl, 130, 143
Sturgeon, Theodore, 181
Sunset Boulevard, 120
Sunset Strip, 50
Super Science Stories, 82
Swift, Jonathan, 82

Tallahassee, Fla., 195–96
Tarzan, 3, 20, 37, 85, 87, 109, 172, 180, 188
Teasdale, Sara, "There Will Come Soft Rains," 107
Thomas, Dylan, "A Child's Christmas in Wales," 50
Thomas, Parnell, 146
Time, 141
Tintoretto, Jacopo Robusti, 95
To Kill A Mockingbird, 28
Tom Swift books, 21
Toulouse-Lautrec, Henri de, 120
Treasure of the Sierra Madre, The, 57–59
Truffaut, François, 41, 73–75, 146, 158–59, 176–77, 178
Tucson, Ariz., 87, 191
Twain, Mark, *The Adventures of Huckleberry Finn*, 52, 160
Twilight Zone, The, 70
2 Live Crew, 142
2001, 154

United Nations, 33, 49, 56
Universal Studios, 175
USA Today, 141, 148
U.S. News and World Reports, 104

Valley of the Dolls, 42
Van Fleet, Jo, 70
Veiller, Anthony, 61, 62
Verne, Jules, 17, 18–19, 21, 37, 48, 52, 53, 59, 82, 98, 104, 110, 117, 120, 172, 180
Verrill, A. Hyatt, "The World of Giant Ants," 21
Vidal, Gore, 124, 155
Vietnam (conflict), 33, 43, 49
Vogue, 161
Vonnegut, Kurt, 157; *Player Piano*, 157

Wald, Jerry, 72
Warhol, Andy, 42
Warlord of Mars, 20–21, 37, 172, 180
Warner, Jack L., 62
Warner Brothers studios, 54, 61, 62, 75, 159
Waukegan, Ill., 21, 22, 30, 111, 133, 135, 163, 178
Webb, Jimmy, 162
Weird Tales, 16, 89, 90
Wells, H. G., 21, 37, 52, 82, 172; *The War of the Worlds*, 17
Welty, Eudora, 149
Werner, Oskar, 74, 158
Wertham, Frederic, 37
Wesso, H. W., 86
West, Jessamyn, 173; *The Friendly Persuasion*, 181
West, Mae, 163
Wharton, Edith, 173, 181; *The Age of Innocence*, 149
Whitman, Walt, 52
Who's Afraid of Virginia Woolf?, 37
Wilde, Oscar, 160; *The Picture of Dorian Gray*, 52
Wildmon, Donald, 142
Will, George, 131
Williamson, Jack, 21
Wiseman, Joseph, 67
Wolfe, Thomas, 38, 48, 52, 72
Wonder Stories, 20, 83
Wright, Frank Lloyd, 43, 137

Yeats, William Butler, 120